EMERSON AND

SELF-CULTURE

EMERSON AND SELF-CULTURE

John T. Lysaker

Indiana University Press

BLOOMINGTON AND INDIANAPOLIS

This book is a publication of

Indiana University Press
601 North Morton Street
Bloomington, IN 47404-3797 USA

http://iupress.indiana.edu

Telephone orders   800-842-6796
Fax orders   812-855-7931
Orders by e-mail   iuporder@indiana.edu

MANUFACTURED IN THE UNITED STATES OF AMERICA

Library of Congress Cataloging-in-Publication Data
Lysaker, John T.
    Emerson and self-culture / John T. Lysaker.
        p. cm.
    Includes bibliographical references and index.
    ISBN-13: 978-0-253-35107-4 (cloth)
    ISBN-13: 978-0-253-21971-8 (pbk.)
    1. Transcendentalism (New England) 2. Self-culture. 3. Emerson, Ralph Waldo, 1803–1882.
I. Title.
    B905.L97 2007
    814'.3—dc22

                                                              2007033668

1   2   3   4   5   13   12   11   10   09   08

For Hilary M. Hart, with whom I am lovingly bound,
and for Ricardo Barragan, Peter Gager,
Michael O'Connor, and Joe O'Grady,
with whom the dream of an Emersonian life first began

CONTENTS

ACKNOWLEDGMENTS

This book owes many debts and aims to honor them, knowing that gifts cannot be repaid. Once again, the department at the University of Oregon has been uniformly supportive, particularly Mark Johnson and Scott Pratt. (The sabbatical was very helpful too.) My time in Comparative Literature, far from over, has also been a boost. Among my many students, I want to thank those who took the three Emerson seminars I offered. I'd also like to thank Carolyn Culbertson and Moshe Rachmuth in particular for their work as research assistants. I wish I had been that smart, careful, and cool when I was a graduate student. I probably was as funny. Thanks also to Ival McMains for enabling me to have Carolyn as a research assistant and indexer and for his generous, thoughtful, and gregarious presence. Steve Brence also read chapters 1 through 5, and our conversation concerning their twists and turns was much appreciated. Michael Sullivan engaged most if not all of the work in various forms, and his comments were both encouraging and helpful at several points. I am also grateful to Terry Hummer, then of *The Georgia Review*, for publishing a version of chapter 1. His enthusiasm helped fuel the project. Several audiences also gave me the sense that I wasn't completely crazy, including folks at the Society for the Advancement of American Philosophy, the Society for Phenomenology and Existential Psychology, Kenyon College, Utah State University, and the University of Colorado at Denver. I am also grateful for being able to offer an Emerson seminar at the Summer Institute in American Philosophy. Those in attendance drew out work that has proven integral to this project. An NEH seminar regarding Emerson, convened and hosted by Russell Goodman and Steven Affeldt, was a downright blast and a great point from which to begin this project. (Special thanks to Maurice Lee, Richard Deming, and Erin Flynn for letting an old guy hang out and for continuing to greet me in public.) And then, most recently, my manuscript improved under the care and support of Dee Mortensen and John Stuhr. I am grateful for their keen advice and trust.

Less interpersonally, but nevertheless importantly, my venture into Emerson follows certain leads, particularly Stanley Cavell's three decades of work. Cavell's cumulative insights prove the following: "There is always room for a man of force, and he makes room for others" (*CW6*, 31). I repeat Emerson's remark from "Fate" because my essay ambles along a path that Cavell's writings have helped clear, and for that I am grateful in a way that I hope my gait conveys. Barbara Packer's work, both *Emerson's Fall* and her magisterial history of Transcendentalism, gave me a much better sense of where I was putting my foot. Likewise, Cornel West's opening essay in *The American Evasion of Philosophy* first reminded me that Emerson is fair game and fine nourishment for philosophers. And his presentation at the NEH seminar, down to its Beethoven-like synthesis of freedom and forms, showed me how the term "eloquence" could apply to Emerson's entire project.

A few other acknowledgements touch the heart of this work. The first lies with my mother, whose life I quote with reverence and gratitude on a daily basis. Second, given that I never had as much as an undergraduate class devoted to Emerson, let alone a graduate seminar in philosophy, I began this project wondering what the hell I was thinking. Luckily, Bill Rossi, a genuine scholar and reader and an indulgent colleague and friend, showed a degree of enthusiasm and support that enabled me to believe in myself. His generosity manifested itself in various ways--from not asking me to leave his office, to an initial reading group on some early lectures (thanks, too, to Jim Crosswhite), to our "Figures of Friendship in Emerson and Thoreau" conference, a remarkable gathering of scholars whose reflections were a joy and benefit to receive as I was preparing chapter 6.

My lifelong friends, Ricardo Barragan, Peter Gager, Mike O'Connor, and Joe O'Grady, were and are presences of a different order. I first encountered Emerson at fifteen, sure of a dinner and truly boon companions. With that going for me, or rather, surrounding me, I took "Self-Reliance" to heart. I doubt I would have had the force to do so, however, if I didn't think these lads had (and have) my back. More recently, Hilary Hart agreed to share her life with me, an event that has enriched my days beyond measure, making plain how two can be one while remaining two. Without her love I think I'd survive, but in a much diminished way. I thus dedicate this essay to her and to those four whom I've called friend for some thirty years, as a glimmer of the gratitude I feel whenever I catch myself in the sublime spectacle of their presence, near and far.

ABBREVIATIONS FOR
CITATIONS FROM EMERSON'S WORKS

CW1-6   *The Collected Works of Ralph Waldo Emerson.* 6 vols. to date. Edited by Robert E. Spiller et al. Cambridge, Mass.: Harvard University Press, 1971–.

CS1-4   *Complete Sermons of Ralph Waldo Emerson.* 4 vols. Edited by Albert J. von Frank et al. Columbia: University of Missouri Press, 1989–92.

CE1-12   *The Complete Works of Ralph Waldo Emerson.* Centenary Edition. 12 vols. Edited by Edward Waldo Emerson. Boston: Houghton Mifflin, 1903–1904.

CEC   *The Correspondence of Emerson and Carlyle.* Edited by Joseph Slater. New York: Columbia University Press, 1964

EL1-3   *The Early Lectures of Ralph Waldo Emerson.* Edited by Stephen E. Whicher et al. Cambridge, Mass.: Harvard University Press. 1959–72.

EAW   *Emerson's Antislavery Writings.* Edited by Len Gougeon et al. New Haven, Conn.: Yale University Press, 1995

JMN1-16   *The Journals and Miscellaneous Notebooks of Ralph Waldo Emerson.* Edited by William H. Gillman et al. Cambridge, Mass.: Harvard University Press, 1960–82.

LL1-2   *The Later Lectures of Ralph Waldo Emerson.* 2 vols. Edited by Don Bosco et al. Athens: University of Georgia Press, 2001.

CL1-10   *The Letters of Ralph Waldo Emerson.* 10 vols. Edited by Ralph L. Rusk et al. New York: Columbia University Press. 1939–95.

MMF1-2   *The Memoirs of Margaret Fuller Ossoli.* Edited by Emerson, Clarke, and Channing. Boston: Phillips, Sampson. 1852

PN   *The Poetry Notebooks of Ralph Waldo Emerson.* Edited by Ralph H. Orth et al. Columbia: University of Missouri Press, 1986

TN1-3   *The Topical Notebooks of Ralph Waldo Emerson.* 3 vols. Edited by Ralph Orth et al. Columbia: University of Missouri Press, 1990–94.

EMERSON AND

SELF-CULTURE

ONE

Taking Emerson Personally

All the right steps in Human Culture are made by listening to the voice of the Eternal in the heart of the Individual.

—*EL2*, 310

In your study of the great books, I should say, read a little proudly, as if one should say to the author, 'tis of no account what your reputation is abroad: You have now to convince Me, or I leave you.

—*LL2*, 314

In its widest scope, as far as I can see, turning in each direction, this work pursues *Bildung*, what I regard as a practice of self-culture, a studied, even labored effort to cultivate one's life.[1] Along Emerson's path, which I will explore, interrogate, mostly champion—and, I hope, advance—self-culture centers us, more *and* less. Responding to and reworking character, both in terms of its habits and its incalculable genius, Emersonian self-culture opens us to horizons of growth expanding in each of their degrees. A bit more precisely, though only barely, my focus is the organic, even divine mechanics of self-culture, an ensemble of events and activities that enable what I will call an "eloquent life," one that I have in some sense fashioned myself and that expresses who I am in my diversity and, to the degree that they exist, my coherencies. Thus, even though my focus will be many texts signed "Ralph Waldo Emerson," this pursuit of *Bildung*, my pursuit, perhaps our pursuit, if you will, is more than a meditation on a nineteenth-century concern: my intention is to articulate and defend, by way of Emerson, a living conception of self-culture.

To the contemporary American ear, the notion of *Bildung* has an exotic ring, and not solely because the word is German and polysemic: physiological formation and development; creation in the sense of establishing or founding; formal education and training, with connotations of cultural refinement; and so on. No, the thought rings oddly, given contemporary . . . what shall we call them? . . . perhaps "mindsets," along the lines of "headsets." As noted, "culture" currently denotes a state of affairs, an existential background coextensive for some with the lifeworld. However, if culture is a given, perhaps even an ineliminable facet of any given, it is difficult to think of culture as an activity, a pursuit that admits of failure and success. But that is what *Bildung* entails—a pursuit that might come up short, a task whose completion is far from secure. Furthermore, the reigning (albeit opposed) ideals of self-expression and character development that govern the eyes and ears of many of my students, though not only they, are hostile to the kind of work that vigorous self-culture proposes. Those bent toward self-expression, self-consciously "liberal," regard tuition of any sort as invasive, an affront to native genius. Or they dismiss rigorous, challenging reflection as "academic," favoring instead self-authorizing discourses like relativism. That one has to doggedly fashion a self worth expressing, or that expression is an art of sorts, well, this thought strikes many as absurd, even totalitarian. For the other hand, a self-consciously "conservative" fist, character development entails little more than internalizing prevailing norms, for example, upholding compulsively heterosexual family values or acquiring practical virtues at the expense of intellectual ones, thus transforming courage and common sense into willful refusals to consider the ends our lives rush toward. In the scales that such a mindset reproduces, it often proves unimaginable—hence, the right's fondness for mockery and derision—that an actualizing self might be led, even driven, to throw down most of its cultural inheritance, to reject what is offered as exemplary in favor of what may still lack sufficient exemplification. Such a hand could never have recorded, as Emerson's did in 1839: "We not only affirm that we have few great men but absolutely speaking that we have none, that we have no history; no record of any character or mode of living that entirely contents us" (*JMN7*, 296).

If my sense for some of my students and peers is right, then a call to self-culture is somewhat untimely. But how can that be? Aren't we always compiling and weaving a life that announces our character wherever we go, in our affirmations, negations, and even omissions? How do you choose to dress? What would you have your clothing say? And if you can't be bothered, isn't that itself a stance to take among those who may be overly bothered? I'll defend these assertions later, in chapter 3, but for now, let me state that I find Emerson compelling when he insists in "Spiritual Laws" that "human character evermore publishes itself. The most fugitive deed and word, the mere doing of a thing, the intimated purpose, expresses character" (*CW2*, 90). And if that is right, then however we respond to what befalls us says something about us. "The world is full of Judgment Days," Emerson proclaims in the middle of his *Human Culture* lectures, "and into every assembly that a man enters, in every action he attempts, he is gauged and stamped" (*EL2*, 301).

But I think many already know this, and, at least in certain corners of their lives, take it to heart. Here's a personal example that suggests, I think, that self-culture is a rather intuitive affair, one we all pursue to varying degrees. My teenage years, distinguished mostly by their privileges and my size thirteen sneakers, were marked by a strong devotion to what was then alternative pop music. Buying and listening to albums, as well as not buying and not listening to others, was a pressing concern. I wanted to be sure my selections and omissions reflected and manifested who I was, for they were extensions of my person and mirrors for my self-conception. They needed to have an edge, but not too sharp an edge, perhaps one blunted with a bit of irony. Thus, I was drawn to Devo's yellow suits, nerdy aura, and prescient contempt for what later became the 1980s. Similarly, I embraced The Smiths' rejection of crotch rock riffs and their unique emotionalism, at once ironic and genuine. But I was put off by The Dead Kennedys' intemperate masculinist rage—too cocksure, too unconcerned with the travails of reconstruction. I was also enamored of records that were lyrically or formally smart. I dug Elvis Costello's vocal lines, seemingly too long for verse/chorus singles. I also grooved to King Crimson's minimalist melodies built around odd time signatures—the effect lulling *and* off-putting.

In part, then, I became a fan of various artists, and those associations presumably said something about me. But I didn't want to be a genre junky. I wasn't interested in being anyone or anything's disciple, a foot soldier trotting about in a uniform of rat-tailed hair or torn jeans and Chuck Taylors. I was thus also drawn, perhaps a bit obsessed, with

David Bowie's continual changes, particularly *Scary Monsters,* though I recoiled when he put on his red shoes and danced the blues. (Actually, I liked *Let's Dance* when it appeared in 1983, although I no longer know why—that is, I no longer recognize that part of me that found it compelling. Now, however, I can acknowledge it as the affirmation of a self that has ceased becoming, and so let it go at that.)

Interestingly, some of the records I loved also thematized my approach to them, albeit not very subtly. Joe Jackson's "Don't Want to Be Like That," an aggressive condemnation of over-privileged, unreflective pleasure hounds, was a reliable source of righteous indignation whenever I needed buoying. Air guitar riffs firing, hearing that record helped me believe that I wasn't being like that, but thinking, resisting, trying to find my own way. Similarly, some years later, in more confident moods, Devo's "We're Through Being Cool" paced my morning preparations for school. Bopping around my bedroom, I was telling myself—and purportedly proving—that I was just too hip to be hip.

Deep affection for records may strike you as a trivial example in a discussion purportedly connected with *Bildung,* yet another example of an American mind closing quickly. But the phenomenon I'm describing is a complex affair. In taking my records as seriously as I did, I was led to consider why I chose those discs in particular. And why records at all? Why not other things, if even things? And outside of the sphere of preference, mighty as it might be, what enabled my passion? Without too much effort, a number of contributing forces became apparent over time: money from my parents, money I earned in a mall, record shops I frequented, their workers who were loose and casual in a studied kind of way, vinyl, workers producing vinyl, the hydrocarbon materials and brine-derived chlorine needed for vinyl, trucks transporting records on highways, ships transporting records overseas, artists/performers, recording engineers, and so on. Quite a sea of forces kept that early obsession afloat, and so rose another concern: what was I affirming and supporting whenever I acquired a record?

Along a related but different line, I also had to explore my relationship to those records I chose. Was my playback system part of the equation? Since it was, I had to ask: Do I love music, or am I an audiophile? And how should I care for my records? I was already wary of throwaway culture, and I wanted them to sound their best, but there were other questions, less easily answered. Was I a "collector"? Were the vinyl discs investments? What was I laying on my turntable's platter? Was this a work of art in the age of mechanical reproduction or just a commodity?

From a third and broader viewpoint, I also had to consider whether records were the sole or even the most important facets of my self-culture. How else was I working with and on myself? And how did these struggles relate to the kid who saved his money, boarded a train to New York City, and hunted through Greenwich Village for bootlegs and 7 inches? As I was also pretending to understand Carl Jung, writing all-too-real, awful poetry, and diving across the goalmouth of a soccer field, I had to negotiate, every now and then, the diversities that each manifest passion and pursuit threw into relief; that is, I felt, in each case, that *I* was at stake, that each was a moment of self-culture, each a partially elected manifestation of who I was becoming.

A complex affair, then, the steps, even the adolescent steps, we undergo in pursuit of self-culture. As I hope my anecdotes have shown, each step rises with and responds to many first- and second-order questions regarding our who, whom, what, and why (which includes our whereto). And it is to those steps that I would direct your attention. Or I should say, I hope to focus your attention as you follow out your own steps, even here, reading this book, for it seems that despite the apparent exoticism of self-culture, these are steps that any reflective person takes. Who do I find myself to be in this undertaking, and is this someone I wish to continue being? If so, how can I help bring it about? If not, what must I do to bring this chapter to a close? I assert the ubiquity of self-culture at this point in order to forecast a claim that I will later expand and defend. Humans are, they exist, as problems for themselves. Who we are is not an assured thing. Rather, for us, you and me, being is a task, and an irreducibly personal one at that. This is not to say that it is a solitary task, only that it involves performances that no one else can do for us, not I for you, or any of you for me. Given this, self-culture is part and parcel with how a human life unfolds, a vocation beneath the more common distinction between vocation and avocation. The question is thus not *whether* to pursue self-culture, but how best to do so.

With precisely this last question in mind, I have elected to focus my energies on Emerson. Allow me to defend my choice. Throughout his career as a public speaker and writer and across his journals, the task of self-culture unfolds as theme and practice. One finds early lectures explicitly devoted to the theme (e.g., "Human Culture" [1837–38] and "Human Life" [1838–39]). *Conduct of Life* (1860), derived in part from the lecture series of the same name (delivered between 1851 and 1853), not only contains an essay entitled "Culture" but reflects throughout on the forces that self-culture confronts and wields (e.g., "Fate," "Wealth," "Power," and "Illusion") as well as the practice in which Emerson finds it consummated: "Worship." Similarly, the two series of *Essays* (1841 and 1844) address the issues and spheres of life around and in which self-culture moves: "Self-Reliance," "Friendship," "Art" and "The Poet," "Manners," "Gifts," "Nature," and "Experience." Even his reflections on national temperaments, *English Traits* and the 1843–44 lectures on *New England,* engage principal axes of self-culture: "Manners," "Character," "Wealth," "Religion," and "Literature."[2] Finally, references to self-culture are spread across the journals, from an 1832 reflection on the importance of "Self-Education" (*JMN4,* 50) to a late worry that self-culture had become little more than amoral affectation (*JMN16,* 140).

Wherever one turns, then, self-culture is at issue in Emerson, though not always as a theme. For the author of the famous line, "I will also essay to be," writing carries out self-culture, performs it in the words chosen, the sentences constructed, the essays assembled (*JMN7,* 13; *CW1,* 103). It is thus no exaggeration to say that wherever one turns in Emerson, self-culture is at issue; that is, it is a matter of concern and a product, an effect, an issue.[3] Finding, then, the ubiquity of the concern, I have elected to use Emerson as a springboard for my own meditations. Or rather—and the strictness of this language will become apparent later—I have elected to pursue self-culture in a quotation of the practices, insights, and problems that one encounters in pursuing the question of self-culture alongside Emerson.

At this point, you may be wondering: Why take up the theme of self-culture through any thinker? Isn't this best pursued on one's own? But what, precisely, marks the region of "one's own"? If it turns out that the historicity of our condition renders us beings who are inextricably bound to the thoughts and words of others, then entering into dialogue with one of those others will remain truer to our "own" than proceeding as if the project of our being is a solitary affair. Likewise, if conversation with others allows us to return more thoroughly to ourselves, then again, a rich dialogue with another, particularly one to whom self-culture is so dear, seems a boon, not a hindrance. Not that I have argued for these positions. That will have to wait for chapters 2 and 6. But I alert you to them now in order to underscore that my dialogue with Emerson is as much a matter of performing self-culture, from its quotations to its objections, from its endnotes to its examples, as it is one of articulating the ways in which his work offers us self-culture.

Now, in electing Emerson for my interlocutor, I am not claiming that he alone should concern those interested in self-culture. First, if what I said about the history of our condition is right, then the phrase "he alone" makes little sense. Second, such a claim would require a comparative study and defense of likely fellow travelers, and I've barely room to do partial justice to Emerson. My claim is thus only that Emerson is a worthy partner in such exercises, even a magnificent one, and not only because self-culture remains at issue throughout his corpus. Emerson's work also enables us to see how a thoroughly relational and dependent creature nevertheless is faced with the task of achieving what I've called an *eloquent* life, one that expresses a character in part self-fashioned through irreducibly personal labors like self-trust, commitment, perseverance, letting go, and so on. His work thus takes us outside the withered playing field of liberal atomism (which denies our relatedness or misconstrues it as contractual in nature); social construction (which leaves us mere functions of larger, impersonal events); and utilitarian collectivism, socialist or capitalist (which neglects the personal in favor of the illusory, unified subject of social engineering).[4]

In providing us with a feel for an eloquent life, Emerson's work also moves us past the so-called death, or more precisely, the "absolute dispersion of man," a sequence of events, announced by Foucault and others, that disclosed: (a) the illusion of transparent, juridical subjectivity; (b) the vested interests that inform supposedly open dialogue and debate; and (c) the incipient violence inflicted by the metaphysics of human nature (Foucault 1970, 385). In a sense—and this will become evident across the second and third chapters—Emerson's deference to genius and its involuntary perceptions contributes to the "death of man." And yet, Emersonian self-culture nevertheless leaves us with a strong sense of who emerges in the wake of that death, a being unfolding in what I will present as (and in) an irreducibly personal project, both bound to and dependent upon relations that stretch into the corners of the cosmos.

In employing the rhetoric of the "personal," I feel compelled to explain why I have not relied on terms like "individual" or "private." First, for better or for worse, "individualism" deeply connotes liberal atomism, the belief that persons are fundamentally ontologically independent, juridical subjects.[5] Second, again by connotation, "individual" appears wedded to a wish for autonomy; that is, it seems to valorize self-legislation. Since Emerson resists both of these commitments, I find the notion of individualism unwieldy in the context of his work. Third, in the history of metaphysics, "individual" denotes a particular existence as opposed to the generality of its concept or the unity of its ground. As such, it suggests, although not necessarily (Hegel is an exception), that being an individual is a state rather than an activity admitting of success or failure. But self-culture is precisely something at which one can fail, and thus I've been led to think of it as something other than "individuation" and to regard its issue as something other than an individual.[6]

In figuring self-culture, I have also steered away from notions of privacy and a private life. Again, the terms connote a liberal atomism, standing as contrasts to sociality and political life. While Emerson has little interest in directing self-culture through state apparatuses, he conceives of self-culture as a practice of solitude *and* sociality, and in a marvelously complex way that the connotations surrounding "privacy" threaten to overwhelm. Second, privacy has distracting epistemological connotations. Earlier I suggested that the personal names what others cannot undergo for us, even though they can enable or hinder us. Now, this is not to say that another cannot know what I understand. Rather, it is to say that another cannot understand *for me*. In other words, my interest in self-culture concerns the events and actions constitutive of persons and their lives, not the intersubjective accessibility of their lives.

Given the nature of Emerson's writing and the history of his reception, I'll begin my reading with a series of hermeneutic orientations, the first of which is negative. This is not an exercise in source criticism. My concern is not Emerson's sources, whether within his corpus—for example, tying together journal, lecture, and essay passages—or without—for example, determining what precisely Emerson drew from Coleridge, Kant, and de Stael regarding genius. Nor am I much concerned with Emerson's influence on later thinkers, for example, Nietzsche.[7] I admire such work, but with some impatience, if only because I am keen to take a text personally, to receive it as it bears upon my own life. A historical treatment of a text stands aloof from such issues, however. Instead, it regards the text as a function in a casual series, and it works to locate that text's contributions to the series, discerning contingencies and effects. Again, valuable work, but not the kind I'll pursue here.

My essays in self-culture also are not principally comparatist, and for a similar reason. While it is genuinely instructive to compare how Emerson and Thoreau received the *Bhagavad-Gita,* unless we eventually champion or decry aspects of the how and what of their reception, we are left with artifacts whose place in self-culture is merely ornamental. Again, valuable scholarly work, but not the work of self-culture and thus not the kind of work I want my reading of Emerson to do.

More generally, I must also note, perhaps with too much force, that in engaging Emersonian self-culture, we should abandon the moorings of "method." Methods are the kinds of engagement that purport to be particularly appropriate to the matter at hand. Readers are drawn to methods because they seem to ensure that one's forays will be more than a series of fallible steps along paths opening within hermeneutic circles. But one cannot elude such circles, and thus reading is always a matter of double reading, of beginning by quoting another reading, of reading a text against a previous construal, be it one's own, another's, or the pre-reflective construal that one's socio-psychological background conditions instantiate.

For those who find this glib, let me add that a text is readable only on the basis of certain preconditions, in the least, literacy (including cultural literacy), and an implicit or explicit theory of textuality, one that delimits meaning, for example, with reference to authorial intent, unconscious projections, class struggles, genres and forms, literary devices like enjambments, and so forth. Given those conditions, one proceeds by tracking the interplay of textual elements—say, formal, thematic, or performative—until meanings such as ubiquitous and unstable metaphysical oppositions, Plato's esoteric doctrine, or Nietzsche's self-overcoming inquiry into truth become apparent. And it is over that tracking that interpretations clash. Or, said otherwise, an interpretation succeeds to the degree that it shows how some set of elements articulate certain meanings rather than others. Now, this tracking of meanings is not a random activity. As Adorno insists in "Lyric Poetry and Society," and I only paraphrase, all readings, even sociological readings, must vindicate claims in and through the text (Adorno 1991). I take this to mean, in part, that as-

[9]

certaining a con-text is not the same as interpreting a text, just as looking up a word in a dictionary is not the same as tracing its meaning within a poem. This is not to say that texts generate their own meaning, only that whatever meaning is *found* there, whether it involves class struggle, sublimated desire, or authorial intent, must be found *there*, even if one regards its origin as extra-textual.

With meanings in hand, one returns to the text for corroboration or refutation and compares one's efforts with those of others, real or imagined. And so one continues until one thinks one has it well in hand. Now, if one could secure from the outset the propriety of those conditions that make a text readable in the first place, conditions that include the elements whose interactions produce meaning, one might imagine the process of vision and revision coming to an end. But those initial steps are part of the interpretation, and thus they are equally susceptible to revision. To put it another way, every interpretation, even longstanding ones, may find themselves in the scene that opens Emerson's "Experience":

> Where do we find ourselves? In a series, of which we do not know the extremes, and believe that it has none. We wake and find ourselves on a stair: there are stairs below us, which we seem to have ascended; there are stairs above us, many a one, which go upward and out of sight. But the Genius which, according to the old belief, stands at the door by which we enter, and gives us the lethe to drink, that we may tell no tales, mixed the cup too strongly, and we cannot shake off the lethargy now at noonday. Sleep lingers all our lifetime about our eyes, as night hovers all day in the boughs of the fir-tree. All things swim and glimmer. Our life is not so much threatened as our perception. Ghostlike we glide through nature, and should not know our place again. (*CW3*, 27)

Because this fate might befall any interpretation, no reader, methodologically armed or not, will convincingly lay hold of criteria able to categorically distinguish better from worse readings, say, on the basis of a theory of textuality. I have thus abandoned the language of method and have, epistemically speaking, decided to make do with a persistent interrogation along the lines of "where and how does it say that?"

Without much precision, I would say at this point that I'm hoping more to work with Emerson than to talk about him. I'm thus not all that hot about what one might call Emerson's considered views on matters of longstanding concern like freedom and determinism. First, I'm mistrustful of the authority of so-called considered views. As readers of extant work, authors are just that, readers, and not necessarily the best. Focusing on a supposedly considered view might very well obscure thoughts and/or implications whose brilliance eluded the author's considerations. Second, I prefer to focus on problematics, not on theses or views. What grabs me is that to which a text or corpus responds, what Heidegger would term its *Sache*. Moreover, my principal concern is what to think about the matter at hand, not which view Emerson eventually elected.

After so many negations, you have a right to ask for a more positive account of what I have to offer. Let me begin by saying that I find it necessary to approach Emerson as he approached Shakespeare—"The Genius draws up the ladder after him, when the creative age goes up to heaven, and gives way to a new, which seeks the works, and asks in vain for a history" (*CW4*, 119). But what does this entail, and must any such reading prove ahistorical? I think not, but it will take some time to show you why.

In seeking works instead of authors, I am not supposing that works simply await our gaze, or that one can demarcate them without reference to authorial activity. Moreover, I concur with Emerson's assertion in the *English Literature* series of 1835–36: "Reading must not be passive. The pupil must conspire with the Teachers. It needs Shakspear, it needs Bacon, to read Shakspear and Bacon in the best manner" (*EL1*, 214).[8] And, in *Representative Men,* he wrote: "Shakspeare is the only biographer of Shakspeare, and even he can tell nothing except to the Shakspeare in us, that is, to our most apprehensive and sympathetic hour" (*CW4*, 119). Odd thoughts. Let's see if we can't position ourselves so as to apprehend their claim.

In comporting myself toward Emerson's texts through something like the Emerson in me, I am approaching them as their secret addressee, to invoke a figure offered by Osip Mandelstam in 1916 (see Mandelstam 1979, 67–73). This is not narcissism. I am not presuming that Emerson wrote with my specific, empirical subjectivity in mind. Rather, to engage a text as its secret addressee is to respect a dimension of its performativity. Every speech-act, no matter its content, no matter its form, has a second-person facet—it is addressed to another. And so too the essay and the lecture. Just like the poem, they have an audience. Mandelstam on his mind, Paul Celan writes in 1958: "The poem can be, because it is a manifestation of language and thus dialogical by nature, a letter in a bottle sent with the faith—certainly not always full of hope—that it might sometime and somewhere wash ashore, perhaps on the land of the heart" (Celan 1983, 3:186). So when I say that in reading Emerson I am taking him personally, this is to say that I hear or read him interpersonally, that I am reading a speaker as his or her addressee, or to defer to his language: "Happy is he who looks only into his work to know if it will succeed, never into the times or the public opinion; and who writes from the love of imparting certain thoughts & not from the necessity of sale—who writes always to *the unknown friend*" (*JMN10*, 315). Emerson's texts are thus not merely outcroppings on the mountain of objective spirit, although they are certainly part of our cultural record. They also address us with a second-person liveliness, and our reception of them should register that, just as one should acknowledge a friend's criticism as a criticism and not simply as the product of socio-psychological forces.

You may be thinking: So you're interested in Emerson's claims? I am. I reject Emerson's recurrent theodicy, his belief that a divine being orders history in a way that is ultimately and thus persistently just; and I'm cheered by his insistence that self-culture is intrinsically dependent on enabling conditions. But a claim is not merely some proposition floating in an ideal space somewhere between our ears, ascribing predicates to subjects or offering predictions. Nor is it simply a premise and/or a conclusion, a logically determinate rung in the ladder of an argument.

Now, I am not suggesting that Emerson fails to offer arguments or that his claims do not have what has come to be called "propositional content." He has arguments, and his remarks refer to states of affairs: emanations, inspirations, and moods. My point, rather, is that Emerson's claims are not reducible to that content or to the logical forms in which they are presented. Moreover, any reading that proceeds by way of such reductions misreads the claims that Emerson advances, ignoring both the intersubjectivity of Emerson's address and other performative dimensions opening within the genres of the lecture and essay.

Much has been said about the genre of the essay, from its individuality to its spontaneity and its fragmentary nature, and much of that discussion applies to Emerson's own essays.[9] What I would stress here is that Emerson's essays are concentrated versions of his lectures. This is not to remind us that many of Emerson's essays had their first run at the lectern. Rather, my point is that what Emerson sought in his lectures, "an eloquence that can agitate," also orients his essays (*JMN12*, 503). Or, as he says in Journal U: "When I address a large assembly, as last Wednesday, I am always apprised what an opportunity is there: not for reading to them as I do, lively miscellanies, but for painting in fire my thought, & being agitated to agitate" (*JMN9*, 70).

We can elaborate this point with a longer entry from a journal of 1839, where Emerson writes: "Is it not plain that not in senates or courts or chambers of commerce but in the conversation of the true philosopher the eloquence must be found that can agitate, convict, inspire, & possess us & guide us to a true peace? I look upon the Lecture room as the true church of today" (*JMN7*, 277). To my ear, this passage holds a key to the door through which we might responsively receive Emerson's claims.

Emerson's essays and lectures are agitating in the broad sense—they start us thinking, in irritation or excitement. They thus not only ruminate, as William Gass (1982) has suggested, but they nip and gnaw at what passes for truisms, for example, that consistency is a virtue, that Jesus was an unsurpassable moralist, or that an exemplar cannot be great and flawed. Not that they tell us to be agitated or give us imperatives, although at times they do. Rather, they are agitating performances, rhetorically provoking us, say, with the kind of overstatement we just witnessed. "Is it not plain that not in senates or courts or chambers of commerce but in the conversation of the true philosopher the eloquence must be found that can agitate?" Once we set this appeal to plainness alongside Emerson's ubiquitous call for self-reliance, it dangles more like bait, a hook that might drag us to determine the matter for ourselves.[10]

Emerson's writings are also full of accusation. For example: "We are afraid of truth, afraid of fortune, afraid of death, and afraid of each other" (*CW2*, 43). Such remarks convict us directly, driving us to recall (or hope for) postures that rise above cowardice. At times we find ourselves convicted less directly, however, particularly in inspiring passages.

> What is it we heartily wish of each other? Is it to be pleased and flattered? No, but to be convicted and exposed, to be shamed out of our

nonsense of all kinds, and made men of, instead of ghosts and phan-
toms. We are weary of gliding ghostlike through the world, which is
itself so slight and unreal. We crave a sense of reality, though it come
in strokes of pain. (*CW3*, 161)

Here Emerson is baiting us with our own desire to grow, to improve, to
leave dross and moss behind. And as I thrill to the thought—and I do,
even now—I realize that most of the time I don't desire this, at least not
strongly, but live "afraid of truth, afraid of fortune, afraid of death, and
afraid of others." And so, in my affirmation of that with which Emerson tempts me, shame rises, as I realize how often I do not live the life
I really want. In passages such as these, therefore, it is less that Emerson accuses me than that he enables me to accuse myself, thus drawing
out of me what he so often demands of me: self-reliance.[11]

While provocative, Emerson's lectures and essays ultimately resist
indoctrination. In "Considerations by the Way," he writes: "Although
this garrulity of advising is born with us, I confess that life is rather a
subject of wonder, than of didactics" (*CW6*, 130). And as he tells an audience in a better-known passage: "Truly speaking, it is not instruction, but provocation, that I can receive from another soul" (*CW1*, 80).
Socratic rather than encyclopedic in their orientation, Emerson's remarks seek to "possess" their addressees with something other than
doctrine. But what else is there?

Recall how "Experience" opens:

Where do we find ourselves? In a series, of which we do not know the
extremes, and believe that it has none. We wake and find ourselves
on a stair: there are stairs below us, which we seem to have ascended;
there are stairs above us, many a one, which go upward and out of
sight. But the Genius which, according to the old belief, stands at the
door by which we enter, and gives us the lethe to drink, that we may
tell no tales, mixed the cup too strongly, and we cannot shake off the
lethargy now at noonday. Sleep lingers all our lifetime about our
eyes, as night hovers all day in the boughs of the fir-tree. All things
swim and glimmer. Our life is not so much threatened as our perception. Ghostlike we glide through nature, and should not know
our place again. (*CW3*, 27)

The essay opens with the thought that the steps that have brought us here
are not what we took them to be, while the steps that lie ahead may buck

and sway and topple us should we attempt to ascend them on the basis of what we know. Perhaps our theories may fall flat. Or, more powerfully, young boys and girls, men and women, some our children, might perish and leave us both empty across years we imagined would be full and guilty that we were able to live on without them. Full in the swim and glitter of this uncertainty, the essay proceeds to probe and test the "lords of life" whose march the prefatory poem marks as defining moments of a day, and all in the hopes of securing a foothold. But Emerson's reckoning, speculative and incisive as it is, fails to call these lords (e.g., illusion, temperament, surface, and surprise) to order. Instead, in the third to last paragraph, he confesses: "I know better than to claim any completeness for my picture. I am a fragment, and this is a fragment of me." (*CW3*, 47). And he accepts, in both a theoretical and practical way, the moral this insight imposes: "I know that the world I converse with in the city and in the farms, is not the world *I think*. I observe the difference, and shall observe it" (*CW3*, 48). The essay thus fails to overcome the impasse with which it began. This is not to say the essay fails, however. It seeks an "eloquence that agitates." Thus, if it brings us to this step and leaves us there (and it leaves us there in the speaker's commitment to observe, as one might observe a holiday or a ritual, the distinction between appearance and reality), then the essay succeeds insofar as it prods us to determine for ourselves, in and through our observances, what we need in order to move on, to ascend the steps experience lays before us.

A proper reception of Emerson's texts thus not only requires an acknowledgement of the challenges they pose—challenges to our beliefs, habits, and character—but also a willingness to assume the tasks they set, conclude them as we will. *Conduct of Life* is thus not simply the title of one of Emerson's late collections. It names that which his claims consistently invoke as a matter in question for both speaker and addressee.

In stressing the performative aspects of Emerson's texts, I am not suggesting that their claims are provocations without content, as if we could translate each into one stern command, say, "Think for yourself." Emerson's lectures and essays offer numerous thoughts purporting to be insights. And while he never systematically binds them together, this does not mean that they are offered ironically, that is, in order that their speaker might be taken for what he is not, to borrow Barbara Packer's words (1982, 19). When Emerson tells us, "In our way of talking, we say, 'That is yours, this is mine'; but the poet knows well that it is not his; that it is as strange and beautiful to him as to you," he is offering a phenome-nologically astute account of thought (*CW3*, 22–23). Likewise, anticipat-ing what Heidegger later termed *Geworfenheit* (throwness), he aptly de-scribes our more general condition: "Man is a stream whose source is hidden. Our being is descending into us from we know not whence" (*CW2*, 159). Emerson's claims thus seek to possess us not only with the problems they set before us but also with touchstones from which we might address those problems, touchstones we might ourselves essay, that is, make an experiment of, try out, venture.

At this point I seem to be at odds with some of Emerson's promi-nent readers. Cavell seems insistent that Emerson gives his readers "no other source of companionship or importance, either political or reli-gious or moral, save the importance of philosophy, of thinking itself" (2003, 27). And in this he finds Emerson akin to Wittgenstein; he offers no teaching. Similarly, although he admits that Emerson offers would-be insights, Kateb insists that "his aim is not to get us to agree with his judgments but to persuade us to take a chance and think for ourselves" (2002, xlii). My thought is that thinking for ourselves, whereby we take up the call for thinking, is something we can do while taking a chance on what Emerson offers. Said otherwise, the mood of philosophy sus-tains both the offer and embrace of ventures like "Man is a stream whose source is hidden." Now, I am not denying that Buell is right to term Emerson a sage who addresses us as an anti-mentor (2003, 292). This should be evident in what follows. What I am resisting, however, is the more general thought that one offers either authoritarian procla-mations that seek converts or pure provocations to think for oneself. On my reading, Emerson offers a good deal of intellectual companion-ship in the form of purported insights into the human and more-than-human condition. But these are essays, and offered as such. If we agree with them, therefore, this is only to say, we will share in their venture.

I have been outlining what Emerson would regard as a "manner," a way of behaving, here, a way of reading, of receiving and responding to claims and provocations. At this point I need to add that Emerson's claims are not offered on his behalf, as if some person "Emerson" were trying to convince us of something in order to have convinced us, in order to have won an argument or even a convert. Instead, they seek our attention on behalf of some matter that has compelled them. Lec-turing on Chaucer, Emerson writes: "But the wise man and much more

the true Poet quits himself and throws his spirit into whatever he con-
templates and enjoys the making it speak that it would say" (*EL1*, 272–
73). I conclude from this that the so-called propositional content of
Emerson's claims is something to which they have been driven to bear
witness, and our reception of them is lacking if we overlook this responsive pathos, one that is quite evident in Emerson's feel for lecturing: "But only then is the orator successful when he is himself agitated
& is as much a hearer as any of the assembly" (*JMN7*, 224–25).

By tuning the notion of claim with the notion of witnessing, I am
underscoring the debt that any claim owes to that which is witnessed.[12]
What goes by the name of propositional content is neither the possession
of an Emersonian claim nor something entirely produced by an Emersonian text. Rather, Emerson's claims are responses to what has been given
to them, made evident. For the time being, one could state it this way: It
isn't that an Emersonian remark lays claim to the matter at hand, but
that that matter claims it. In still other words, Emerson's claims become
such because they have been called as witnesses for some matter. Taking
Emerson personally is thus not only a matter of receiving his claims as
provocative interpersonal addresses, replete with tasks, but also one of
attending to the witness and testimony at work in those addresses, and
all in order to bring it to the shorelines of one's heart, that is, to receive it
as having the potential to claim one as well.

A passage from "New England Reformers" should help us better see
what it means to bring an Emersonian claim to the shorelines of one's
heart. Emerson writes: "As every man at heart wishes the best and not
inferior society, wishes to be convicted of his error, and to come to himself, so he wishes that the same healing should not stop in his thoughts,
but should penetrate his will or active power" (*CW3*, 162–63). This is a
remarkable line, one that sketches a landscape those readings must tra-
verse if they wish to join Emerson in pursuit of self-culture. At its close,
the line suggests that we keep the company we do (including collections
of essays, I would think) because it promises a deepened self-knowledge
whose translation into practical power provides a life more fully lived,
that is, one with richer and deeper relations. To his readers, then, Emerson seems to be saying—Isn't this why you are here, to come to your-
selves? And: Aren't these the stakes of your reading—a kind of healing,
even empowerment? Or: Aren't you here for self-culture? Now, we
needn't agree with the assertions embedded in these rhetorical ques-

tions. But in receiving them, we must nevertheless consider why we have sought their company, and that seems Emerson's deeper concern—that we engage him on terms we have thematized and affirmed, that we have a good sense for why we are here, reading, reflecting.

Consider next the opening moments of Emerson's sentence: "As every man at heart wishes . . . " In venturing a description of what goes on in our hearts, the line provokes the reader to search out his or her heart, to pose another question, less Why am I reading this? than What do I really believe? As it continues, the line also predicts what one will find in one's heart: a wish for good, ennobling company. For now, my concern is not whether this thought, one recurrent throughout Plato's early dialogues, merits our assent.[13] Rather, I want to direct your attention to how Emerson figures the heart: with a wish, a longing for what is not in our control. In Emerson's implicit instruction to consult our hearts, this figure of the wish instructs us on how to consult our hearts. Our concern should not simply be what we are willing to defend in an agon of debate. Rather, he directs his readers to those matters that have claimed them, those matters on whose behalf they might bear witness, matters they might themselves essay and possibly advance. In his claim about what lurks in our hearts, therefore, Emerson is also tuning his predictive assertion with what we could call the terms of the heart, with the wish, an inclining toward something that has claimed us and has drawn an emphatic response.

I think we are now at a point to make better sense of Emerson's claim that the best reader of Bacon needs Bacon, that one should approach Shakespeare from the Shakespeare within. Put simply, I think we find the Shakespeare within when we personally attend to the matters to which Shakespeare's claims bear witness and to the tasks those claims initiate, for then we begin to see what it would mean to think in this way, what it might mean to be Bacon, to be Shakespeare, to be the bearer of these thoughts, which is not to say their creator, but one who takes them to heart.

Let's parse this process. First, this is not simply a passive reception. Preparation is required, for "books are good only as far as a boy is ready for them" (CW6, 75). After all, to read well, one must be literate, have time, be willing and able to concentrate, be open to having one's mind changed, and so forth. And note that this is in part a matter of mood or attunement. I can recall preparing to teach a different range of authors, and what it takes to get inside them. I need to rev up for Adorno's anger, store patience for Derrida's playfulness, and embrace Emerson's enthusiasm. In Emerson's own words: "We animate what we can, and we see only what we animate. It depends on the mood of the man whether he shall see the sunset or a fine poem. There are always sunsets, and there is always genius; but only a few hours so serene that we can relish nature or criticism" (*CW3*, 30). But even then, I need to stay close to what I find on the page in order to actually find the author within. Close reading is thus an irreplaceable activity in this regard, although only in the sense of one that is attentive to whatever can be found there, as opposed to a reading, via some method, that knows it's keeping close to the text's true meaning.

In keeping close, we cannot forget, however, that a text is also a witness to what has claimed it. In attending to its ins and outs, therefore, we must keep a lookout for that to which it is a response. Such matters can be quite evident; for example, throughout his life, Emerson rejects the leveling authority of commerce. But they can also be barely perceptible; for example, in championing intuition and conversation, Emerson both instantiates the philosophy of the subject—which regards every thought as a presentation of self-consciousness—and pushes past that paradigm into a more intersubjective one that regards every thought as also presented to an interlocutor.

But given the mooded nature of these explorations, isn't one likely to find only what one puts into the reading, thus belying any language of discovery? As a reminder that we often need to read against ourselves, I find this question well placed. Just about one hundred years later, Heidegger will say that reading is a struggle against ourselves, a "*Kampf gegen uns*," in which we attempt to translate ourselves into the fundamental mood and language with which a work addresses us (1980, 22). Concretely, I take this to mean that reading is a response to questions that return us again and again to what is found there. Where and how does it say that? Or, What else might it say? Or even, How might someone else take these words? In other words, we won't succeed in finding the Bacon within unless we multiply our self against itself in the heat of our hermeneutic grappling.

Finally, we must also imagine the prospects that await us should our own active power be claimed by the thoughts we find. For example, if it is the case, for the attentive, that sublimity is always lurking ("We are all very near to sublimity," one finds in Journal G), then we must begin to imagine what it would mean to live the sublimity of a conversation, a meal, a quick trip to the store, a morning shower, and so forth (*JMN8*, 51). Of course, prospecting is a risky business. A given claim might forecast a future at odds with the manner in which the claim first arrived. For example, Emerson's trust in self-trust, in self-reliance, is empowered by the purportedly divine ground of our involuntary perceptions. But once so empowered, involuntary perceptions may turn against that ground, even venture dæmonic futures without it. Mining prospects thus may broach changes that not only follow from certain claims but also double back on them, exposing a tenuous force field where, at least initially, there had been simplicity.[14]

These efforts—preparation, close reading, ascertaining that to which the text is a response, taking up the struggle against ourselves, and prospecting—amount to conspiring with our teachers in an apprehensive and sympathetic hour. Not that our assent is required, as if sympathy necessitated agreement. Rather, the task is to take the claim to heart and apprehend it such that it *might* also claim us for its own, perhaps even in a new manner, one more Bacon than Bacon. In other words, one who conspires with a text might at some point realize, as Emerson seems to have: "We heard in their words a deeper sense than the speakers put into them, and could express ourselves in other people's phrases to finer purpose than they knew" (*CE8*, 197).

In taking Emerson personally, in receiving his responsive address on the shorelines of one's heart, in conspiring with him, one eschews a strictly historicist regard for textuality. Such readings limit a text's illocutionary reach to its peers. But if I am to receive that address on the shoreline of my heart, then I must also be implicated in what Emerson essays. And if I am implicated in those experiments, then I too am called to attend to that to which they bear witness. But is it the case that I can only share in that witness if I bind the intension of Emerson's claims to concepts extant at the time of their articulation or to then-current situations to which a thought or phrase would be a response? I doubt it. Such a position underplays what we might term a text's prospective force, the ways in which its dynamics, even while employing extant forms, bring new meanings to worn tropes. (Consider the fate of "transcendental" in Kant, "experience" in Dewey, "*Sinn*" and "*Dasein*" in Heidegger, "writing" and "text" in Derrida, and "ordinary" in

Cavell). Moreover, such emergences may only come to light, given the altered presumptions of future readers, of unknown friends. Emerson himself says: "The fame of a great man is not rigid and stony like his bust. It changes with time. It needs time to give it due perspective" (*EL1*, 145). And, a bit more to the point: "It was not possible to write the history of Shakspear until now. For it was on the translation of Shakspear into German by Lessing that 'the succeeding rapid burst of German literature was most intimately concerned.' Here certainly is an important particular in the story of that great mind yet how recent! And is this the last fact?" (*JMN7*, 116). In short, historicism seems to preclude the ways in which a text may prove untimely, or rather, timely for a later set of readers who know that the "past has a new value every moment to the advancing mind" (*JMN9*, 87).

I should stress that by embracing Emerson's address as a living provocation and challenge, I am not receiving it ahistorically. If anything, I am receiving it with a finer feel for historical occurrence than historicism provides. In "History," Emerson writes: "The student is to read history actively and not passively; to esteem his own life the text, and books the commentary. Thus compelled, the muse of history will utter oracles, as never to those who do not respect themselves" (*CW3*, 5). This insistence is well grounded for at least three reasons. First, insofar as histories are not only told but also received, some activity on the part of the recipient is required. To deny this, to skulk about one's own receptions, to conceal oneself within the repetitions that propel our lives, is tantamount to a kind of self-denial that estranges us from the dimensions of our being that enable us to be historical, what we will later explore as a matter of quotation. Moreover, such denials are hermeneutically suspect. Not only are they naively positivistic, as if historical events were ascertainable without interpretation, but they conceal the purposes prompting and orienting their interpretations, the kind of *teloi* that accompany all practices. This kind of concealment troubles me less for the biases it might introduce than for the way in which it obscures the commitments and contributions that orient and follow from a reckoning with history that is itself part of history's unfolding. In receiving Emerson's claims, therefore, we need to bring those commitments and effects within the folds of self-culture, both to better apprehend who it is we are becoming and to consider whether those ends and results square with our deepest wishes.

In refusing the limits of historicism, in treating Emerson as if he were in some sense my contemporary, my reading enters into a perplexing time signature. Let me again make my way with the help of Celan: "For the poem is not timeless. Certainly, it raises a claim to the infinite, it seeks to grasp it through time—but through, not over and above it" (1983, 186). In receiving Emerson outside the hermeneutic sensibility of historicism, I am not setting these texts or their reception outside of time—neither event is *Zeitlos* (literally, 'without time'). The texts, full of quotations, explicit and implicit, are repetitions, the paper of the centenary edition at least one hundred years old. And my readings are no less repetitions of my own inheritances, some named (e.g., Mandelstam and Cavell), some not (e.g., Habermas), and still others unknown to me even though they are in some sense more me than my reflective self-presentations. But in receiving the texts of Emerson, I am receiving an address that lays claim to the infinite, and in the following sense: it lays claim to a perpetual now in which it speaks. This is not the infinite of indefinite duration or the omnipresence of what is at once alpha and omega, beginning and end. Rather, it is a perpetually living present, one that arrives with every reception of the work. This is not to say that Emerson's texts are about infinity, although some are. Rather, they grasp the infinite in the performativity of their address, in the hand they extend to their secret addressees, in the bottle cast into the sea to which they've entrusted their fate. As he writes in a journal of 1839: "A lecture is a new literature, which leaves aside all tradition, time, place, circumstance, & addresses an assembly as (pure) mere human beings,—no more" (*JMN7*, 224). And a bit later, again reflecting on lecturing: "I am to invite men drenched in time to recover themselves and come out of time, & taste their native immortal air" (*JMN7*, 271).

Readers of the essay "History" may find my line of thinking oblique, given: "When a thought of Plato becomes a thought to me, when a truth that fired the soul of Pindar fires mine, time is no more. When I feel that we two meet in a perception, that our two souls are tinged with the same hue, and do, as it were, run into one, why should I measure degrees of latitude, why should I count Egyptian years?" (*CW2*, 15). But one mustn't receive this claim concerning the cessation of time too passively. In the same essay, some pages later, Emerson states: "No man can antedate his experience, or guess what faculty or feeling a new object shall unlock, any more than he can draw to-day the face of the person whom he shall see to-morrow for the first time" (*CW3*, 21). Read back into the earlier remark, this dependence on the temporality of experience draws the reception of Pindar's fire into a present moment, one that is always potentially novel, even shocking. Emerson's position is thus closer to Celan's than one might have thought. His move to the point beyond Egyptian years is one that moves through the time of experience and thus, strictly speaking, it is not *Zeitlos,* without time. Rather, its arrival, temporally marked, offers something other than a preserved but lifeless mummy—if I take the qualifier "Egyptian" alongside this assertion from "The Method of Nature": "The power of mind is not mortification, but life" (*CW1*, 121). What we have in an Emersonian essay is thus a matter still living, still speaking, still seeking a secret addressee.[15]

In accepting the infinite offer of Emerson's texts, one enters, perhaps, what Walter Benjamin (2003) regards as the *Jetztzeit,* the "now-time," in which a past might be citable in all its moments, in which nothing is lost and everyone has their say. But what does this mean for reading? Benjamin takes the *Jetztzeit* to interrupt the histories of the victor, histories that are told in order to vindicate the privileges and choices of those with the power to tell (and/or publish), histories that murder victims a second time. In our context (to the degree we know it), to receive the provocative offer of an Emersonian claim within the *Jetztzeit* of its address is to resist the reckoning of the victor who claims figures as his or her own, like spoils of war, or consigns them to the graves of the defeated. More concretely, this entails not insisting that Emerson is principally one kind of thinker to the exclusion of another: a proto-pragmatist, a neo-Hegelian, a Vedantist, or an American original. Likewise, it requires that we struggle against ourselves to receive all that claims our attention in his texts, everything to which his texts bear witness, all the moments marked on the list just given, as well as others gone missing.

In setting Emerson's essays and lectures within the context of Benjamin's and Celan's remarks, I am intensifying the stakes erected in William Gass's "Emerson and the Essay." Gass regards an Emersonian essay as a convocation of writers quoted and invoked for the purpose of pleasure, praise, and a confirmation of the "continuity, the contemporaneity, the reality of writing" (1982, 339, 341). A convocation of pleasure and praise, while it may evidence the enduring value of writing, nevertheless lacks the responsive pathos of the Emersonian essay. For Emerson, the reality of writing (and of reading, for that matter) is a reality of witness and provocation, and thus a reality unwilling to celebrate itself on its own behalf. Emerson's writing clamors for our attention so that we might also essay the matter at hand, whether friendship, gifts, or worship. For readers of Emerson, this means that we should care less that Emerson is citing the Koran, Goethe, or himself, and attend instead to the prospects that await one should she or he take a remark to heart. As Emerson says at the outset of *Representative Men,* "But I find him greater, when he can abolish himself and all heroes, by letting in this element of reason, irrespective of persons, this subtilizer, and irresistible upward force, into our thought, destroying individualism;—the power so great, that the potentate is nothing" (*CW4,* 14).

If one receives Emerson's texts within the now of their address, his corpus undergoes an amazing transformation—it assembles into one long, multifaceted collection of essays, lectures, journals, letters, and sermons. Or, to put it another way, reading Emerson in the now of his address is a matter of moving among one massive conversation, each remark a message in a bottle, signed RWE. Now, this is not to presume that the whole presents a unified view. Contemporaneity in no way insures congruence. In fact, the artificial unity sometimes imposed on a corpus by the author function fractures when every claim is admitted. Thus, in the now of their address, it may prove easier to critically engage Emerson's claims—for example, his occasional racial determinism—because they arrive alongside others—for example, his denial in "Experience" that temperament is in any way final or fixed (*CW3,* 32). But more importantly, essaying Emerson's corpus as a contemporaneous phenomenon allows its manifold witness and challenge to be shared and taken up, pruned and possibly deepened. As Emerson says: "The Past is for us; but the sole terms on which it can become ours are its subordination to the Present" (*CE8,* 204).

Infinite addresses, personal responses—you may be troubled. The view I am offering is not as crazy as it sounds. The address of an Emersonian text is ever present, always asking to be taken to heart, to be taken personally, and in the fullness of its responsive provocations. His efforts are thus no exception to a rule he so rightly recounts: "A good sentence, a noble verse which I meet in my reading are an epoch in my life. From month to month from year to year they remain fresh & memorable" (*JMN7,* 299). I first read "Self-Reliance" with Mary Capello, a first-year teacher of high school literature from Dickinson College, if my memory serves. Now, more than twenty-five years later, its address persists; that is, it awaits me, perpetually arriving, even though I am no longer that boy and it is no longer that text for me or anyone else, except perhaps with regard to that time-signature I have been calling "Emerson." I am still its secret addressee, and so I'll be whenever I read: "I read the other day some verses written by an eminent painter which were original and not conventional" (*CW2*, 27)

In closing this chapter, I must stress that I am not claiming that Emerson's texts offer secure, timeless truths. "Circles" puts this most forcefully: "There is not a piece of science, but its flank may be turned to-morrow; there is not any literary reputation, not the so-called eternal names of fame, that may not be revised and condemned" (*CW2*, 183) What is eternally now is not some propositional content but the now of the event of our reading, the meeting of speaker and addressee, the now in which we might find ourselves upon a stair, upon a series of steps of which we do not know the extremes. This is the now in which self-culture unfolds, conspiring with teachers, one in which we might meet ourselves and change our lives or, more likely, the now in which we prove afraid of ourselves, of one another, of fortune and death. This is the now of agitation, of an inspiration that convicts us of being something less than inspired and inspiring. In short, this is the now of crisis, a turning point, an unstable moment that no one can resolve for us.

TWO

The Genius of Nature

The only objection to spiritism is, that it is in the wrong hands. New powers are to be looked for. Who has found the limits of human intelligence?

—*JMN14*, 112

Where to next? Whereto in this task of taking Emerson personally, of self-culture sought through another's, of articulating the space of an eloquent life in the spaces his articulations throw into relief, even open? Wherever, it will be a venture that must prove itself by way of the Emerson I find, for I cannot know ahead of time the order in which I should ascend or descend the topics that await me, particularly since several staircases lead from the threshold that I have called "taking Emerson personally." Here is one from "History": "His power consists in the multitude of his affinities, in the fact that his life is intertwined with the whole chain of organic and inorganic being" (*CW2*, 20). The thought in an earlier form is even sterner:

> Nothing but God is self-dependent. Every being in nature has its existence so connected with other beings that if set apart from them it would instantly perish. An ear of corn is very far from being a simple nature; it is a composite one; it is a cord of many strands which light, heat, water, air, carbon, azote compose. Is a man less complex? On the contrary.
>
> Man is powerful only by the multitude of his affinities, or because his life is intertwined with the whole chain of organic and inorganic being. (*EL2*, 17)[1]

Given our concerns, this is a remarkable thought: the self of self-culture is not just me, or even solely mine, but it is intertwined with others, even with inorganic life. How then am I to cultivate a life that eloquently manifests my character? What all is being cultivated? And who or what is doing the cultivation? The questions become even thornier when we find in the same course of lectures, *The Philosophy of History*: "Always life is to be administered by the new and fresh action of the soul" (*EL2*, 166). How does one think a fresh action of the soul in terms of multiple affinities?

The questions above will occupy us for some time. Before responding by way of Emerson's texts, let me underscore that what follows, in how and what it considers, interprets in order to inherit. It thus asks you to take stock not only of my interpretation but also of what it portends for our pursuits of lives that say well who we take ourselves to be.

Let us begin with this notion of the soul's "action." Consider again a line from "The Over-Soul": "Man is a stream whose source is hidden. Our being is descending into us from we know not where" (*CW2*, 159). On the one hand, this is a phenomenological claim about the ways in which our being is manifest to us. Whether we consider thoughts, desires, or sallies of the imagination, in each instance, reflection undergoes these events rather than producing them. The sun sets on the brick façade of an art museum, and I find it beautiful. I'm perplexed by how best to explain to a student why graduate school isn't an appropriate choice for him, and the words suddenly come to me. I'm unsure whether to repair a fractured love affair, and quite suddenly, I know I'd be a fool if I didn't. I can't for the life of me fathom what the "earth" means in Heidegger's "Origin of the Work of Art," and then I get it and am stunned. From the vantage point of reflective inquiry, therefore, our source is hidden, and phenomena like thoughts and desires are what I would term "events" rather than the accomplishments of a discernable agent. To use a Heideggerian idiom, the soul's action is "thrown" into conditions that envelop, delimit, and enable the project of self-culture. "I conceive of a man as always spoken to from behind and unable to turn his head and see the speaker," to return to Emerson. "In all the millions who have heard the voice, none ever saw the face" (*CW1*, 129).

In order to develop this claim regarding the throwness of our condition, let's focus on a passage from "Self-Reliance" (paragraph 21) and explore the "stream" of our being in terms of four currents: involuntary perceptions or intuition, quotations, moods, and temperament. As we'll see, together these currents amount to what Emerson regards as the "essence of genius, of virtue, and of life," and they do a fine job at laying out one side of the scene in which self-culture commences (*CW2*, 37).

Many of the first twenty paragraphs of "Self-Reliance" charge us with and praise the task of doing our own work. From paragraphs 21 to 26, however, the incalculable mechanics of the soul's fresh action are invoked, what Emerson terms "involuntary perceptions" as well as "Spontaneity or Instinct," adding: "We denote this primary wisdom as Intuition, whilst all later teachings are tuitions" (*CW2*, 37).[2]

In writing of "perceptions," Emerson has in mind an awareness of various subject matters such as the viciousness of commerce, the boorishness of zealots, or the trustworthiness of a friend. As instances of primary wisdom, these perceptions open and mark the vanguard of self-culture, offering the touchstones from which one essays to be. Consider a journal entry from November 1822. Reflecting on an earlier entry that reviewed several arguments on behalf of slavery, Emerson asserts:

> To establish by whatever specious argumentation the perfect expediency of the worst institution on earth is *prima facie* an assault upon Reason and Common sense. No ingenious sophistry can ever reconcile the unperverted mind to the pardon of *Slavery*, nothing but tremendous familiarity, and the bias of private *interest*. Under the influence of better arguments than can be offered in support of Slavery, we should sustain our tranquility by the confidence that no surrender of our opinion is ever demanded and that we are only required to discover the lurking fallacy which the disputant acknowledges to exist. (*JMN2*, 57–58)

I have chosen this passage because it offers a thought, something like "slavery is an abomination," that reflection seemingly cannot undermine.[3] It thus functions for Emerson as a "primary wisdom" to which later reflections, here arguments regarding slavery, are matters of "tuition," that is, matters of elaboration and instruction rather than discovery. Presuming this identification, perceptions like these, though intuitions, are far from vague presentiments or hunches. Instead, they have the form and force of conclusions, of insights that settle disputes. I would thus suggest that involuntary perceptions arrive as completed judgments, asserting some matter as settled.

I don't want the example to say too much, however. I am not claiming that all involuntary perceptions are moral judgments. They may equally involve predictions, for example: "But do your work and I shall know you" (*CW2*, 32). Or they may involve social-theoretical issues, for example: "Society is a wave. The wave moves onward, but the water of which it is composed does not" (*CW2*, 49). Or they may provide practical maxims: "Whoso would be a man must be a non-conformist" (*CW2*, 29). They can even concern one's self, for example, when one realizes that one has something like a vocation. Involuntary perceptions are thus not limited to certain kinds of judgments. Rather, they can concern any number of affairs—the rightness of an action, the principles or forces organizing an event, the nature of someone's character, and so forth. In each case, however, there is that which is perceived, and thus we can conclude, I think, that involuntary perceptions have an intentional structure, or, to use James's and Dewey's language instead of Husserl's, involuntary perceptions are double-barreled, involving a perceiving and a perceived.[4]

In terming these perceptions "involuntary," Emerson is underscoring the prereflective way in which what is intuited is manifest. What Emerson says of the artist in Journal U, 1844, also applies here: "But I speak of instincts. I did not make the desires or know anything about them: I went to the public assembly, put myself in the conditions, & instantly feel this new craving,—I hear the voice, I see the beckoning of the Ghost. To me it is vegetation, the pullation & universal budding of the plant of man" (*JMN9*, 71). The passivity of reflection in the face of involuntary perceptions is underscored by Emerson's use of "intuition," an event to be contrasted with the explicit application of a concept like "mammal" to a particular case like "platypus." In these latter instances, I locate the rules governing the use of the concept—has hair and births live young—and decide what they direct in this particular case. With involuntary perceptions, however, I less arrive at a conclusion than am struck by one: "Slavery is an abomination." Or "Clay is a true friend." As Emerson suggests in "The School": "But a thought has its own proper motion which it communicates to me, not borrows of me, and on its winged back I override and overlook the world" (*EL3*, 43).

The passage from Emerson's Journal U suggests something else concerning involuntary perceptions. Not only are they logically intentional, they are responsive as well—"I went to the public assembly, put myself in the conditions, & instantly feel this new craving." The primary wisdom upon which we essay to be is thus not categorically distinct from what Emerson terms our affinities, and thus self-culture takes its leave from relations with the world. So it is not the case that self-culture simply prepares one for worldly engagements. Rather, worldly engagements are already percolating within the explosive core of self-culture.

At this point it is worth adding that Emerson also holds the more general view that self-reflection is always parasitic on experiences it does not produce out of itself: "That which each can do best [or do at all—JTL], none but his Maker can teach him. No man knows yet what it is, nor can, till that person has exhibited it" (CW2, 47). In other words, like Kant and later Fichte, Emerson denies that we have direct, intuitive access to our own nature. Rather, we encounter ourselves in our encounters with what we are not. Self-culture is thus thoroughly dependent on affinities, for our affinities are keys to ourselves. In "The American Scholar," Emerson writes: "So much of nature as he is ignorant of, so much of his own mind does he not yet possess. And, in fine, the ancient precept 'know thyself,' and the modern precept, 'study nature,' become at last one maxim" (CW1, 55). I take this as a worthy maxim for self-culture. In place of would-be intellectual intuitions, we should attend to the kind of character we show in our engagements and collisions. In other words, we should seek our sense of whom we would cultivate through our relations. Or, more strongly, the suggestion is that we should pursue relations, for therein we will experience ourselves in new, perhaps startling ways. "Whatever he does," Emerson proposes in *Human Culture*, "or whatever befalls him, opens another chamber in his soul,—that is, he has got a new feeling, a new thought, a new organ" (EL2, 200).

Say I take up rock climbing (which I have, thanks to Bret, but only once, although Peter has tempted me to try again). The activity awakens me, among other things, to the weakness of my hands, the inflexibility of my hips and hamstrings, my willingness to take physical risks, my struggle to work through failure, and my trust in others to hold fast the rope should I fall, among other things. Note also that all of these discoveries are not limited to this one event. Instead, once thought, they continue on with me, that is, they expand who I am. As Emerson says of the varieties of human conduct, which he terms "manners": "They are instantly affected by whatever affects them" (EL2, 130).

In highlighting the opportunities for self-discovery and growth that novel interactions offer us, I am not suggesting that Emersonian self-culture is based on a study of nature instead of the rush of involuntary perception. Recall that our primary wisdom is responsive. New relations thus may offer new involuntary perceptions. A passage from "The American Scholar" offers this very thought: "The world,—this shadow of the soul, or *other me,* lies wide round. Its attractions are the keys which unlock my thoughts, and make me acquainted with myself. I run eagerly into this resounding tumult" (*CW1,* 59). Emerson's provocation to take up thoughtfully and expansively our manifold relations is thus a provocation to risk the arrival of new involuntary perceptions rather than a suggestion to replace them with some other source of insight.

Thus far I have suggested that involuntary perceptions involve the prereflective and responsive apprehension of what seem to be unlimited ranges of possible subject matters. I would now add that involuntary perceptions appear to be epistemically charged, and inextricably so. In the third lecture from the series, *Mind and Manners of the 19th Century,* Emerson writes of instinctive thought: "It is not in our will. That is the quality of it, that, it commands, and is not commanded" (*LL1,* 181). And a bit earlier in the lecture, one finds: "Ask what Instinct declares, and we have little to say; he is no newsmonger, no disputant, no talker" (*LL1,* 175).

"Slavery is an abomination!" "Clay is a true friend." "I should be a teacher." Such perceptions arrive as if their validity were secure. This is not to say that reflection is certain of their validity. Rather, the validity one apprehends is part of the intuition, not a concept added to it by a later judgment. To say it with greater felicity, in an involuntary perception, reflection is overwhelmed by the perception it undergoes. One can find no distance from which to assess what is disclosed therein. As Emerson says in the Introductory to lectures on *English Literature:* "There are no walls like the invisible ones of an idea. Against these no purpose can prosper or so much as be formed. Rebellion against the thought which rules me is an absurdity. For I cannot separate between me and it" (*EL1,* 218). In the moment that I realize that Clay is a true friend, my awareness of the intuition and the intuition are one, and I am compelled to receive him as such.

Because involuntary perceptions deny me any reflective distance from their occurrence, they are, in a phenomenological sense, indubitable. They must be given as such, however; that is, no reflective judgment can ever confer that quality upon them. As Emerson says later in the lectures on *English Literature,* culling a line from his Italian journal: "For a good sentence is not merely a proposition grammatically stated, but one which contains in itself its own apology, or the reason why it was said. A proposition set down in words is not therefore affirmed. It must affirm itself or no propriety and no vehemence of language will give it evidence" (*EL1,* 349; *JMN4,* 106).

Now, it may seem that I have imported too much into Emerson's notion of an involuntary perception. Perhaps, but then again, I am also defending the view and thus cannot help but amplify it. That said, if involuntary perceptions provide primary wisdom, then as "wisdom," they must have the force of validity in one form or another. If not, if their claim to validity is only added after the fact, then they cannot stand as an instance of primary wisdom but only as a candidate for wisdom, much as a hypothesis is only a candidate for knowledge. Emerson is quite clear, however, that reflection plays cart to the horse. "Always our thinking is an observing," he writes. "Into us flows the stream evermore of thought from we know not whence. We do not determine what we will think" (*EL2,* 250). On his view, even when we come to rethink matters, to lean toward a new course, we remain dupes of new involuntary perceptions. "We must always be prisoners of Ideas which we are just beginning to apprehend; when by and by we understand them and see how we were guided and led we are already following another clue, or tyrannized over by another Ruling Thought, which we can no more see around" (*EL2,* 170).[5]

Appreciating the epistemically charged nature of involuntary perceptions, that they contain their own apology, allows us to make some sense of Emerson's assertion that they shine forth as stars "without calculable elements" (*CW2,* 37). My claim has been that involuntary perceptions are akin to flashes of insight, judgments that, at birth, are articulate and self-legitimating. Phenomenologically speaking, involuntary perceptions arrive altogether, that is, they do not involve rulebound applications of concepts to subject matters. In fact, in these instances apperception seems to fold into perception and be swept away by it. In their givenness, then, involuntary perceptions are "without calculable elements."

But why is it that they mark the "last fact behind which analysis cannot go"? And is he right to also insist: "If we ask whence this comes, if we seek to pry into the soul that causes, all philosophy is at fault" (*CW2*, 37)? I do not understand Emerson to be claiming that under no conditions can one analyze involuntary perceptions. The phrase itself combines two terms, after all. Moreover, its logical structure (perceiver and perceived) as well as the activity/passivity distinction implicit in "involuntary" leads us to look for at least three logically discrete moments: the perceiver, the perception, and the perceived. But in proceeding in this way, one risks losing the integrity of involuntary perceptions as they occur. Not only do they reach reflection fully clad, their claim to validity part of their meaning, but they also take reflection into their care, even their tuition, thereby eliding any fundamental distinction between perceiver and perception.

Look carefully (with added emphases) at what Emerson says. "If we ask whence this comes, *if we seek to pry into the soul that causes,* all philosophy is at fault." I think that "prying" here marks an imposition of an order of reflection on those aspects of our lives on which reflection cannot help but remain dependent. Just as, in its own fashion, grass unfolds in blades, our life unfolds, albeit not exclusively, in involuntary perceptions, in actions of the soul to recall other words. But we lose that life and that action if we set the perceiver aside from the perceiving, just as we lose the grass if we clip every blade and stare intently at the roots.[6]

Here is another, more telling example. In instructing us not to "pry into the soul that causes," Emerson is also beginning to delimit what we could call, after Kant, a more felicitous use of the concept of causality. To put it another way, "causality" may itself pry where it shouldn't. Emerson's efforts to this end are perhaps most apparent in the punning favor he shows for the term "casual." "We thrive by casualties," he writes in "Experience." "Our chief experiences are casual" (*CW3*, 39). And later in "Nominalist and Realist," he claims that nature "punishes abstractionists, and will only forgive an induction that is rare and casual" (*CW3*, 139). While the term "casualty" assumes added significance in "Experience," for now, I want to focus on what I take to be an argumentative strategy that is critical in spirit. When we turn back into the ground of our own causal judgments, circumspect, inductive generalizations about their origins are not forthcoming. Instead, we find the "rare" (which I take to name the exceptional as opposed to the typical), and the "casual" (which I take to name what "comes to pass without design and without being foreseen," to paraphrase Webster's 1828). In other words, our own generalizations—for example, objects of class A are occasioned by the interaction of objects from class B and C—are driven by what is both exceptional, hence not rigorously classifiable, and unpredictable, hence never the simple result of antecedent conditions. If so, philosophy is at fault when it brings the figure of causality into the heart of what we have been calling, following Emerson, involuntary perception; that phenomenon requires a different mode of apprehension, or better still, reception.

"Now wait," you might say, "Emerson nevertheless speaks of 'the soul that causes,' not the soul that does something other than causes." Fair enough, he does; and thus I think the delimitation is more about felicity than the avoidance of a category mistake. Emerson, unlike Kant, would not replace a physiology of the understanding with a transcendental deduction of its categories, and not just because the latter conforms to established tablature. Rather, in orienting oneself toward a phenomenon by way of causality, and now I simply repeat a point I made earlier regarding historicism, one keeps it at arm's length and thus resists its claim on us—or rather, subjects that claim to terms that might very well not prove responsive to what is dawning on us. With regard to the figure of causality, therefore, the fault of philosophy lies less with a descriptive or predictive miscue than in what amounts to a kind of pragmatics of self-and-other-world-relations. And this why I've claimed that involuntary perceptions require a different mode of apprehension, or better still, reception.

Given their prereflective sources, their responsive nature, and the way in which they manhandle reflection in their arrival, involuntary perceptions are best marked as impersonal at the point of genesis; that is, they should not be regarded as the personal achievements of solitary subjects. And yet they are thoroughly personal in that no one can undergo an involuntary perception for another. In its givenness, "Slavery is an abomination!" overruns the reflection of particular persons, and so too does "Clay is a true friend." Involuntary perceptions thus mark a kind of personal impersonal at the heart of self-culture, for if I essay to be on their bases, that which stands at the center of my self-culture isn't mine, strictly speaking. "What has my will done to make me that I am?" Emerson asks those attending his *Human Life* lectures. "Nothing," he answers. "I have been floated into this thought, this hour, this connexion of events, by might and mind sublime" (*EL3*, 40).

At this point, we have a sense for one lengthy side of Emersonian self-culture. Rather than entailing willful self-legislation, the Emersonian life takes up the flurries of involuntary perception and cultivates a life around what they disclose. "Slavery is an abomination!" not only orients me toward slavery per se but also toward those points where it is manifest—in the cotton shirts one can wear, or the sugar one might buy. Similarly, if it strikes me, convincingly, that "whoso would be a man must be a non-conformist," my life should manifest a kind of nonconformity, and at each point—in my friendships, my dress, even in my relation to slavery.

In attending to our involuntary perceptions, we should be careful not to ignore the quotations that Emerson regards as another aspect of our condition. Nor should we categorically distinguish the former from the latter. As we'll see, the two are difficult to distinguish, and to the degree that involuntary perceptions are, to varying degrees, actually matters of original quotation. But first, consider Emerson's conception of *quotation:*

> Man is made;—the creature who seems a refinement on the form of all who went before him, and made perfect in the image of the Maker by the gift of moral nature; but his limbs are only a more exquisite organization,—say rather—the finish of the fundamental forms that have been already sweeping the sea and creeping in the mud; the brother of his hand is even now cleaving the Arctic Sea in the fin of a whale. (*EL1*, 32)

> Old and New set their seal to everything in Nature. The Past makes the warp, the Present makes the woof in every web.... All things wear a luster which is the gift of the Present; a tarnish which they owe to time. (*EL2*, 158)

> All our literature is a quotation, our life a custom or imitation, and our body is borrowed like a beggar's dinner from a hundred charities. (*JMN9*, 126)

> But the inventor only knows how to borrow.... Every book is a quotation; and every house is a quotation out of all forests and mines and stone-quarries; and every man is a quotation from all his ancestors. (*CW4*, 24)

All minds quote. Old and new make the warp and woof of every moment. There is no thread that is not a twist of these two strands. By
necessity, by proclivity, and by delight, we all quote. We quote not
only books and proverbs, but arts, sciences, religion, customs and
laws; nay, we quote temples and houses, tables and chairs by imitation. (*CE8*, 178–79)

It is inevitable that you are indebted to the past. You are fed and
formed by it. The old forest is decomposed for the composition of the
new forest. . . . So it is in thought." (*CE8*, 200)[7]

Emerson's point is that a human life is never *sui generis,* but follows the lead of its inheritance, whether in: (a) the language we speak
(which Emerson terms a "poetry that no man wrote," and a "city to the
building of which every human being brought a stone"); (b) the traits
we manifest; (c) the perceptions we register; or (d) the potentialities
our labor draws out of our environment (*CE8*, 193, 199). Alongside involuntary perceptions, one could thus add quotation as an action of
the soul that underlies and informs our condition.

Given the linguistic cast of a trope like "quotation," it is important
to stress that the term extends well beyond the literal senses of quoting,
referring, and citing. In "The Poet," Emerson writes: "Things admit of
being used as symbols, because nature is a symbol, in the whole, and in
every part. Every line we draw in the sand has expression; and there is
no body without spirit or genius" (*CW3*, 8). I take this to mean something very particular. Nature is symbolic because, in a Spinozistic
sense, it expresses those forces that produce the phenomenon in question. This is why Emerson is so adamant that there is nothing mean in
nature. A tree tells a tale of sunlight, soil chemistry, rainfall, a deer's
teeth, or the claws of a puma, and so on to the depth and degree of our
literacy. Similarly, our bodies, "borrowed like a beggar's dinner from a
hundred charities," tell tales of gravitational fields, atmospheric composition, climates, the chances of natural selection—or, more personally, of falls, collisions, nutritional choices, social histories of sexuality,
and so forth. Quotation is thus an event of expression, one wherein the
relations girding us appear in and through us.

Recall, if you please, my brief account of the activity of rock climbing and how I am manifest there, weak of hand, trusting, and so on. At
this point, we should add that the activity that sparks these realizations

is not self-activating. The rock and other enabling forces—and this includes the air, the earth, the sun, my companions, the food I ate, the events that marked the rock face with pockets and ledges—afford me these discoveries and are present therein, if only obliquely at first. In our quotations, a kind of depth thus opens, even a sublime depth insofar as the number of relations to which we are bound runs beyond the reach of available concepts as well the figurative power of the imagination. In Journal E, Emerson states: "In all my lectures, I have taught the infinity of the private man" (*JMN7*, 342). To my ear, this doesn't testify to the solitary depths of subjectivity, but to the lines of exteriority running through our very interiority. That is, given what we've seen regarding quotation, the infinity of the private man is a matter of infinite affinities, some evident, most not.

Alongside involuntary perceptions, quotation names, I think, a figure of our condition, one that directs us toward the breadth and depth of our inheritances, what we have been thinking in terms of "affinities," taking this word from Emerson's "History," though less in the sense of a liking or sympathy than in the sense of a tendency among certain chemicals to compound with one another, or, drawing on another sense of the term, to marry, to join in a shared life. In these affinities, our being bears witness to those beings or even forces that Emerson in *Nature* terms "NOT-ME," forces that are not simply modes of my being even as they are intertwined with it. Note that "affinity" in part speaks of this trace of alterity in our being. Its Latin root, *affinis,* means not only 'relation by marriage,' but 'bordering upon,' thus underscoring the difference that persists in the bond. I find this difference significant, not only because it indicates lines of relation and dependency in the projects of self-culture but also because it preserves the thought of our singularity within our affinities. In my terms, "affinity" preserves the space of the "personal." Like involuntary perceptions, quotation has a personal-impersonal quality to it. Nothing else, no one else, can quote for me, can replay and express those facets of the world that course through my being. Thus, while they are not "mine" at their point of genesis, quotations are nevertheless mine in their point of intersection with me, thereby offering me the beginnings of a personal life.

Another valence moves within Emerson's sense of "affinity," although not etymologically. In "Culture," Emerson announces: "You cannot have one well-bred man without a whole society of such" (*CW6,*

79). While this suggests many things, including a kind of sociality in the labor of self-culture, for now I want to underscore that by tying our powers to affinities, Emerson is marking us as dependent beings, to adopt the kind of language favored by feminist theorists like Eva Kittay.[8] A passage from Journal G explicates this powerfully.

> I have a tree which produces these golden delicious cones called Bartlett pears. . . . The pear tree is certainly a fine genius but . . . it will very easily languish & bear nothing, if I starve it, give it no southern exposure, & no protecting neighborhood of other trees. How differs it with the tree planter? He too may have a rare constructive power to make poems or characters, or nations perchance but though his power be new & unique if he be starved of his needful influences, if he have no love, no book, no critic, no external call, no need or market for that faculty of his, then he may sleep through dwarfish years and die at last without fruit. (*JMN8*, 9)

And so too this insistence from *The Present Age* lectures:

> Is his nurture less compound? Who has not,—what has not contributed something to make him that he is? Art, science, institutions, black men, white men, vices, virtues, of all people; the church; the prison; the shop; poets; nature; joy; and fear; all help, all teach him. Every fairy, and every imp have brought a gift. (*EL3*, 251–52)

I stress this because the self of self-culture neither stands nor proceeds alone, but only with the support of others. Moreover, it intensifies the observation that self-culture should look to our relations in order to find ourselves coming and going. Consider the famous line from "Self-Reliance" where Emerson offers the "nonchalance of boys who are sure of a dinner" as the "healthy attitude of human nature" (*CW2*, 29). Given the dependency of our condition, it is not incidental that they are sure of their dinner. Without that security, they would be forced to beg from those they now regard with little deference, thus rendering eloquent only their obsequiousness. Self-culture is thus as much a material practice as it is an intellectual one, and should we wish our lives to be eloquent, we must begin to wonder what would render those webs of relation eloquent in the many ways in which we quote them.

In setting quotation alongside involuntary perceptions in the crucible of our condition, I don't want to overly distinguish them. In other words, involuntary perceptions themselves entail quotation. First, like all events, they "quote" or express that to which they are responses and all that enables them. "We are to each other results," Emerson observes. "As your perception or sensibility is exalted, you see the genesis of my action, & of my thought, you see me in my debt & fountains, & to your eye instead of a little pond of the water of life, I am a rivulet fed by mills from every plain & height in nature & antiquity & deriving a remote origin from the foundation of all things" (*JMN8*, 26). Second, involuntary perceptions can also involve repetitions of previous thoughts. When reading, one is often struck by the utter rightness of what one reads, that is, in the words of Journal U: "The writer goes my way & better mounted than I . . . and so we proceed as directed, seeking in their wake a tuition that does them justice" (*JMN9*, 82). In other words, self-culture can make use of inherited texts and thoughts without fear of self-effacement, presuming, of course, that we quote well.

Let me provide an example, drawing tuition from Emerson's thought of the ubiquity of quotation in our lives. Insofar as we are creatures of relation, insofar as that insight assumes the role of a primary wisdom, learning about ourselves requires that we learn about ourselves in relation. This deepens, I think, the line from "The American Scholar" cited earlier. "So much of nature as he is ignorant of, so much of his own mind does he not yet possess. And, in fine, the ancient precept 'know thyself,' and the modern precept, 'study nature,' become at last one maxim" (CW1, 55). The point is not just that the rest of the world helps us discover ourselves and transforms the self that we are discovering, but also that the self at stake in the inquiry is thoroughly bound to the world it would know, and thus to explore nature is to explore webs of relation to which we belong and on which we are dependent. Setting relation at the heart of self-culture, I thus find myself agreeing with Emerson's assertion in his Introductory to the lectures on *Human Culture:* "He exists and the world exists in a new relation of subject and object, neither of which is valid alone, but only in their marriage have a creative life" (*EL2*, 215).

Permit me another point of tuition. Finding ourselves always already in relation further requires that we come to think of the self we would cultivate as a relational self, and that which we would cultivate as relations rather than as traits or characteristics of isolated selves. My hairstyle is thus not only a matter of my hair and my desire to appear in certain ways, but as an object of self-culture, it entails all those relations that go into the style I adopt. Likewise, my domestic space is not just domestic, but all of what supports it. Self-culture is thus a matter of affinities in its inception and in its products, although it will take us until the end of the book to mine the tuition contained in this thought.

One more conclusion from Emerson's striking thought of quotation. The relations it introduces into the heart of our being mark not only a path for self-culture but an end as well. As we are relational beings, that life which does justice to our being should manifest our place in these relations. That is, an eloquent life should speak like the poet "who re-attaches things to nature or the Whole" (CW3, 11). This is a powerful thought, for it suggests that self-culture is less an inward journey than a journey along the many axes through which we come to ourselves and are constituted. I am thus led to agree with this strong, if orientalist assertion in *Society and Solitude:* "Do you think any rhetoric or any romance would get your ear from the wise gypsy who could tell straight on the real fortunes of the man; who could reconcile your moral character and your natural history; who could explain your misfortunes, your fevers, your debts, your temperament, your habits of thought; your tastes, and, in every explanation, not sever you from the whole, but unite you to it?" (CE7, 107–108). Not that we know what such a disclosure would entail, concretely. But at this point in our reflections, it does seem clear that self-culture is a practice bent on finding ways of cultivating a life attuned to the connections often sundered in our experience, reflection, and intellectual traditions.

We are investigating the cellar of Emersonian self-culture, its bases, shifting and slippery as they are; and we have begun with a particular action of the soul, what Emerson terms involuntary perceptions, thoughts impersonal in genesis and wholly personal in arrival that overrun reflection and provide us with touchstones from which we might essay to be. "Slavery is an abomination." "'For my perception is as much a fact as the sun." "Our best thought came from others." We have also seen how this action bears the impress of untold affinities with nature. On the one hand, our relations with the world ignite involuntary perceptions. An open sky filled with stars whose light has traveled toward us for stretches that exceed the life of humanity might impress upon us the nearly incalculable minuteness of our perspective. Or a large city, strewn with trash and teeming with people oblivious to suffering, might occasion the thought, *pace* Aristotle, that while we do delight in knowledge, we only seek it in limited doses and occasionally turn a deaf ear to the clamor of troublesome thoughts.

On the other hand, involuntary perceptions can involve intimate repetitions of extant thoughts that profoundly open us to ourselves—say Plato, Plotinus, and de Stael. Or, less directly—and this is true not only of involuntary perceptions but the whole of our being—human life unfolds as a witness to those other lives with which it's bound. Here and now, addressing you, who could count the enabling events, past and present, that have brought us together? Who could attend to and say all that we here express? Thought in terms of all that we express, human beings are multifaceted significations, announcing at once their own being as well as the being of that which sparked or enabled the expression she or he is, and in perpetuity, all things being equal. And one bent on Emersonian self-culture needs to learn to read along such lines, for they offer self-culture roads into the nexus of relations that she or he would render eloquent. But before we probe deeper into the activities that further Emersonian self-culture, we need to return to the actions of the soul that delimit the reach and scope of those activities, for we have yet to do justice to all that we face when take up the task of an eloquent life.

"Life is a train of moods like a string of beads," Emerson asserts in "Experience," "and, as we pass through them, they prove to be many-colored lenses which paint the world their own hue, and each shows only what lies in its focus" (CW3, 30). Like Cavell, I take *mood* to name temporary sensibilities—as opposed to discursive judgments—that illumine facets of self and world (Cavell 2003). On cool, clear days, optimism usually rules me, and I see possibilities for growth, even enrichment in the least likely encounters—a chat on a bus, committee meetings, some old paper I had set aside in the hope of never finding again. But drunk and melancholy at 3 a.m., I find everything en route to failure—my current essay, the plight of higher education, the eco-systemic health of the planet. Because they are disclosive, one can regard the train of moods that Emerson invokes as perceptual and practical forces. They over-determine not only how we perceive but also how we engage the world. Optimistic, I try to repair a relationship bruised by disagreement and oversight. Melancholy, I add another person to the list of friends once known.

The flow of mood not only washes over general situations, however, but also those objects that we encounter: "The secret of the illusoriness is in the necessity of a succession of moods or objects," we are informed (*CW3*, 32). Put yourself in a forest and move about it, keyed by various moods, attending to what might appear there and then. In an aesthetic mood, one receptive to aesthesis and able to tarry there, one can find an abundance of textures and sounds amid depths of field and color, and come to regard one's ordinary experiences as dull, stunted, even drowsy. Led by the mood, one might employ polarized lenses in order to neutralize the glare that bleaches the spectrum of our light. That is, the mood, as a perceptual and practical power, not only gives us a range for an object but also leads us to engage the object along that range. Shift now to an inquisitive mood, one that seeks order in a house, however temporary. One focuses on a particular species, or, binoculars in hand, the feathers of different birds. Or, test tubes along for the ride, one analyzes the soil to better understand variations in the flora. In an inquisitive mood, one pushes past the line at which an aesthetic mood halts and seeks the causes of what has been brought under the reign of various concepts. And one might, fixed upon that causal web, see oneself as a potential bull in a china shop and attend all the more to what one's presence sets in motion. Try one more mood, perhaps the acquisitive one that Emerson (rightly) feared would win the soul of his country. Here a forest falls into acreage containing a timber yard in training, and the whole quickly dissolves into capital that might feed one's greed or demonstrate one's power. As Emerson says, reflecting upon New England—and I take him to be invoking a mood in its perceptual and practical power—"Commerce has no reverence" (*LL1*, 37).

Life is always mooded, a "train of moods" according to Emerson, a thought with which Heidegger could find common ground. We never find ourselves without some general sensibility like a keen interest, wonder, boredom, hunger, greed, melancholy. And this holds as well for epistemic states; that is, Emerson runs counter to the notion that knowledge takes place only when we banish the affects. On his view, moods focus, bringing some facet of the world to the fore, recessing some other facet. And so too in the labors of self-culture. Moods are part of every action of the soul, even involuntary perceptions. In "Experience," Emerson asks, rhetorically: "Who cares what sensibility or discrimination a man has at some time shown, if he falls asleep in his chair? or if he laugh and giggle? or of he apologize?" (*CW3*, 30). In a silly mood, we often cannot take ourselves seriously, and thus the passion with which we denounce the leveling power of global commerce strikes us as silly, even if the involuntary perception, "unbridled capital sets things in the saddle" is rattling about our heads. Or, if we are in an apologetic mood, unsure that our intuitions merit anyone's respect, we might hide from the insistence with which we think that "there is imitation, model, and suggestion, to the very archangels, if we knew their history" (*CE8*, 180). Or, and let this be the last example, one might cling to a "circular wave of circumstance,—as for instance, an empire, rules of an art, a local usage, a religious rite" in order to "hem in life" in its infinite affinities, that is, to refuse the expansion that an involuntary perception suggests, to use terms from "Circles" (*CW2*, 181).

Given the force of moods in our condition, self-culture needs to engage them profitably, riding their disclosive powers, resisting their distracting forces, and learning how to finger their blind spots. But that is not all, for moods also are often at odds with one another. "Our moods do not believe in each other," Emerson writes in "Circles" (*CW2*, 182). And, as he exclaims in "Nominalist and Realist," "If we could have any security against moods!" adding at the close of the paragraph: "I am always insincere, as always knowing there are other moods" (*CW3*, 144 and 145). Making use of them is thus something of a puzzle, since it seems more the case that they make use of us, or rather, to be more precise, that reflection is parasitic upon them.

Thus far, we have been thinking of moods in a functional manner, naming them by way of their force and role in self-culture. We've seen that they are sensibilities that carry us into different worldly relations and establish general situations (recall the examples of optimism and melancholy) out of which particular objects of experience are given, including quotations and involuntary perceptions. This is not to say, however, that all moods carry equal power across a given life. "It is not enough to say that we are bundles of moods, for we rank our mental states. The gradation is exquisite. We are not a bundle but a house" (*JMN9*, 70). One may have moments of generosity but not be a generous person, just as one may occasionally notice aesthetic phenomena, but rarely, and without any sustained feel for them. On my reading, at stake here is the difference between mood and temperament, the latter being the "iron wire on which the beads [i.e., moods] are strung" (*CW3*, 30). As Emerson says at greater length: "In the moment, it seems impulse; in the year, in the lifetime, it turns out to be a certain uniform tune which the revolving barrel of the music box must play" (*CW3*, 31). As a phenomenon of recurring moods (and thus as a matter that is functionally similar to mood), temperament names less a passing sensibility than a character trait, though I would rather use the language of capacity, given that temperament is a disposition to perceive and engage the world along certain lines, not something like eye or hair color.

Imagine a range of philosophical temperaments. On the one hand, I've met analytic and synthetic thinkers. The former have a nose for semantic and syntactic ambiguities and the refined aspects of logical entailment; while the latter sniff out an author, era, or tradition's broader, often understated substantive commitments. On another hand, there are those thinkers who undermine positions and those who meliorate them. The former look for where and how a position fails, and they are adept at locating and loosening hinges. The latter, when a wheel squeaks, prefer to meditate on how one might right it so that it can continue on.[9] With a third hand, we also could mark those of a metaphysical versus a moral bent. For some, the question of how things hang together, what Emerson regards as the matter of "our place in nature," is the most agreeable and stimulating arena of philosophical concern; whereas for others, the fate of those lives lived among and through relation fires the mind.

Because it orients our thought and action in the world, temperament, like mood, names a perceptual and practical power. But it is an enduring one, so I think we can regard temperament as coextensive with what Emerson also terms "talent," a "certain constitutional apparatus determining him on some one activity which is easy and delightful to him" (*LL2*, 202).[10] As such, it anchors a central facet of our condition, keying us, marking us as characteristically attuned to and concerned with a certain range of phenomena. But this is not to say that our temperament exhausts our condition. Emerson is adamant that involuntary perceptions can outstrip temperament:

> True growth is spontaneous in every step. The mind that grows could not predict the times, the means, the mode of that spontaneity. God comes in by a private door into every individual: thoughts enter by passages which the individual never left open. (*EL2*, 250)

> For when I see the doors by which God entereth into the mind and that there is no sop nor fop nor ruffian, nor pedant, into whom

thoughts do not enter by passages which the individual never left open, I can expect any revolution in character. (*EL3*, 35)

> On its own level, or in view of nature, temperament is final. . . . But it is impossible that the creative power should exclude itself. Into every intelligence there is a door which is never closed, through which the creator passes. (*CW3*, 32)

These passages are remarkable for several reasons, beginning with the figure of the door, that which vanishes as it closes behind us, to recall the opening passage of "Experience." For now, though, I only note how they recast the conditions of and for self-culture. On Emerson's terms, we are beings that are always mooded, and with regard to one or two moods, constitutionally so. Moods and temperament are perceptual and practical forces in our lives, illuminating facets of the world and enabling certain relations while discouraging others. But then, we also fly past ourselves. This suggests that at heart, the heart we must attend to in taking Emerson personally, our being is both molded and ecstatic, thrown into a determinate shape and then occasionally, perhaps rarely, thrown again beyond itself, and to the degree that Emerson is driven to insist: "The results of life are uncalculated and uncalculable" (*CW3*, 40).

In Emerson's hands, genius names both facets of our condition, what we could term our probabilities and improbabilities. On the one hand, it is synonymous with the talents that temperaments bring, with our recurring quotations, and thus we can speak of a native genius. Continuing a discussion of involuntary perceptions, Emerson tells those attending his *Human Life* lectures:

> In the next place, this [involuntary perception—JTL] in its primary and mysterious combination with the nature of the Individual makes what we call distinctively the *genius* of the man or the peculiar quality that differences him from every other;—a susceptibility to one class of influences;—a selection of what is fit for him; a rejection of what is unfit. And this evidently determines for each soul the character of the Universe. As a man thinketh, so is he; and as a man chooseth, so is he, and so is Nature. (*EL3*, 36)

Or, later in the course:

> Genius, a man's natural bias or turn of mind, as when we say, consult the boy's genius in choosing his trade or work; where it signifies the

spontaneous turning of every mind to some one class of things and relates to practice. (*EL3*, 70–71)

In this sense, genius denotes temperament or talent, that mooded way of engaging the world, a sensibility, to use Kantian language, which one has never chosen but into which one has been thrown. Our genius is our affinity for and with certain facets of the world, such as aesthesis or causal relations, as well as our dullness to the other classes of influence, such as dependencies or suffering. And this giant accompanying our every step (to recall a figure from one of Emerson's cautionary tales about traveling), enables us to find some sense in the world. Lecturing in the late 1840s on "Men of Thought," Emerson remarks: "Peter is the mould into which every thing is poured, like warm wax, and be it astronomy, or railroads, be it French revolution, or botany, it comes out Peter" (*LL1*, 178). Or, in the language of the earlier lecture, *Human Life*: "A man is a method; a progressive arrangement; a selecting principle, gathering his like to him wherever he goes" (*EL3*, 36–37).

But genius also denotes something else, call it ecstasy, what Emerson regards as a "spontaneous perception and exhibition of the truth," a phrase that recalls the phenomenological indubitability of involuntary perceptions (*EL3*, 71). In the lecture "Men of Thought," shortly after noting Peter's wax-molding power, Emerson adds: "But genius is as weary of his personality, as others are, and he has the royal expedient to thrust nature between him and you, and perpetually to divert attention from himself, by the stream of thoughts, laws, and images" (*LL1*, 178). Genius thus also marks the ways in which thought, or better yet, an involuntary perception, leaves temperament and talent behind. In this sense it is as improbable as temperament is probable. As Emerson says in "Genius" from the *Human Life* series: "It always surprises. It is the distinction of genius that it is always inconceivable: once and ever a surprise" (*EL3*, 79).

In my hands, then, genius marks two sides of the condition of Emersonian self-culture. On the one hand, it stands for an inherited or native temperament or talent that is both a power and a limit because the affinities it affords are complemented by an indifference and even obliviousness to other regions of self and world. On the other hand, it stands for those times when we unexpectedly, or better, involuntarily, transcend that inheritance. In a line that also recalls the image of the door through which the Creator passes, Emerson terms ecstatic genius the "continuation of the divine effort," the recreation of that fold of nature that we manifest or even quote (*LL1*, 180).

I invoke the figure of "nature" here because strictly speaking, genius, in both of its senses, is the work of nature. My point is not that, like Kant, Emerson regards works of genius as akin to the products of natural processes, or that, like a design theologian, he regards natural processes as akin to works of art, though Emerson espouses both views. "In our purest hours nature appears to us one with Art; art perfected; the work of genius and the fertility of both is alike" (*EL3*, 79). My point, rather, is that genius, down to its most psychological flashes, is nature unfolding. This identification is initially evident in Emerson's decision to term various events "facts," that is, natural events, for example, our perception, philosophy, even human life itself (CW2, 38; *CW1*, 108; *CW1*, 128) But the identification is even more apparent when he declares to the students and faculty of Middlebury College (and later at Amherst) that genius is an "emanation of that it tells of" (*LL1*, 96). And then, more straightforward still is this remark from a lecture of 1861: "The power of genius is the power of nature. It is the same nature working through man which made man and the world" (*LL2*, 207). Genius is thus a disclosive event in at least two ways. It presents a facet of its referent and expresses, qua fact, that constellation of natural forces that enable it.

Let's explore this suggestion in terms of the paragraph from "Self-Reliance" (21) that earlier commanded our attention:

> For the sense of being which in calm hours rises, we know not how, in the soul, is not diverse from things, from space, from light, from time, from man, but one with them, and proceeds obviously from the same source whence their life and being also proceed. We first share the life by which things exist, and afterwards see them as appearance in nature, and forget that we have shared their cause. (*CW2*, 37)

One can read this passage in a number of ways, one of which is epistemic, another ontological The former leads one to highlight the insistence found a few lines below that those who appreciate the distinction between voluntary and involuntary know that to the latter "a perfect faith is due." Those who stress the ontological dimensions of the claim are drawn to the paragraph's closing testimony: "For my perception is as much a fact as the sun" (CW2, 38). Of course, the two could be complementary if we suppose that involuntary perceptions deserve our "perfect faith" because they arise out of a prereflective commerce with the world and thus replay what to them is an unmediated given. But given what we've seen regarding mood and temperament, namely, that there is "an optical illusion about every person we meet," it seems unlikely that we should simply combine the epistemic and ontological readings of these sentences (CW3, 31) This combination seems all the more unlikely if we introduce a line from "Circles": "The result of today which haunts the mind and cannot be escaped, will presently be abridged into a word, and the principle that seemed to explain nature, will itself be included as one example of a bolder generalization" (CW3, 181).[11]

From this perch, it seems that reflection knows too well that what inspires today proves insipid tomorrow. This is not to say that the invocation of a "perfect faith" is ironic, however. Rather, it means we have to think the "perfect faith" that involuntary perceptions are due outside of an epistemic horizon wherein we adduce, from a point beyond their momentary grip, why involuntary perceptions are reliable. But what else is there? Well, there is the notion of phenomenological indubitability introduced earlier and glossed in the passage from "Circles" that refers us to thoughts that "haunt the mind and cannot be escaped." On this reading, to claim that involuntary perceptions are due a perfect faith is simply to recognize what they in their givenness call for and effect: spontaneous affirmation. Moreover, and I won't be able to vindicate this fully until the next chapter, Emerson is also claiming that involuntary perceptions deserve a perfect faith because only that depth of commitment or abandonment allows us to essay them and undergo the prospects they hold in store. This is not say, however, that a "perfect faith" embodies what Peirce regards as the method of tenacity—it's true cuz I want it to be, real bad like (1960, 5.378). Instead, a perfect faith (or a "will to believe") ventures forth on the basis of an involuntary perception, come what may, including new perceptions. "I unsettle all things," Emerson writes in "Circles." "No facts are to me sacred [including the fact of my perception—JTL]; none are profane; I simply experiment, an endless seeker, with no Past at my back" (CW2, 188).

In paragraph 21 of "Self-Reliance," therefore, the claim is not that prereflective commerce with the world gets nature right, but that one finds nature on both sides of the subject/object divide. "We first share the life by which things exist," Emerson tells us, even in thought. It is only in reflection that we ontologically exile our thoughts from the world and take them to be appearances as opposed to realities, mind as opposed to matter, or culture as opposed to nature. Recall a passage cited earlier concerning instincts: "To me it is vegetation, the pullation & universal budding of the plant of man" (*JMN9*, 71). And five or so years later, Emerson also writes: "In the growth of the plant, cell grows out of cell, the walls bend inwards, and make two. In the instinct of progress, the mind is always passing—by successive leaps—, forward into new states, and, in that transition, is its health and power" (*LL1*, 168). As the passages from "Self-Reliance" and the Middlebury address show, however, the relation here isn't merely analogical—genius is an emanation of that of which it tells. Our genius is thus the genius of nature; our work, nature's work. "We can never be quite strangers or inferiors in nature," Emerson announces in "The Method of Nature." "We are parties to its existence; it is flesh of our flesh, and bone of our bone" (*CW1*, 123).

In tethering genius to nature, both in its native and ecstatic senses, Emerson aligns it with yet another figure recurring throughout his texts: race. Cornel West writes: "As a trope in his discourse, race signifies the circumstantial, the conditioned, the fateful—that which limits the will of individuals, even exceptional ones" (1989, 31). Whereas I would rather say that race, alongside other figures, exemplifies a slice of fate for Emerson, I nevertheless find West's observation on target; Emerson is a racialist, which is to say, one who regards race as a significant variable in accounting for the makeup of a human being. I say this because Emerson often presents race as a kind of collective temperament or a "native knowledge," as he says in a lecture of 1845. Praising the emancipation of slaves in the British West Indies, he announces: "The civility of the world has reached that pitch, that their [Africans—JTL] more moral genius is becoming indispensable, and the quality of this race is to be honored for itself" (*EAW*, 31). Similarly, in remembering Thoreau, Emerson begins by identifying him as the "last male descendant of a French ancestor who came to this country from the Isle of Guernsey. His character exhibited occasional traits, drawn from this blood, in singular combination with a very strong Saxon genius" (*CE10*, 451). In both instances, Emerson aligns race with genius, which suggests to me that belonging to a race brings with it a certain cast of mind, for instance, an acute moral sentiment as opposed to the Saxon genius that Emerson figures as the "hands of mankind," what marks the English as the "wealth-makers" (*CW5*, 42).

Of course, all things with Emerson are more complicated than they initially seem. In the essay "Race," chapter 4 of *English Traits*, Emerson denies that races are either pure or stable and asserts, contra Knox, that "though we flatter the self-love of men and nations by the legend of pure races, all our experience is of the gradation and resolution of races, and strange resemblances meet us everywhere" (*CW5*, 27). In fact, after examining the *doxa*, Emerson proves to be a nominalist with regard to race: "We must use the popular category, as we do by the Linnaean classification, for convenience, and not as exact and final" (*CW5*, 29). I take this to mean that Emerson finds it useful, if not exact, to gauge his character and that of others with some regard for race, as he does in this entry into a journal of 1864–65: "The genius of a race or family is always equal to itself and if the present tenant fishes it too much, the next tenant will find the stream poor. . . . Hence we say, a great man has not a great son. But this proverb has marked exceptions" (*JMN15*, 415).

For Emerson, then, just as knowledge of a family might give one a clue to a member's character, so too might familiarity with his or her race. But one should stress this "might." As a nominalist regarding race, Emerson is not ascribing to race any enduring or universally distributed foundations, and thus, should the category prove misleading over time, that is, should it not do much by way of indicating the character of the person in question, it is easily dropped. This caveat is not unimportant for inheritors of Emersonian self-culture, for it allows one to inherit the figure of race in such a way that setting it aside requires few if any hermeneutic contortions. In fact, one can leave the figure aside by simply pointing out that its supposed conveniences were greatly exaggerated and its harms all too apparent, from the role it played in justifying slavery to the way the notion of a collective temperament can lead folks to believe that what claims them entails that they, racially speaking, are monsters, living out lives that are wildly incongruous with the order to which they belong.[12]

In this chapter, my goal has been to chart some of the conditions of and for self-culture, thus marking a range of resources and challenges. Recall that self-culture seeks a life that manifests one's character, and in a way that evidences the fruit of labors that, in some meaningful fashion, can be said to be mine. The result is what I am calling an eloquent life that bears witness to the full range of who I find myself becoming and am able to affirm.

At the heart of this project, I have set what Emerson terms genius, a twofold figure of probabilities and improbabilities, of predilections and rebirths. On the one hand, one's self-culture must engage the temperament and talents into which one has been thrown, a kind of native affinity for certain ranges of the world, affinities that Emerson racializes, but we needn't. On another hand, self-culture responds to the incalculable sallies of life-changing insight that Emerson terms "involuntary perceptions." Third, as creatures of relentless quotation, we have also discovered that our genius is one of relation, both in terms of what sparks and enables it, and to the point that we are an event of nature that is partially legible to those reflexive enough to read their perceptions as facts, which is to say, as symbols. So conditioned, self-culture concerns our relations with and as nature, and so its successful pursuit brings about a sense for how we fit among these relations, that is, it re-attaches us to nature in the sense that our relations become intelligible, whereas before they were only obliquely apparent. Eloquence, should it be ours, is thus a matter of allowing the vastness of our being, as much a fact as the sun, to articulate itself wherever our character is announced.

THREE

Reflecting Eloquence

It is essential to eloquence that somewhere you let out all the length of all the reins.

—*JMN6*, 134

Somewhere, not only every orator but every man should let out all the length of all the reins; should find or make a frank and hearty expression of what force and meaning is in him.

—*CW2*, 83

My concern is self-culture, the pursuit of a life that, thanks in part to our own labors, eloquently manifests our character. For better or for worse, I have taken up the project in terms somewhat summarized by Emerson around 1844–45: "A man should be a guest in his own house, and a guest in his own thought; he is there to speak for truth, but who is he? Some clod the truth has snatched from the ground & with fire has fashioned to a momentary man: without the truth he is clod again" (*JMN9*, 120). This passage, like many in Emerson, testifies to our dispossession. We do not command our best thoughts, but they us; that is, they come when they will, epistemically charged, and it is the insights they bring that open the paths down which self-culture travels.

By way of review, let me sketch our guesthouse. First, we are creatures of a twofold genius, some part native temperament and talent, some other part, incalculable to its roots, the ecstatic play of involuntary perceptions. Both sources overdetermine reflection with thematic leads such that they, not self-conscious inquiry, are the principal forays of self-culture. Second, moods accompany us, and as perceptual and practical powers, thereby shaping the world we encounter and engage, and that includes native and ecstatic genius. Third, our condition is one of per-petual quotation. We exist and experience ourselves through what we are not. Or, to put it positively, we are relational beings through and through. Rather than existing solely through ourselves, we are depen-dent on a host of beings and forces: family, friends, a language, social in-stitutions, a deep physiological and ecological history, and so forth.

In a very thorough way, then, the condition for the possibility of self-culture is, on Emersonian terms, a condition of existential dispos-session, although one could equally term it, inclining toward affirma-tion, a condition of possession. "I should say of the memorable mo-ments of my life," Emerson notes, "that I was in them & not they in me" (*JNM9*, 419). But in articulating this condition, I cannot help but wonder what Emersonian self-culture actually accomplishes and how. Two passages press the issue. The first is from "Fate":

> I seemed, in the height of a tempest, to see men overboard struggling in the waves, and driven about here and there. They glanced intelli-gently at each other, but 'twas little they could do for one another; 'twas much if each could keep afloat alone. Well, they had a right to their eye-beams, and that was all. (*CW6*, 10–11)

Note first that the waves in question not only include our many colli-sions and embraces but also our own unfolding being: temperament, moods, and involuntary perceptions. But doesn't that kind of tempest, whirling inside and out, turn self-culture into little more than a prac-tice of keeping afloat or, more precisely, one of simply noticing (as op-posed to shaping) our being as it unfolds?

Here is a second passage, this from "Self-Reliance":

> Man is timid and apologetic; he is no longer upright; he dares not say "I think," "I am," but quotes some saint or sage. He is ashamed before the blade of grass or the blowing rose. These roses under my window make no reference to former roses or to better ones; they are for what they are; they exist with God today. . . . Before a leaf-bud has burst, its whole life acts; in the full-blown flower, there is no more; in the leafless root, there is no less. Its nature is satisfied, and it satisfies nature, in all moments alike. (*CW2*, 38 –39)

This passage presents a different problem. Often by way of contrast with what he terms "quadruped life," Emerson images self-culture as the attempt to stand upright. And I take the suggestion to be that the blade of grass and the blowing rose have something to teach us in this regard.[1] But a rose or blade of grass cannot help but manifest its nature, full-blown, root and blade, stem and petal. I say this because the rose does not strive to be a rose as opposed to a daisy, and grass never flirts with the idea of leaving suburbia in order to urbanize its roots. I thus wonder what lesson these beings have to offer. If they embody the ideal of self-culture, then we face, I fear, a project that may not even involve rapt regard for our unfolding, let alone self-creation. The goal, recalling Rilke's self-styled epitaph ("Rose, oh pure contradiction! To be no one's sleep under so many lids,") may be the complete erasure of self-consciousness (in Mitchell 1982, 278–79; translation modified). But this is a paradoxical task, one whose very pursuit produces its failure, for in taking it up we evidence a gap in the life that would be whole and thus fall short from the outset. In other words, our striving to be like roses and grass only indicates our inability to be them. Moreover, and this simply makes the point in reverse, if the goal is simply manifesting our character without reflective mediation, how could we fail, given that, according to Emerson, our character is always manifest? "Men imagine that they communicate their virtue and vice only by overt actions and do not see that virtue and vice emit a breath every moment" (*CW2*, 34). My fear is that roses and grass are better suited to mark the grave of Emersonian self-culture than its consummation.[2]

In order to address these two worries and to prepare for a discussion of the activities of self-culture, we need to locate the place and purpose of reflection in Emersonian self-culture. While introducing the notion of instinct in the lecture "The Tendencies and Duties of Men of Thought," Emerson says: "Consciousness is but a taper in the great Night; but the taper at which all the illumination of human arts and sciences was kindled" (*LL1*, 175). At this joint in the lecture, his overriding point is now familiar. "Instinct," a term invoked "in the despair of language" (and one I have set under the title of "involuntary perception"), is the lead horse in the carriage of self-culture, a "brain of the brain," a "seminal brain." (*LL1*, 175). But what of consciousness? In a journal passage that sets consciousness into the efflux of nature, he similarly claims: "Introvert your eye & your consciousness is a taper in the desart of Eternity. It is the Channel, though diminished to a thread through which torrents of light roll & flow in the high tides of spontaneity & reveal the landscape of the dusky Universe" (*JMN9*, 66). As in the previous passage, Emerson gestures toward the work of consciousness—here a channel through which inspiration flows, there a light that initiates art and science.

We can say more if we tarry with the figure of the "taper," a small candle or even the light that such emits. (According to Webster's 1828 dictionary, taper can mean either.) Of the two meanings, I prefer the latter, "a small light," because it marks consciousness as part of the onset of illumination. In other words, presuming that illumination arrives as an involuntary perception, its arrival is tied in some small measure to consciousness. I prefer this in part because it recalls a point implicit in my earlier claim that involuntary perceptions, though impersonal in origin, are nevertheless personal in their occurrence. They occur to or for particular persons, and one cannot undergo such a thing for another. Second, it suggests that the event of our being involves—or more humbly, can involve, should we be up to it—an awareness of those events, that is, they can be explicitly undergone. Not that this reading of "taper" throws that much light on our quandary. Since part of our worry is that reflection is only a spectator in the labor of self-culture, setting consciousness into the intentional structure of involuntary perceptions won't abate our concern if consciousness simply looks on from the sidelines. Still, the passage marks a site wherein reflection might contribute something to the ways in which our character manifests itself.

With greater import, Emerson states toward the close of "Intellect": "The thought of genius is spontaneous; but the power of picture or expression, in the most enriched and flowing nature, implies a mixture of will, a certain control over the spontaneous states, without which no production is possible" (*CW2*, 199). Presuming we take art and science to be a kind of production, namely, of tuition, an insight-based mode of instruction, then I have a right to regard this passage as continuous with the two above. Natively or ecstatically—and in either case, spontaneously—genius supplies guiding thoughts, but they only inform production when reflection enters the equation, thereby effecting what Emerson terms a "conversion of all nature [including the nature of our lives—JTL] into the rhetoric of thought, under the eye of judgment, with a strenuous exercise of choice" (*CW2*, 199).[3]

Think now of self-culture. It too is a kind of production, the production of a life that eloquently manifests one's character. I do not term it so because it issues in a discrete product (a "life" is not like a shovel), or because it involves what Gadamer (1981, 92) terms the "acquired skill of the expert that Aristotle names *techne*," but because it involves efforts that can go well or poorly, that can succeed or fail. "So many promising youths & never a finished man," Emerson notes in Journal G, though the line also appears in "The Transcendentalist." "'Tis strange," the journal passage continues, "but this masterpiece is a result of such an extreme delicacy, that the most unobserved flaw in the boy will neutralize the most aspiring genius & spoil the work" (*JMN8*, 30). This suggests, I think, that self-culture is a kind of labor, and a delicate one at that. And if consciousness plays a crucial role for Emerson in the inception of art and science, then, given this analogical pairing of the "finished man" with a work of art, consciousness will also play a role in the craft of self-culture, though we still have little sense for what that involves.

No doubt some would have me distinguish production from practice, leaving the former to *techne*, while inflecting the latter with *praxis*, which involves the "actuation of a life" lived according to free decisions (Gadamer 1981, 90–91). But I am not employing the connotations of production in order to draw self-culture under the auspices of an expert knowledge whose ends are set, say, by Emerson or genetics or wealth-max analysts. (In fact, this chapter is struggling to articulate what the *prohairesis*, the "free decision" of self-culture looks like.) Rather, I have chosen to retain the language of "production" in order to emphasize that a certain kind of industry and labor is required in order to achieve the fruits of self-culture. "Labor hides itself in every mode and form," Emerson says in "Perpetual Forces," continuing a few sentences later: "It is in dress, in pictures, in ships, in cannon, in every spectacle, in odours, in flavors, in sweet sounds, and in works of safety, of delight, of wrath, of science" (*LL2*, 294). But this is something I can barely hear in the contemporary English connotations of "practice," which conjures up either a *techne* or a kind of training. In other words, in this *praxis* of mine, I have elected to give myself in part to the rhetoric of "production" in order to underscore that self-culture labors.

The thought that I am slowly developing concerns the kind of work that a life overdetermined by mood, temperament, quotation, and thus reliant on equally thrown moments of ecstatic genius requires. Our feel for this kind of work will thicken if we turn to "Culture": "But over

all, culture must reinforce from high influx the empirical skills of eloquence, or of politics, or of trade, and the useful arts" (*CW6*, 85). I read
this as insisting, "over all," that self-culture must bring the sallies of
genius into the various activities of life, thereby giving them proper direction, our direction; for as Emerson says elsewhere, "Man thinking
must not be subdued by his instruments" (*CW1*, 67). But the point is
not simply to subordinate the hand to the head, but to begin the "true
romance which the world exists to realize, the transformation of genius into practical power," namely, a kind of power over our lives, the
kind which marks our lives as somehow ours (*CW3*, 49). In other
words, the point is to bring our lives under the sway of our best moments, to realize the potential that sometimes rises up within us, what
Emerson, in "The Method of Nature," terms "a power to translate the
world into some particular language of its own; if not into a picture, a
statue, a dance,—why then into a trade, an art, a science, a mode of living, a conversation, a character, an influence" (*CW1*, 128).

I am collecting passages because they are providing us with the
terms of reflection: "transformation," "translation," "conversion."
These mark events wherein the sallies of genius, native or ecstatic, are
carried into something that is continuous with but nevertheless exceeds them, such as modes of living or character, in order that a life be
re-wrought. (Note that conversion principally names a "turning or
change from one state to another," as when ice becomes water or we
convert currency.) These terms thus compress and figure a significant
facet of the labor of self-culture. Stressing the distance a translation
must travel, its "across," we could say that these terms mark a bridge
between what we have come to be and the possibilities lit up by the
flares of our condition, some no doubt brighter than others. And this
is the bridge that self-culture must travel, exercising a *certain control
over spontaneous states,* if we are to have a life of our own, one that eloquently manifests a character to which we have given ourselves. It
would seem, then, that if we are to articulate the place of reflection in
Emersonian self-culture, we'll have to more or less specify the steps required to cross the bridge that render one's genius, native and ecstatic,
a power practical enough to shape a life.

In "The American Scholar," Emerson terms the activity that effec-
tively summarizes (or "comprises") the duties of the scholar "self-trust"
(*CW1*, 63). And in "Self-Reliance" he opens the third paragraph with:

"Trust thyself: every heart vibrates to that iron string" (CW2, 28). I take self-trust to mark a multifaceted step along the bridge that self-culture travels, although, at least initially, it is a less a step than a matter of standing firm in the face of rival claims to our affirmations. Self-culture demands self-trust because: "Society everywhere is in conspiracy against the manhood of everyone of its members" (CW2, 29). While Emerson's remark is overstated (several of our peers, Emerson included, call for something other than conformity), the claim is onto something. On the one hand, there are those who, chained to habits, regard the advent of the new as a threat and treat it with scorn or a "chuckle of selfgratulation," either because they are convinced they are right—"Difference from me is the measure of absurdity"—or because they lack the energy to push past themselves, if only to consider (let alone essay), other paths (CW4, 14). On the other hand, institutions are built on practices, and our participation in them involves a fair amount of role-playing, the parameters of which are set without heed for our native genius and the fluctuation of our moods, let alone our ecstatic moments. This is why, over time, we "do not use things but are used by them" (LL1, 231). Or, in words used in "The American Scholar": "The tradesman scarcely ever gives an ideal worth to his work, but is ridden by the routine of his craft, and the soul is subject to dollars" (CW1, 53). Variously, therefore, social life, at points of persons and practices, draws us away from whatever intuitions might well up, and an Emersonian self-culture mustn't be carried away by those drafts.

But maybe we should be less concerned with overstatement than with the metaphorics of masculinity scoring Emerson's conception of self-culture. Why, and with what import, is it that society conspires against the "manhood" of its members? The worry is that a characterization of self-reliance as the "nonchalance of boys" banishes women from the province of self-culture (CW2, 29). On my reading, that kind of sexism is foreign to the author, who, in lecture and essay, admonishes women to grow into their own being beyond the reach of their predecessors. On Emerson's view, she, like everyone, "has a new and unattempted problem to solve, perchance that of the happiest nature that ever bloomed" (E12, 336/CW2, 153). Moreover, she should do so with the same "pathos of distance," to use Nietzsche's language, that marks the self-reliance of youthful masculinity. "The fair girl, who repels interference by a decided and proud choice of influences, so careless of pleasing, so willful and lofty, inspires every beholder with some-what of her own nobleness" (*E12*, 336/*CW2*, 153).

This is not to say that Emerson's texts are therefore free of any kind of sexism. He often identifies women with emotion—"the bias of her nature was not to thought, but to sympathy" (*CW3*, 88). At times he admires their beauty above other traits—"It reaches its heights in woman" (*CW6*, 158). And, prefiguring the opening lines of *Beyond Good and Evil*, he even regards women as profound figures of sem-blance—"Women, more than all, are the element and kingdom of illu-sion" (*CW6*, 168). His works thus reproduce and perpetuate the stereo-types of his day on several occasions.

In a more elusive way, the feminine may also mark something of a constitutive outside for the elaboration of Emersonian self-culture, in-dicating that which self-culture ought not to embrace. With this worry in mind, I recall Barbara Packer's discovery of an "endless obsession with issues of manliness" among many Transcendentalists. Interest-ingly, though, she marks "servility," not "effeminacy," as its contrasting term (in Bercovitch 1995, 430). The problem proves more complicated, however, in that Emerson often aligns the feminine with figures that draw near to servility. For example, he regards the inability to act as ef-feminate (*CW1*, 59; *LL1*, 88; *CW6*, 127) and terms mob revolt, which entails "man voluntarily descending to the nature of the beast," a "fem-inine rage" (*CW2*, 69 and 33). Or, in a more indirect example, he terms the heart the "basis of the nature of Woman," and precisely as an organ of deference to the needs of others.[4] Now in men such deference can be noble, but Emerson finds that it renders women "charming" (*EL2*, 281–83). And while charm is a power of sorts, one doesn't find Emerson de-scribing Luther and Napoleon as charming.

I thus find Emersonian self-culture idealizing itself as something other than womanly (at least as "woman" is understood on Emerson's terms). And this compromises the invitation to self-culture that he ex-tends to women, for it seems that, at least on his terms, women may never be able to realize its goals and remain women. And yet this too is a complex matter. In "Manners," Emerson seems acutely aware of woman's alterity, and precisely within the strivings of self-culture. Re-marking upon "Woman's Rights," he states: "Certainly, let her be as much better placed in the laws and in social forms, as the most zealous reformer can ask, but I confide so entirely in her inspiring and musical nature, that I believe only herself can show us how she will be served" (*CW3*, 88). Lines like this suggest, I think, that Emerson's texts are not of one mind on the matter of masculinity and femininity, and I take this to indicate that Emersonian self-culture is more than a masculinist enterprise, or rather, we can inherit it as such insofar as we do not fall prey to the inertia of all of its figurations.

I am addressing the question of masculinist figurations because I am wary of conforming to trajectories that I would rather not inherit, trajectories that might retract, along gendered lines, the invitation I take this study to be. And I pause here, now, because conformity plagues the heart of the activity that is self-trust. In "Self-Reliance," Emerson regards self-reliance as an aversion to conformity, a refusal to defer one's affirmations to the "names and customs" of social life (*CW2*, 29). In worrying about the fate of the feminine in Emersonian self-culture, I am trying to exemplify an aversion we can align with self-trust. Among several meanings, *aversion* denotes "looking away," as when we avert our eyes. Self-trust looks away from names and customs that seek our conformity, for example, from "Emerson" and his gendered tropes, and in order to avert a kind of disaster, one in which we become "mendicant and sycophantic" and thus fall away from the life to which our genius calls us, say, a life led beyond the dichotomies of active masculinity and passive femininity.

To say that society conspires against us is to say that many voices lay claim to our affection. By setting aversion within this din, Emerson marks it as an act whereby we say "no" to those forces that would override the affirmations of our being. Because it requires a self-conscious striving, one through which we might, for example, "shun father and mother and wife and brother, when my genius calls me," it thereby falls within reach of reflection's flickering taper (*CW2*, 30). So it marks us as a bit more than a rose. I only say "a bit" because the involuntary cast of our condition also manifests, at points, the genius of nature, as I argued in the last chapter. And yet it does seem that our condition also requires us to husband what involuntarily claims us, that the bridge of self-culture requires, in part, that we turn away from what contravenes our genius.

Aversion to conformity is not the only reflective act integral to self-culture. It has a cousin, call it *aversion to apology*. In apology we less defer to the authority of rival claims than simply do not feel entitled to live out our own. An early line from "Self-Reliance" says this well:

A man should learn to detect and watch the gleam of light which flashes across his mind from within, more than the lustre of the firmament of bards and sages. Yet he dismisses without notice his thought, because it is his. (*CW2*, 27)

For now, focus on the final line. The worry is that instead of embracing our own illuminations, we divest ourselves of any authority. Perhaps we lack sufficient energy or courage. Or, and this also engages our discussion of masculinist metaphorics, perhaps our cultural inheritance insinuates or boldly declares that not only are we not entitled to our genius, but we are not entitled to even regard ourselves as inflected by genius. But self-culture requires this sense of entitlement: "To believe in your own thought, to believe that what is true for you in your private heart is true for all men—that is genius" (*CW2*, 27). Rather than apologize to the world for our involuntary perceptions, thus giving way to it, we should expect that the world has something to learn from what has welled up from within.[5]

I keep to the language of expectation because it is not as if one knows once and for all that what has claimed one is in fact true for all. "I would write on the lintels of the doorpost, *Whim*," Emerson writes, invoking a host of provocative images. "I hope it is somewhat better than whim at last, but we cannot spend the day in expiation" (*CW2*, 30). And a bit later, in "Circles," he converts this anxiety into a mode of comportment: "But lest I should mislead any when I have my own head, and obey my whims, let me remind the reader that I am only an experimenter" (*CW2*, 188). Recall that involuntary perceptions are phenomenologically, as opposed to reflectively, indubitable. We thus have no assurance that what strikes our fancy is more than fancy. And yet we must trust in what flashes across our minds if we are to realize our genius when it strikes, that is, translate it, convert it. Moreover, what other grounds have we upon which to proceed? Even in deferring to another we still must affirm that to which we defer. Either way, then, conforming or not, we regard ourselves as a source of insight worth acting on. So why not do so explicitly and come back to our selves on plainer, more focused terms? As Emerson insists:

> There is a time in every man's education when he arrives at the conviction that envy is ignorance; that imitation is suicide; that he must take himself for better, for worse, as his portion; that though this

wide universe is full of good, no kernel of nourishing corn can come to him but through his own toil bestowed on that plot of ground which is given to him to toil. (*CW2*, 27–28)

I regard the kind of trust that shuns the posture of apology as another reflective act, something along the lines of not being overcome by the kind of doubt that gnaws at our confidence and leads us to ask, But who am I to think such thoughts? For Emerson, and for me, self-trust is the act that insists that having a thought is sufficient warrant for its venture, for its essay. "Few and mean as my gifts may be," he writes, "I actually am, and do not need for my assurance or the assurance of my fellows any secondary testimony" (*CW2*, 31). This also means that we needn't manufacture doubts in order to ensure that our involuntary perceptions are worth prospecting. I have in mind here freedom from the kind of doubt that Peirce regards as abstract, namely, those without affective force in our private hearts, for example, as to whether this is the same computer I used yesterday and the day before. Not that I couldn't come to have real doubts about such matters, but unless I really find myself wondering whether this is the same computer, I needn't first prove that it is in order to have a right to my affirmation.

Alongside epistemic anxieties, there also lies the matter of self-worth. In the arrival of genius, we might regard deferral to our involuntary perceptions as an indulgence. But Emerson will have nothing of this: "I do not wish to expiate, but to live. My life is for itself, and not for a spectacle. . . . I cannot consent to pay for a privilege where I have an intrinsic right" (*CW2*, 31). "Expiate" is a powerful word in this context. Usually it means to atone or to make reparations for some kind of transgression—in this context, attending to the dictates of one's genius as opposed to the many needs of the world. Emerson is thus refusing to atone for deferring to his genius, say, with socially recognized "good works" offered as penances for a little "me time." Thus, to use more current language, self-trust must be willing to withstand the charge of selfishness, which I mark as a reflective act in the heat of the accusation.

Note also that "expiate," at least according to Webster's 1828 edition, means "to avert the threats of prodigies." This is fabulous, suggesting that Emerson's refusal to expiate for that to which he has an intrinsic right, his genius, is also a refusal to turn away from the futures to which one's genius might give birth, namely, a life lived according to the dictates of genius, a life of self-culture. I say this because "prodigy," again from Webster's 1828, names something out of the ordinary, even something monstrous that portends, which recalls Emerson's treatment of genius as an omen of the method of nature in the essay of the same name (*CW1*, 128). Moreover, genius names extraordinary, disclosive events that, once translated into practical power, threaten to overturn established orders. "The new statement is always hated by the old," we find in "Circles," "and, to those dwelling in the old, comes like an abyss of skepticism" (*CW2*, 181). In choosing life over expiation, Emerson thus not only affirms the insights pressed on him by involuntary perceptions but also their progeny, extraordinary as they may prove and selfish as that may seem.

I should also note that aversion to expiation is not the same as aversion to the needs of others. In fact, we might find ourselves involuntarily directed to help those who prove to be *our* poor.[6] But, we should not turn to them "as an apology . . . [for] living in the world" (*CW2*, 30). Instead, whatever we do, it should be carried out as our birthright, as if we were born to the manner that is its translation into practical power. "I shall endeavor to nourish my parents, to support my family, to be the chaste husband of one wife," Emerson announces, "—but these relations I must fill after a new and unprecedented way" (*CW2*, 42).

In the unfolding of self-culture, reflection is marked by events like translation, transformation, and conversion. Emerson's notion of self-trust offers us a first step into this phenomenon when we read it as an act of negation, of *not* deferring to the views of others, of *not* giving in to self-doubt, and of *not* setting aside one's life because one has no right to such a thing. Self-trust can also be read in an inverse manner, however, as a kind of inner obedience, even abandonment. A passage from "The Method of Nature" articulates this well, and in a familiar context:

> I conceive of man as always spoken to from behind, and unable to turn his head and see the speaker. In all the millions who have heard the voice, none ever saw the face. As children in their play run behind each other, and seize one by the ears and make him walk before them, so is the spirit our unseen pilot. That well-known voice speaks in all languages, governs all men, and none ever caught a glimpse of its form. If the man will exactly obey it, it will adopt him, so that he shall not any longer separate himself in his thought, he shall seem to be it, he shall be it. (*CW1*, 130)

Involuntary perceptions are at issue here, those that, in their arrival, seem to deny reflection any distance from which to call them into question. In returning to them now, it seems as if that says a bit too much, for it appears that we are often simultaneously claimed by other thoughts that would draw us away from what announces itself in moments of inspiration. Self-trust is thus required to ensure an identification between reflection and an involuntary perception, a trust that not only says "no" to rival claims and thus averts them, but also obeys what involuntarily announces itself.

Now, I take obedience, insofar as there are rival tugs and tussles, to mark another reflective act, less a giving over to involuntary perceptions than a giving in to them, an "Ah, here it is, let's go." This is the moment of diving into the wave, of setting off in pursuit of an opportunity, of venturing. In this sense of obedience, then, what we bring to the venture is an "I will" or even a "So be it." As the bridge of self-culture opens before us, we proceed, accepting it as ours, come what may. Not that obedience lays down our road, however. "Power ceases in the instant of repose," we are told in "Self-Reliance"; "it resides in the moment of transition from a past to a new state, in the shooting of the gulf, in the darting to an aim" (*CW2*, 40). Without the coursing power of our genius, growth is hard to come by. But so too in reverse; that is, if we prove false to our genius and the path it clears, if we deny our genius a perfect faith, our conversions will stall, and we will fail to shoot the gulf between who we have been and who we might yet be.

As a kind of abandonment, self-trust is as much a coming into ourselves as a departure. In abandoning ourselves to our genius, we abandon our habitual life and, perhaps, the many expectations of our peers. And that to which we abandon ourselves eventually will also be abandoned. "If we were not of all opinions!" Emerson exclaims in "Nominalist and Realist," "if we did not in any moment shift the platform on which we stand, and look and speak from another! if there could be any regulation, any 'one-hour-rule,' that a man should never leave his point of view, without sound of trumpet. I am always insincere, as always knowing there are other moods" (*CW2*, 145). The crisis broached here concerns the unfolding of nature that is our own unfolding, one that "confounds the saint with the rogue, shoves Jesus and Judas equally aside" (*CW2*, 40). Yet rather than forgo self-trust altogether, Emerson simply cautions us not to overly valorize the act of obedience: "To speak of reliance, is a poor external way of speaking. Speak rather of that which relies, because it works and is" (*CW2*, 40).

This second line is oblique. The temptation is to read "that which relies, because it works and is" as "that which one relies upon, because it works and is." There is good reason to favor this inflection. Not only does the act of reliance not produce the insight, but also, over time, our enthusiasm appears naïve. Better then to always turn to where new life arrives, to involuntary perceptions. But note that such a venture may say too much. The words "that" and "it" are ambiguous. They refer at once to a reflexive act, a self "relying" as well as to that same self in its aboriginal roots. Now, a reading could decide on one referent instead of another, tying, for example, "that" to a reflexive act and "it" to an aboriginal emanation of nature. But "Self-Reliance," at least as I have been reading it, ventures the thought that wedding ourselves to our genius is a task to be completed again and again. And a crucial part of the task involves an "exact obedience" whereby "he shall not any longer separate himself in his thought, he shall seem to be it, he shall be it," to recall "The Method of Nature." I would thus argue against resolving the ambiguity of this crucial line, at least in an interpretation of the essay, because it exposes the difference between our reflective selves and our genius, thereby marking the distance self-trust must travel in an obedient embrace of involuntary perceptions, an act in which our "so be it" partly enables us to be it.

I have been marking aversion to conformity, aversion to apology, and a kind of wild obedience as reflective facets of self-trust, steps we take in carrying our genius into the various reaches of our lives. This draws my discussion away from George Kateb, who suggests that self-reliance involves a kind of detachment from any particular set of commitments (2002, 4). I reject this reading because it obscures the force of involuntary perceptions in Emersonian self-culture as well as the virtue of obedience that we have just explored. Moreover, it misses a fundamental Emersonian commitment. In "Circles," Emerson speaks of a wonderful life whose way is abandonment (*CW2*, 190). Similarly, both "The Method of Nature" and "Fate" speak of our ecstasies as key features of our being (*CW1*, 127; *CW6*, 22). But these raptures fade from view if we cast self-reliance along the lines of an aloof Cartesian freedom, one grounded in our ability to be dubious. True, this may moderate Emersonian self-culture, but in this regard, I feel compelled to abandon myself to its excesses.

With greater felicity, Lawrence Buell (2003, 64–66) ties self-reliance to several movements, including aversion and self-trust, which he regards as independent moments. This seems right insofar as the virtue of aversion can be in play when abandonment is not. "If we cannot at once rise to the sanctities of obedience and faith," Emerson notes, "let us at least resist our temptations" (*CW2*, 41). But that remark seems bound to instances when our genius leaves us unlit. Should it arrive, however, and if we resist those temptations in favor of involuntary perceptions, we will simply be obeying our genius, with nothing else to command us. I thus see aversion and abandonment as mutually reinforcing events, even of a piece in the ecstasies of inspiration, perhaps two sides of a more general term like courage, or so I think when I read: "Every man has his own courage, and is betrayed because he seeks in himself the courage of other persons, which is not there" (*JMN9*, 112).

Now, one might resolve this squabble of emphases by talking about how various reflective acts are analytically distinct if existentially intertwined. Fair enough, but I would add that we ought not to confuse the taxonomy I am developing with an analytic of discrete acts or faculties. Within the labors of self-culture, the application of concepts occurs within the sphere of a self's relation to itself and others, a relation wherein we try to negotiate the tempest of the world. I thus offer these descriptions and distinctions in order to further self-culture, not to foreground a new psychological typography. Conformity, aversion, abandonment, and self-trust—the value of these terms hinges on their ability to inform and direct our lives. "Power is in nature the essential measure of right," Emerson announces in "Self-Reliance" (*CW2*, 40). In this context, I take that to mean that a term is the right term insofar as it "resides in the moment of transition from a past to a new state, in the shooting of the gulf, in the darting to an aim," to recall a line. Felicity of phrase is thus not first or foremost a matter of correspondence but of enabling an aim. True, it must navigate the world in order to empower, but as to whether it maps on to the world in some deep or ultimate sense, that is, for this set of practices, not a pressing concern.

If you find this shift in register a sleight of hand, turn your attention to the outset of "Fate," where Emerson announces that for him the "question of the times . . . resolved itself into a practical question of the conduct of life" (*CW6*, 1).[7] Note the construction—a question *resolves itself*. Its reflexive voice suggests that as a result of some transformation undergone by the initial question, the questioner now faces a question concerning the conduct of life. In "Fate," therefore, we have less an age in search of its proper name than Emerson finding himself, his conduct, called into question. This leads me to take *resolve* in the sense of "render fluid," hence workable. In other words, in becoming a question concerning the conduct of life, the question of the times becomes a workable question, one the author can begin to essay. Note also that two sentences later Emerson announces, "We are incompetent to solve the times," thereby suggesting that an attempt to "remove" the question or "dissipate it," two meanings of *solve*, is beyond our capabilities. As he says at the paragraph's close, it is "fine to *speculate* and elect our course, if we must accept an irresistible dictation" (*CW6*, 2). I bring emphasis to "speculate" because, like the active voice speaking in the phrase "to solve," it is being displaced in favor of a different mode of response to questions that claim our attention. Once claimed, we are no longer able to set the terms of our condition (as those "discussing the theory of the Age" seem wont to do) but face them as roads to be walked, seas to be navigated. As Emerson says somewhat cryptically in his own "The Spirit of the Times" lecture: "For what is the Age? It is what he is who beholds it"—although I would add, given the inflections of "Fate," that it is what she or he is who conducts it, that is, acts it out, perpetuates it as its conduit, and, perhaps, leads it (*LL1*, 106).[8]

I recall my terminology to the practice and grammar of self-culture because the stakes of our discussion are broader than one might think. In and through Emerson's texts, questions resolve themselves into issues of conduct, and so confronted, we must decide how best to respond, "best" praising that response which enables us to navigate an opening road. I stress this because it evidences a general but decisive point: we are beings who must play along with our condition. Or, to repeat an Emersonian term, we must *conspire* with our condition. "It is very natural to us all, perhaps, to exaggerate the importance of our services," he tells an audience at Worcester assembled to hear him address the problem of slavery, "but it is the order of Providence that we should conspire heartily in this work" (*EAW*, 49–50). Or, as he writes in "Fate":

> I cited the instructive and heroic races as proud believers in Destiny. They conspire with it; a loving resignation is with the event. But the dogma makes a different impression, when it is held by the weak and lazy. 'Tis weak and vicious people who cast the blame on Fate. The right use of Fate is to bring up our conduct to the loftiness of nature. (*CW6*, 13)

Conspiring thus names an active embrace of what we undergo, a making do with it, a "taking of ourselves for better, for worse, as our portion." According to Emerson, then, while we are projects of nature, perpetually possessed and dispossessed by moods, dawning insights, ebbing confidences, and enthusiasms, we are also projects in the sense of tasks that require our participation.

In Emersonian self-culture, "conspire" names something crucial. At the heart of our condition lies a task that no one else can assume for us, one in which we join ourselves to our condition according to terms we have come to accept, even obey. It would seem, therefore, that on Emerson's own terms, we are quite unlike roses, at least insofar as I know them and us. At one level, this is evident in the fact that we undergo our condition as such, as "Fate" announces: "But if there be irresistible dictation, this dictation understands itself," so instituting what "Experience" terms "the fall of man" (*CW6*, 2; *CW3*, 43). At another level, however, our condition resolves itself into tasks that we must take up, say, by way of conformity or not conforming. Our condition is thus riddled with a dimension I earlier termed personal. "It is not to societies that the secrets of nature are revealed," he writes in 1862, "but to private persons, to each man in his organization, in his thoughts" (*EAW*, 102). But whereas the genius of our condition arrives as an impersonal personal, one that possesses us rather than beckons to our call, self-trust is thoroughly personal, a labor unfolding in the arrivals of life. This is not to say that acts of self-trust express our truest selves. We are no less, and most likely we are more, matters of mood and temperament. But I am claiming that self-culture is very much a personal project, and one in which reflection plays a crucial though not the central role.

At the risk of seeming pedantic, I want to underscore that this notion of "the personal" marks what I take to be one of this study's central quotations and conversions. I say this for one principal reason. It marks a limit to what Foucault has termed the "total dispersion of man," without denying that we are fundamentally beings of quotation. Or, to put it another way, it introduces into nature the plight of human agency without in principle isolating us from one another and the planet. Yes, reflection finds itself and human being in general to be parasitic on a vast network of relations. But given that no one else can live out those relations for us, our singularity is an ineliminable part of the larger whole to which we belong. Moreover, since we can quote those relations in varying ways, for example, by averting conformity or not, how we conspire with our condition has something to say about how that whole unfolds, namely, with more or less conforming moments. Our singularity is thus not simply an ontological given but also, to varying degrees, the fruit of self-culture.

One bent on self-culture is thus confronted with a choice, and at every turn. "Perhaps we shall find the mild satisfactions of merely constituting a part of nature, and witnessing, in obscurity the ongoing of the world" (EL2, 301). Or, perhaps we will "[s]hine with real light, and not with the borrowed reflections of gifts" (CW2, 93). As to which one should choose, that hinges on what kind of character one would manifest. What is certain, though, is that one's character will manifest itself one way or the other.

I also take my turn to the personal to offer something of a response to Sharon Cameron's powerful "The Way of Life by Abandonment: Emerson's Impersonal." She concludes: "If one tries to answer the question, What is a person? no answer with any coherent substance can be produced with reference to Emerson's writing" (1998, 31). But is the question, "What is a person?" the right question? It strikes me as too akin to the question of the times, and thus, when I bring it to Emerson's writings, I find it resolved into a question concerning the conduct of life, something closer to Who am I? and What is to be done? Or, as Emerson asks his audience at Middlebury College in 1845, "Who are you? What do you? Can you obtain what you wish? Is there method in your consciousness? Can you see tendency in your life? Can you help any soul?" (LL1, 96). Emerson's personal arises in interrogations like these. Rather than secured by a "coherent substance," Emerson's personal lies with tasks that no one can assume for us, tasks that, once acknowledged, disclose a kind of being, as Heidegger would say, whose being is always in question, and one whose unfolding hinges in part on how she or he conspires with the variegated paths of his or her condition.

I find Emerson underscoring the personal dimension of self-culture when he tells an early audience: "I have as much doubt as any one of the value of general rules. There are heights of character to which a man must ascend alone—not to be foreshown,—that can only exist by the arrival of the man and the crisis" (EL2, 229). I take the various thrown facets of our condition to mark our arrival into a scene in which the conduct of life is in question. And I take "the crisis" to name that gulf that opens with every transition, a gulf we might shoot in a manner true to our arrival or shrink from in order to conform to the contours of the shore. In this chapter, I have been specifying what it might mean to be courageous in the breach or along the bridge that such a transition opens: by trusting what resources we have, by averting conformity, and by presuming that we are worthy of the life suggested in those darting moments.

If we look further into it, I think the notion of weathering the crises that our condition initiates evidences other reflective acts that are an integral part of self-culture: eschewing a foolish consistency, letting go of sclerotic habits, and persisting when the road steepens. As readers of "Self-Reliance" know, Emerson regards consistency as the "other terror that scares us from self-trust" (*CW2*, 33). Here the worry is less social consistency than inner consistency, although the two are intertwined, as Emerson himself notes—"because the eyes of others have no other data for computing our orbit than our past acts, and we are loath to disappoint them" (*CW2*, 33). But the point is not simply one concerning conformity. Habits can be fierce on the one hand and comforting on the other, and thus we may actively resist some of the changes a new thought commences. Emerson imagines just this scenario in "Circles," observing: "For, it is the inert effort of each thought having formed itself into a circular wave of circumstance,—as, for instance, an empire, rules of an art, a local usage, a religious rite,—to heap itself upon that ridge, and to solidify, and hem in life" (*CW2*, 181).[9] While not quite a death drive, Emerson acknowledges that we occasionally shrink from growth, "afraid of life, afraid of death," and thus we need to wean ourselves from those modes of conduct that once provided ballast. In other words, at times, the fingers of our own conventions pinch our taper, and thus, at times, we must avert ourselves.

We are drawn back to our habits because new waves of circumstance often wash us into waters where bearings are hard to come by. Self-trust may thus require us to let go of selves no longer becoming, even should the change strike others as an about face. Like aversion to conformity and abandonment, such transitions require reflective acts. For example, still wanting to be something of the athlete I once was, I may routinely injure myself playing beyond my bounds and thus confront the facts of who I have become and who I can no longer be. Or, once wedded to the possibilities of revolution, I may come to find my-self drawn toward melioration, and so stand before myself as the kind of political thinker I once ridiculed. These are the moments where scle-rotic habits might assert themselves, or where some desire to remain consistent might wing flights just then commencing.

Of course, it is not as if we know exactly what we are getting into when we let go of selves who've ceased becoming, and thus the crisis Emerson notes can prove an ongoing affair, one that calls for a kind of persistence, a staying the course as it unfolds, far as it might take us away from whom we've been. In *Essays: First Series,* Emerson charac-terizes heroism as a mode of self-trust, specifying it in terms of persis-tency (*CW2,* 149). Moreover, in paragraph 14, he does so in a way that ties it to other modes of self-trust:

> All men have wandering impulses, fits and starts of generosity. But when you have chosen your part [with a "So be it," I have suggested— JTL] abide by it, and do not weakly try to reconcile yourself with the world. Adhere to your own act, and congratulate yourself if you have done something strange and extravagant, and broken the monotony of a decorous age.... A simple manly character need never make an apology, but should regard its past action with the calmness of Pho-cion, when he admitted that the event of the battle was happy, yet did not regret his dissuasion from the battle. (*CW2,* 153–54)

"Adhere," "abide"—these terms mark a reflective act, one that re-weds us to a path on which we've embarked, presumably without conformity or apology. Again, I say this because the terms mark responses to cri-ses, responses no one else can offer on our behalf, ones wherein we risk and possibly prove our mettle, at least for the time being.

We'll better appreciate the ways in which persistence is a compo-nent of self-culture if we recall a term from chapter 1: prospecting. I take the term from the final section of *Nature,* "Prospects," where he declares that "there remains much to learn of his [humanity's—JTL] relation to the world, and that it is not to be learned by any addition or subtraction or other comparison of known quantities, but is arrived at by untaught sallies of the spirit, by a continual self-recovery, and by entire humility" (*CW1,* 39). Now such sallies are no doubt bound to flights of genius, but not solely, as "Intellect" suggests: "Every intellec-tion is mainly prospective. Its present value is its least.... Each truth that a writer acquires, is a lantern which he turns full on what facts and thoughts lay already in his mind, and behold, all the mats and rubbish which had littered his garret, become precious" (*CW1*, 197).

Again, we are at the taper of consciousness, though here its light follows out the implications of our inspirations, a process that requires, to return to *Nature*, a "continual self-recovery." I take this to be a continual articulation of who we are becoming, which itself requires an "entire humility," what we earlier termed "obedience." Prospecting thus names imaginative construals of the "sensible effects" of our involuntary perceptions, to use Peirce's language, an activity we find at the close of "Self-Reliance," where Emerson considers, or prospects the "revolution in all the offices and relations of men" that a "greater self-reliance might work": prayer should become something other than begging for success, classification should be read as itself a kind of prospecting, travel should become less intoxicating, and so forth (*CW2*, 44–47).[10]

Prospecting is thus yet another way in which we conspire with our condition and what it affords. And it is an activity capable of generating its own crises; for example, prayer may have become something else if, as Emerson proclaims: "Revelation is the disclosure of the soul" (*CW2*, 167). I note this to underscore that prospecting is not simply the application of spontaneous insights but is itself a revelatory activity, one capable of opening gulfs at every turn whose navigation will require that we abide by what we have chosen, that we not conform to dying trajectories, that we not withdraw with apologies to those we might have left behind.

"Self-Reliance" adds another side to prospecting. "The power which resides in him is new in nature, and none but he knows what that is which he can do, nor does he know until he has tried" (*CW2*, 28). Similarly, "The American Scholar" observes that "he who has put forth his total strength in fit actions has the richest return of wisdom. I will not shut myself out of this globe of action and transplant an oak into a flower pot, there to hunger and pine" (*CW1*, 60). I thus take prospecting to be more than an imaginative affair. It also involves acting on what our genius affords in order to better see what our genius entails. For example, we might travel less, as Emerson would have it, or travel differently, less focused on ruins, more devoted to what "had been negligently trodden under foot by those who were harnessing and provisioning themselves for long journeys into foreign countries," namely, "the literature of the poor, the feelings of the child, the philosophy of the street, the meaning of household life," to quote a list provided in "The American Scholar" (*CW1,* 67). However, again, one should not embark with the thought that what awaits is a museum of the new, anecdotes of future triumphs. The "method of nature," or better, the "genius of nature," never relents. "If anything could stand still, it would be crushed and dissipated by the torrent it resisted, and if it were a mind, would be crazed; as insane persons are those who hold fast to one thought, and do not flow with the course of nature" (*CW1,* 124). So it may be that deep in the heart of a prospect we'll find ourselves redirected, beginning again.

Upon inspection, reflection is proving vital to self-culture. Self-culture, the translation of genius into practical power, entails conspiring with our condition and in ways that accentuate the personal, the region of our being that no other can live for us. Thus far we have specified several such activities: averting conformity, apology, and foolish consistencies; abandoning ourselves to genius when it comes; letting go when habits grow old; prospecting; and persisting whenever we threaten to slide back into those regions out of which our genius has called us. But note also that reflection might play some proactive roles in the labor of self-culture, as Emerson suggests in the summary lecture of his *Human Culture* series. "All take for granted,—the learned as well as the unlearned,—that a great deal, nay, almost all, is known and forever settled. But in truth all is now to be begun, and every new mind ought to take the attitude of Columbus, launch out from the gaping loiterers on the shore, and sail west for a new world" (*EL2,* 359). But how does one "launch out," precisely?

Let us begin with temperament. Like a sprinter into her speed, or a pianist into every finger, we must work our way into and cultivate our native genius: "He is only a well-made man who has good determination. And the end of culture is not to destroy this, God forbid! but to train away all impediment and mixture and leave nothing but pure power" (*CW6,* 71).[11]

One can find this very process at work in Emerson's journals, which manifest a growing power of expression as the years and volumes accumulate. But then, any person of talent can tell you that there were times when they apprenticed themselves to their capabilities so that they might grow, while too many others can tell you tales of gifts squandered. A first step on our proactive voyage thus involves deepening those capacities that give us most powerfully to the world, and the world to us.

Consider next involuntary perceptions, the heaving bedrock of self-culture. Because they are bound to affinities, that is, because our genius rises in response to the provocative address of the world, proactive acts of self-culture should include the pursuit of new affinities. "Culture," Emerson suggests, "is the suggestion from certain best thoughts, that a man has a range of affinities, through which he can modulate the violence of any mastertones that have a droning preponderance in his scale, and succor him against himself" (*CW6*, 72). What is required, therefore, is the search for engagements to spark new thoughts. "The antidotes against this organic egotism [an effect of native genius—JTL], are, the range and variety of attractions, as gained by acquaintance with the world, with men of merit, with classes of society, with travel, with eminent persons, and with the high resources of philosophy, art, and religion: books, travel, society, solitude" (*CW6*, 73).

Of course, nothing will come of our engagements if a spirit of self-preservation rules us. In "Compensation," Emerson pronounces: "The wise man throws himself on the side of his assailants. It is more his interest than it is theirs to find his weak point" (*CW2*, 68). And later, in "Culture": "As soon as he sides, with his critic, against himself, with joy, he is a cultivated man" (*CW6*, 84). "Joy" is a key term here, for it marks the movement of abandonment, one wherein we give in to what another makes possible, even if it marks us a fool. Near the core of self-culture one finds, therefore, ventures and trials, proactive exposures to differences that might ignite us. "And the great man loves the conversation or the book that convicts him, not that which soothes and flatters him," Emerson proclaims in 1840. "For this opens to him a new and great career; fills him with hope; whilst compliments bereave him of hope" (*EL3*, 259–60).

I think two examples will concretize the pursuit of new affinities. "Cities give us collision," Emerson observes, and thus we ought to avail ourselves of their energy and diversity, particularly given that our native genius "will repel quite as much of agreeable and valuable talent as it draws" (*CW6*, 79 and 78). Similarly, in our idle hours, that is, those without the portent of involuntary perceptions, we can find collisions in books. "Novels make us skeptical by giving such prominence to wealth & social position," Emerson records in Journal V, "but I think them to be fine occasional stimulants, and, though with some shame, I am brought into an intellectual state" (*JMN9*, 118). City life, books, these are what Emerson terms "exalters that will bring us into an expansive & productive state, or to the top of our condition," and he is insistent that "[w]e cannot spare any stimulant or any purgative" (*JMN9*, 108–109).

Self-culture requires such ventures because nothing stays still for long.

> Thought is like manna, that fell out of heaven, which cannot be stored. It will be sour if kept; and tomorrow must be gathered anew. Perpetually must we *east* ourselves or we get into irrevocable error starting from the plainest truths, and keeping, as we think, the straightest road of logic. (*EL2*, 93)

Like Kant, Emerson would chasten those speculations that would deduce the world from a thought. And yet, unlike Kant, he is driven to do so, given the world's dynamism, which we must keep pace with, ever inclining toward what is just now dawning on us from some metaphorical eastern horizon. Reflection thus not only enters into self-culture through self-trust and prospecting but also through the use of exalters, activities that raise us up and throw us over the ridge on which our last waves of life have settled.

Of course, we can open the lid once too often and spoil the stew. In Journal W, Emerson records: "Ah we busybodies! Cannot we be a little abstemious? We talk too much & act too much, & think too much. Cannot we cease doing, & gravitate only to our ends? Cannot we let the morning be?" (*JMN9*, 186). One shouldn't presume, therefore, that city life, intense readership, and walks and talks will ever settle us once and for all within a canon, no matter how many voices it tries to score. Genius remains the driving force of Emersonian self-culture, and reflection will always play second fiddle to whatever it natively or ecstatically affords. "As respects the delicate questions of Culture, I do not think that any other than negative rules can be laid down. For positive rules, for suggestion, Nature alone inspires it" (*CW6*, 104). But this is not to say that the play of reflection in self-culture is negligible. As we've seen, our condition demands of us that we prove co-conspirators in our fate, for projected as we might be, if the project does not become our own, it will not come to fruition in what I would now like to elaborate as an eloquent life.

An entry from Journal G, penned in 1841, has led me to regard the end of self-culture as a kind of eloquence:

> I saw a young man who had a rare gift for pulpit eloquence: his whole constitution seemed to qualify him for that office and to see & hear him produced an effect like a strain of music: not what he said but the pleasing efflux of the spirit of the man through his sentences & gesture, suggested a thousand things, and I enjoyed it as I do painting or poetry, & said to myself, "Here is a creation again." (*JMN8*, 35)

Like the preacher's eloquence, self-culture flows less from what is done than from how it is done. In carrying out a vocation or an avocation, in organizing one's home, or in entering into marriage, we can always ask whether we have proceeded without apology and with an aversion to conformity so intense that we stand ready to leave even ourselves behind. Similarly, our "sentences and gestures" should make evident the depth of our abandonment. Others, as well as ourselves, should recognize our offices as ours, and our lives as fit to be so tied. If so, we should prove to be an "acrostic or Alexandrian stanza;—read it forward, backward, or across and it still spells the same thing" (*CW2*, 34).

Viewed more generally, the preacher's "manners" are what Emerson finds so pleasing. Now "manners" might denote some degree of conformity with social etiquette, but Emerson has something more in mind. "The soul which animates Nature is not less significantly published in the figure, movement, and gesture of animated bodies, than it is in the last vehicle of articulate speech. This silent and subtle language is manners; not *what*, but *how*. Life expresses" (*CW6*, 89). Given that self-culture focuses on how we conspire with and conduct our condition, it is a matter of manners so understood. Alert to the flash of one's genius, one's task is that of prospecting and persevering, without apology, even with abandonment, in a life that more than adequately expresses what is found there. In other words, an eloquent life is precisely one that announces its affirmations wherever we flare and flicker.

Consider this brief example. I teach philosophy. And while that is not all I do, it nevertheless is a significant slice of what you could call my manner, though one should do so noting how manifold a manner can be: lecturing, leading discussions, advising, grading, scheduling classes, deliberating with colleagues, working with an office manager, communicating with the registrar, and so forth. The hope of self-culture is that my genius and its dictates will be eloquently manifest across that spectrum: in the texts I choose to teach, in how I respond to sincere but ill-conceived questions, in the depth I bring to the papers I grade, in how I ask for things and provide them, in how I coordinate my efforts with those of my colleagues, and so forth. At each point, a proponent of self-culture should ask, have the dictates of my genius had their way with me? Have I been true to the life I've found flashing, occasionally, across my mind? "Life only avails," Emerson writes in "Self-Reliance," "not the having lived" (*CW2*, 40). In this context, that challenges us to scrape away the manners of selves who have ceased becoming so that other manners, living manners, may burst through and eventually avail us of their own successors. "The world is as rich as ever it was," Emerson tells himself in 1853, "but it cannot live on old corn . . . or in short on its memory, but must have new men, new instincts, new will, new insights, new spontaneities every day" (*JMN13*, 166).

In distinguishing the "how" from the "what" of our manners, I must hasten to add that the "what" of our life is not insignificant to the labor of self-culture. This is in part why Emerson feels so at home in the term "vocation." Genius arrives as a "call" of sorts. "Each man has his own vocation. The talent is the call" (*CW2*, 82). But we allow that vocation to founder if we simply rest in having heard it. "But when the genius comes, it makes fingers: it is pliancy, and the power of transferring the affair in the street into oils and colors" (*CW1*, 128). In other words, genius is inherently praxical, its arrival bent toward determinate ends. Self-culture is thus not just a matter of formal virtues that we hope to exercise wherever we go. Our native genius, which we must repeatedly read and nurture, orients us toward and away from various offices, so the "what" as well as the "how" of self-culture must accord with the promptings of our condition.

Appreciating the "what" of our manners helps me read the claim, offered in "The Poet," that "the man is only half himself, the other half is his expression" (*CW3*, 4). We are only ever half because our genius demands expression, so we must conspire with its dictates to fashion a life that does it justice, though in this regard we rarely prove true. "We but half express ourselves, and are ashamed of that divine idea which each of us represents" (*CW2*, 28). An eloquent life averts such shame, however; and like the young preacher who inspires Emerson, it flows into offices with a pleasing efflux.

Emerson's young preacher is also exemplary in that his conduct "suggested a thousand things," so it gives the "delight that sudden eloquence gives,—the surprise that the moment is so rich" (*JMN14*, 333). In the life of self-culture, this comes to mean that a life driven by genius eloquently announces the affinities of that genius, such that alongside and through one's character, a range of nature speaks. My thin arms suggest writing instead of jackhammering; my pale skin, a life lived indoors; and my way of introducing examples shows one line of influence, say Cavell, while my fondness for lists shows another tied to Whitman. Or push further and see whether you can't find here the paper of a tree, the design of a typesetter and printer, the smell of diesel fuel from the truck that carried this book along a highway that was built by we know not who, the realization marking the limits of our eloquence. Regardless, the point is that the eloquence I am seeking here reaches past a well-appointed assemblage of individual bests. Rather, an eloquent life seeks to express the full range of its migrations, the full life it conducts.

At the risk of wearying you, I will stress, once again, that an eloquent life is an ongoing task. Nothing will sit still for long, and thus, as Emerson notes in "Nature," "Every end is prospective of some other end, which is also temporary; a round and final success nowhere. We are encamped in nature [and thus in ourselves, I think—JTL], not domesticated" (*CW3*, 110). Moreover, an eloquent life born of self-culture should not be equated with a rigorous self-mastery. This truth of "Experience" will not be outstripped: "Man lives by pulses; our organic movements are such; and the chemical and ethereal agents are undulatory and alternate; and the mind goes antagonizing on, and never prospers but by fits. We thrive by casualties" (*CW3*, 39). "Casualties" names, among other things, those selves we do not become as well as the chance nature of our discoveries and redirections. Self-culture will thus never proceed by way of "direct strokes" upon our condition, which enable us to predict and control the futures that await us. Even for the most eloquent among us, "the results of life are uncalculated and uncalculable" (*CW3*, 40).

Though buffeted about by casualties, an eloquent life nevertheless remains a matter of the "transformation of genius into practical power," albeit one whose ends are never set from without or fully grasped from within. And while here I mostly have tried to detail some of the contributions that reflection makes to our conversions, now I would stress the result: "practical power." I do so in order to capture the scope of the Emersonian project, a scope sometimes narrowed by readers like Kateb, who valorize something like "mental self-reliance" over "practical self-reliance" (2002, 166, 171). Not only am I constitutionally averse to oppositions between thought and action, but also the suggestion runs afoul of lines like these from "The American Scholar," which I continually cite: "I do not see how any man can afford, for the sake of his nerves and his nap, to spare any action in which he can partake. It is pearls and rubies to his discourse" (*CW1*, 59). As noted before, genius is praxical, demanding expression, and while thoughts and journals and essays and poems are very much expressions, they fail to do justice to all of our prospects, as this third line from "The American Scholar" says most forcefully: "Does he lack organ or medium to impart his truths? He can still fall back on living them. This is a total act. Thinking is a partial act" (*CW1*, 61).

Now, I am not proposing an inversion of Kateb's distinction, as if the issue were something called life or action as opposed to thought. Celebrating Emerson's writing, Richard Poirier aptly notes: "Thinking/writing is different than thought/texts; thinking/writing shapes itself as an action that *tropes* rather than reveres or mourns the creations of the past" (1992, 64). I emphasize "tropes" because it says much of what "conversion" says, coming from the Latin, *tropus,* itself a translation (or conversion) of the Greek, *tropos,* which says, at once, "to turn" (from *trepein*), as well as "manner and style." To say, then, that writing "tropes" is to say that its conduct or bearing turns or transforms what it quotes, and in a way that conducts prospects as yet unthought (or forgotten) in the course of one's inheritance. Thinking and writing, like walking and gardening, are thus practices that can evidence a kind of practical power, and they can eloquently express one's character, and should, to the degree one's life finds itself in those fields.

Instead of inverting Kateb's distinction, I am displacing it in order to open self-culture to the full range of its entanglements, or rather, to all of our affinities. Self-culture is thus as much a matter of writing as it is of what we redundantly name "home economics," what Emerson takes up in "Domestic Life," an essay from *Society and Solitude:*

Does the household obey an idea? Do you see the man,—his form, genius, and aspiration in his economy? Is that translucent, thorough-lighted? There should be nothing confounding and conventional in economy, but the genius and love of the man so conspicuously marked in all his estate that the eye that knew him should read all his character in his property, in his grounds, in his ornaments, in every expense. (*CE7*, 109)

An eloquent life, unfolding along lines drawn by affinities that feed, even inspire us, is one whose character is legible and articulate across what we mistakenly distinguish as its exterior and interior. "I am not one thing and my expenditure another," Emerson continues. "That our expenditure and our character are twain, is the vice of society" (*CE7*, 109).

In closing this chapter, I want to stress how Emersonian self-culture elides any inevitable distinction between our interiority and exteriority. Self-culture concerns wherever we find ourselves at stake, and that should prove to be everywhere for those with subtle and deep enough affinities. "Our life is consentaneous and far-related," Emerson writes. "This knot of nature is so well tied, that nobody was ever cunning enough to find the two ends. Nature is intricate, overlapped, interweaved, and endless" (*CW6*, 20). As nature ourselves, as one of its generations, so too are we intricate and overlapped. Or, to emphasize the fact that we give as well as take from these uncountable circulations, perhaps I should say instead, so too we overlap and thus intertwine with what might seem at first to simply not be us at all: an understanding, a landfill, a family next door, a paved road, smog, a misunderstanding, and so on and so on.

Because we are so widely at stake, Emersonian self-culture concerns the full range of our person and requires us to *east* ourselves, to peer over and behind ledges established by our native genius, ledges that stand at once as vantage and disadvantage points. And while its core unfolds in casualties, in the sallies of genius, native and ecstatic, we come into our own only if we conspire with our condition by way of conversions that eloquently express conditions we affirm. This is to say that our genius will only become an eloquent, practical power if we commence and recommence with an abandonment that averts conformity and apology and that perseveres even when our prospects threaten to undo not only what we once had in hand but also what we'd hoped for.

FOUR

Divining Becoming

O my brothers, God exists. There is a soul at the centre of nature, and over the will of every man, so that none of us can wrong the universe.
—*CW2*, 81

If Christianity cannot look to us as it looked to our fathers, we must thank Christianity for that very enlargement.
—*LL2*, 388

Conspiring with genius, native and ecstatic, Emersonian self-culture seeks a life that eloquently articulates a character to which we have abandoned ourselves. Eschewing apology and prospecting along the reaches its affinities afford, such a life unfolds a new creation, as much a fact as the sun, though one whose light and heat is cupped and intensified, reflected in and by resistances and ventures. It bears repeating that, given our condition, such a project is not self-generated but carries the mark of impersonal origins in its quotations and inspirations. "His whole frame," Emerson announces in a lecture of 1862, "is responsive to the world, part for part, every sense, every pore, to a new element, so that he seems to have as many talents as there are qualities in nature. . . . Man in Nature is a suction pipe through which the world flows. No force, but is his force. He does not possess them: he is a pipe through which their currents flow" (*LL2*, 293). Such impersonality would seem to rob us of any character we might call our own, but as we saw last chapter, it rather throws us into our own, setting it as a task whose pursuit and fulfillment are personal, which is to say, a matter that no one else can assume for us. Our character is thus borne toward eloquence by how we conspire with the winds that sound us out, with how we respond to our shifting centers and play along the heaving circumferences of our condition. And should we play well, averse throughout to conformity, apology, and foolish consistencies, persevering in our abandonment, and letting go when trajectories fall off, then, for however long, our words and deeds, works and days, should read like a translation of genius into practical power.

In elaborating the contours of an eloquent life, I have returned again and again to the "one fact the world hates, that the soul *becomes*," as well as to its import: "There is no permanent wise man, except in the figment of the stoics" (*CW2*, 40 and 81). From moods that fail to agree with one another to the incalculable sallies of involuntary perceptions, from chance encounters and the illuminations they spark to our own proactive efforts to *east* ourselves, that which one would cultivate and that which orients our cultivations refuses to stay put. In words from 1854: "Our little sir, from his first tottering steps, as soon as he can crow, does not like to be practiced upon, suspects that someone is '*doing*' him; and at this hint, everything is compromised; gunpowder is laid under every man's breakfast table" (*LL1*, 299).

Wherever we turn, therefore, an undoing is announced, although one might also speak of an invitation, as Emerson seems to in "Literary Ethics": "The perpetual admonition of nature to us, is, 'The world is new untried. Do not believe the past. I give you the universe a virgin, to-day'" (*CW1*, 105–106). Note also the source of this admonition: nature is speaking. This suggests to me that the grinding, going round of our condition proves unhandsome not only because we grasp at things but also because they fly. Or, to put it more strongly, nature itself is unsettled.

> Metamorphosis is the law of the Universe. All forms are fluent and as the bird alights on the bough & pauses for rest, then plunges into the air again on its way, so the thoughts of God pause but for a moment in any form, but pass into a new form, as if by touching the earth again in burial, to acquire new energy. A wise man is not deceived by the pause: he knows that it is momentary: he already foresees the new departure, and departure after departure, in long series. Dull people think they have traced the matter far enough if they have reached the history of one of these temporary forms, which they describe as fixed & final. (*JMN9*, 301)

In this chapter I will prospect the knot tied by the law of metamorphosis, one that is manifest in departure after departure: now from now, you from we, me from me, acorn to oak, oak to nurse log, and so on. I pause here because such a law, should we find ourselves under it, is less one that our self-culture should exemplify—how could it not?—than one that our manner might eloquently reflect, and I would know the how of it.

In a favorite essay of mine, "The Method of Nature," Emerson quotes the figure of "emanation" in order to name the law of metamorphosis, a law we can never get around, that is, one we cannot transform into the expression of a vaster law. Two passages from paragraph nine convey the matter.

> The method of nature: who could ever analyze it? That rushing stream will not stop to be observed. We can never surprise nature in a corner; never find the end of the thread; never tell where to set the first stone. (*CW1*, 124)

> Every natural fact is an emanation, and that from which it emanates is an emanation also, and from every emanation is a new emanation. (*CW1*, 124)

I see two claims here. One quotes Neoplatonic thought and Heraclitus. The other figures its epistemic import. Thought together, they read: nature's perpetual changes or appearances leave us unable to circumvent it.

I think we can vindicate this sense of our place in nature. As far as experience is concerned, if that prologue is even necessary, all beings, while enduring to various degrees, transform. Humans and polar bears are born, develop, age, and die. Asteroids fall into orbits, suffer collisions, and assume new shapes in the wake of these encounters. Moreover, in all cases like these such changes initiate eventual changes for other beings, and to systemic levels, as we see when the loss of one species initiates a change reaction in an ecosystem. The universe is a dense whirl, and an interactive one, with ripples rolling around every corner. It thus spells an elusive drama of metamorphosis for its witnesses.

Second, the shifting space-time slice to which we belong conditions the breadth of our witnessing, and on multiple fronts: our selective perceptual apparatuses, our cultural background conditions, our talents and personal experiences, our simple presence in an experimental context, and so forth. Thus, even if the world would slow down and grant us something like a view from everywhere, our path through the suspended thicket would be partial, just as it is with regard to the full range of information that we pre-reflectively process as individuals. With regard to perception, John Dewey was right, selective emphasis is the rule, and thus the whole is something we posit rather than apprehend. True, we can inductively generalize about classes of things and the rules they seem to follow, and we can subsume those classes under more general ones: Bob, human being, mammal, carbon-based life form, matter, and so on. But unless the initial categories are somehow derivable without remainder from the more general ones, to regard the result as an adequate apprehension of the whole is like allowing the phrase "all animals" to pass for a zoology, to repeat Hegel's poignant example. And that's a dangerous undertaking. It may well be that energy can neither be created nor destroyed, but heads, like melons, are less resilient. As Emerson says, nature "punishes abstractionists, and will only forgive an induction which is rare and casual," which is to say, enjoy our predictive power, but don't claim too much more on its behalf (*CW3*, 139).

So braided, this thought of an effusive and thus insurmountable nature is a central if wobbly axis of Emersonian self-culture. Early in 1827 he observes: "We are the changing inhabitants of a changing world. The night & the day, the ebbing & flowing of the tide, the round of the seasons, the waxing & waning moon, the flux & reflux of the arts & of civilization of nations & the swift & sad succession of human generations, these are the monitors among which we live. . . . An unsubstantial pageant. The ground on which we stand is passing away under our feet" (*JMN3*, 72–73). In 1838, he announces in the concluding lecture of the *Human Culture* series: "We dwell on the surface of nature. We dwell amidst surfaces; and surface laps so closely on surface, that we cannot easily pierce to see the interior organism. Then the subtlety of things! Under every cause, another cause" (*EL2*, 358). In 1845, he records: "The Universe is like an infinite series of planes, each of which is a false bottom, and when we think our feet are planted now at last on the Adamant, the slide is drawn out from under us" (*JMN9*, 295). With different emphases but to an analogous end, he suggests while praising Shakespeare: "The translation of Plutarch gets its excellence by being translation on translation. There never was a time when there was none" (*CW4*, 115). Later, lecturing in 1858, he notes: "What baulks all language is the broad, radiating, immensely distributive action of nature and of mind. If it were linear, if it were successive, step by step, jet by jet, like a small human agency, we could follow with language, but it mocks us by its ubiquity and omnipotence" (*LL2*, 74). Then, in *Conduct of Life*, published in 1860, "Fate" offers: "The knot of nature is so well tied, that nobody was ever cunning enough to find the two ends" (*CW6*, 20). And "Illusions," the essay that closes the collection, offers: "All is riddle, and the key to the riddle is another riddle" (*CW6*, 167).

It is important to appreciate both threads of this braid. Our inability to plumb nature, to plant our feet on adamant or see the interior organism pulsing in nature's creatures, ourselves included, does not simply result from our dimness, one that would erect a Kantian divide between things as they are in themselves and things as they appear to those like us. Rather, nature, as an event of appearing, is too much with us, of us; and thus, in the sublime breadth of its relations, and in the dynamism of those relations, we are overwhelmed—"The world rolls, the din of life is never hushed" (*CW6*, 167). In other words, Emerson's point is not that nature is inaccessible, as if our life were elsewhere, but that lacking the view from every where and every time, we forget that "as much as man is a whole, so is he also a part; and it were partial not to see it" (*CW3*, 139).[1]

And yet, like Kant's phenomenal/noumenal distinction, Emerson's figures of surface, emanation, translation, and becoming delimit the scope of efficient causality. This is perhaps most evident in the 1838 remark that under every cause one finds another, a discovery that opens an ontological deployment of efficient causality to an infinite regress. And this, as Kant has shown, sets reason at odds with itself whenever it wishes to halt the train. Now, one might propose that a term like "emanation" tries to name what causality in its so-called efficient sense misses, perhaps something more organic, something more like petals emerging from flowers than billiard balls crashing into one another. I don't think this is what Emerson is after, however, as his equal penchant for "surface" suggests. Rather, given that emanation suffers the same regress that causality does—and "The Method of Nature" makes this explicit—one should read "emanation" as a "none shall pass" concept, one less interested in furthering an order of explanation than in riddling it, thereby delimiting it.

Now, to delimit an order of explanation is not the same as calling for silence on the matter. After all, "emanation" is still offered to an addressee, and in a meaningful speech-act. But the act in question is not an explanation. Rather, I think we would do better to receive it as a provocation and redirection; that is, "emanation" doesn't explain something "efficient causality" bungles, but asks one to approach the matter differently.

> It will not be dissected, nor unraveled, nor shown. Away profane philosopher! Seekest thou in nature the cause? This refers to that, and that to the next, and the next to a third, and everything refers. Thou must ask in another mood, thou must feel it, and love it. . . . Known it will not be, but gladly beloved and enjoyed. (*CW1*, 125)

My claim is that in Emerson's hands a figure like "emanation" says, in part, "Away profane philosopher!" But not only that, for it also calls us toward some other mode of engagement: what, via "enjoyed" and "love," I take as modes of abandonment that exceed analysis, receptive modes whereby we conspire with our condition.

Let me see whether I can be more precise. Please recall a point from chapter 2. In disclosing the casualty in which the very thought of causality arises, Emerson draws the bottom out from under this would-be ontological linchpin. But that is not all; in terming our own judgments unmasterable, Emerson redirects our relation to them, turning us away from architectonics toward a conspiring reception of unpredictable sallies. I think "emanation" plays out a similar drama, though across all of nature, and that includes our own pulsing bodies and lives. I say this because moods, involuntary perceptions, aversions, and reversions are emanations of our being, which is itself an emanation of a network of relations, which itself . . . I think you get it.

"Emanation" thus highlights a casualty in every event, or rather, it prods us to be ready, even to look for surprise. Whereas efficient causality fuels dreams of mastery predicated on our increasing ability to predict and thus control the cosmos, a rushing, nonlinear terrain of successive emanations without bottom, a self-translating thread without end, and a series without beginning remains elusive to the point that one forgoes a search for beginnings, bottoms, and ends in order to play (or conspire) with the hands that are dealt.

In receiving the directions lurking within a term like "emanation," one shouldn't mistake it for an understated, categorical maxim along the lines of Thou shalt accept what rushes past. Rather, the provocation directs us toward where our work begins, namely, in and as the throwness of our condition, a Heideggerian phrase I've assembled to translate a line from "Self-Reliance": "Accept the place the divine Providence has found for you: the society of your contemporaries, the connexion of events" (*CW2*, 28). My claim, then, is that Emerson's essays provocatively delimit the scope of efficient causality in two ways: the language of "casualty" reorients us with regard to our own inspirations, whereas "emanation" marks us and the world of a kind, such that the tasks of self-culture are matters of living with, in, and as nature, that is, matters of conduct. As Emerson writes, "Nature who made the mason, made the house" (106).

I think the close of "Experience" testifies to the kind of redirection I have been describing, so I'll return to a reading introduced in chapter 1. The final paragraph begins: "I know that the world I converse with in the city and in the farms, is not the world I *think*. I observe that difference, and shall observe it" (*CW3*, 48). What strikes me first is what Emerson avoids, namely, the Kantian distinction between things as they appear and things as they are in themselves. Instead, the distinction concerns two ways in which we engage the world, ways we could term, following Dewey: (a) primary experience, that is, our ongoing conversation with persons, places, and things; and (b) secondary experience, that is, our reflective thinking about that which we undergo.[2] This is notable because the essay's first paragraph opens a scene of epistemic turbulence wherein "our life is not so much threatened as our perception. Ghostlike we glide through nature and should not know our place again" (*CW3*, 27). One might therefore expect the essay to secure our place with grounding gestures that either name things as they are in themselves or, like Kant, unveil the necessities that organize the world as it appears to us, thus providing us with a transcendental philosophy of nature; but it does not. However, neither does it give way to skepticism. Instead, Emerson closes the piece by way of a reflective observation that locates his life in a movement between primary and secondary experience, a movement predicated on a difference (or "discrepance") that he then promises to observe as one would observe a holiday.

I want to describe this redirection as a shift from observation toward observance, the latter naming a way of conspiring with our condition that recognizes and respects the difference between primary and secondary experience. But what does that entail? The final paragraph of "Experience" suggests several things. First, it tells us: "I have not found that much was gained by manipular attempts to realize the world of thought" (*CW3*, 48). I take this to mean that utopian exercises that would instantiate a world of unmoored reflection "make themselves ridiculous" because they fail to respect how thought, if hypostatized, freezes a life that will not stay still. Recall that, for Emerson, "Life only avails, not the having lived" (*CW2*, 40). No longer circulating among the disclosures afforded us by our affinities and the proceedings they enable, the world of thought becomes the world of the having lived, which thereby hems in life, to recall the language of "Circles." An observance of the difference between primary and secondary experience is thus, in part, a matter of repeatedly returning to the bottomless and tempestuous proceedings that are our condition, lest our manna grow stale.

Such observances have other effects as well. One is patience in the face of loss and frustration:

> Patience and patience, we shall win at the last. We must be very suspicious of the deceptions of the element of time. It takes a good deal of time to eat or to sleep, or to earn a hundred dollars, and a very little time to entertain a hope and an insight which becomes the light of our life. (*CW3*, 49)

In the context I've assembled, one point is that we should not expect an immediate and eloquent translation of our inspirations into the fullness of our lives. First, "Insight is not will, nor is affection will," as we find in "Fate" (*CW6*, 16). Genius may indicate futures, but those only come about if we conspire and our condition cooperates. Second, such translations take time, and we should not be deceived by deferral and lose heart, but should persevere along the roads opening with involuntary perceptions.

Time deceives in more than one way, however. It takes but the instant of an involuntary perception to open our lives onto new vistas. We should thus be equally patient in our long, dull stretches, in those wherein our taper seems about to gutter. Periods like these loom like a rule without exception, but they are not. Ecstatic genius might visit at any time, and we should be prepared for it, ready to "detect and watch that gleam of light which flashes," for it offers rebirth. As Emerson remarks in Journal CD: "Every thing teaches transition, transference, metamorphosis: therein is human power, in transference, not in creation; & therein is human destiny, not in longevity but in removal. We dive & reappear in new places" (*JMN10*, 76).

I find Emerson's observances near the end of "Experience" so remarkable because they return observation to the conduct of life. Rather than remain in the sphere of reflection and bemoan the fact that primary experience exceeds the reach of secondary experience, as skepticism would, Emerson reconfigures his conduct, given the "evanescence and lubricity of all objects"; that is, he makes do with what he has been allotted, thus remaining true to the spirit of "Self-Reliance": "Accept the place the divine Providence has found for you: the society of your contemporaries, the connexion of events." Putting it another way, "Experience" closes with an admittedly timid step into a world ruled by the law of metamorphosis, one wherein the connection of events cannot be rendered causally transparent, and one wherein nature is carnivalesque:

> For flowing is the secret of things & no wonder the children love masks, & to trick themselves in endless costumes, & be a horse, a soldier, a parson, or a bear; and, older, delight in theatricals; as, in nature, the egg is passing to a grub, the grub to a fly, and the vegetable eye to a bud, the bud to a leaf, a stem, a flower, a fruit; the children have only the instinct of their race, the instinct of the Universe, in which, *Becoming somewhat else* is the whole game of nature, & death the penalty of standing still. (*JMN13*, 408)

But then, this is also a timid entry into experience itself, or better yet, a timid acceptance of how we unfold, the "so be it" of an abandonment. Sensation, discursive judgment, imagination, memory—each converts what it quotes, and thus what it quotes becomes something else in its hands. The difference between the world of thought and the world with which we pre-reflectively converse is thus our difference, part of our very nature, and thus our part in the whole game. To observe it is thus to come to our selves or to the selves that begin and end there, and to live in an observance of that difference is to remain alert to those comings and goings.

I have worked this carefully with the law of metamorphosis because it further elaborates the condition in which self-culture arises and proceeds, underscoring the mortality of the project. But in confronting that mortality, we have also come to a richer sense of ourselves. For all the despair of "Experience," its observances give us a place in the whirlwind, one in which the dispersions of time also bring us back to ourselves, and in a way that calls us to conspire with what we find there.[3]

But Emerson is not always so sanguine in the face of metamorphosis. While "Experience" suggests that the tempest of our condition threatens our perception more than our lives, the figure of "casualties" says otherwise, as Emerson himself observes in the face of little Waldo's death. Under the law of metamorphoses, there is death and loss, as this journal entry of 1826 attests:

> It is the business of the moralist to shew there is no evil, neither sin nor sorrow, neither imperfection nor vice which has not its corrector, to shew that compensation is complete.
> But it is plain that in the present state this system is not entire. There are griefs as the loss of friends, the disappointment of parents in their children, which do not admit of atonement in this world. (*JMN3*, 5)

And though he there belittles those who fear it for themselves, the early lecture "Tragedy," delivered in 1839, notes the central role that loss plays in our condition: "And here the spectre Death, as it breaks up all the fittest particulars of life and the habits of mutual leaning and furtherance, to say nothing of all the imaginary hopes its shivers" (*EL3*, 108–109). Finally, in 1854, he observes that our place in nature is not final: "First, innuendoes; then, broad hints, then smart taps are given, suggesting that nothing stands still in nature but Death; that the creation is on wheels, in transit, always passing into something else" (*LL1*, 298–99).

These passages evidence that throughout his life Emerson took death to mark a central concern, one his thought had to confront. But this should come as no surprise, given the losses he suffered.[4] Born in 1803, he lost a brother in 1807, his father in 1811, a sister in 1814, his first wife Ellen in 1831, another brother in 1834, and his son Waldo in 1842. Nor was he without a sense of his own infirmity. He survived early bouts of rheumatism that required two surgeries and had his own struggles with tuberculosis. I stress this for two reasons. First, readers of Emerson tend to focus on the enormity of Waldo's loss to the point that we forget how, since boyhood (if we are to believe "Compensation"), he aspired to carry out the "business of the moralist" and utter, as best he could, another law, a "law of compensation" whose aspiration inversely testifies to the suffering it would abate (*CW2*, 57). As Joel Porte puts it, "It is his *positive* facts that sound ominous" (Porte et al.,

1979, 167). Not that Waldo's loss was incidental, or that it didn't transform Emerson's outlook on life, but I am suggesting that it less introduced Emerson to an entirely new order of thought than intensified
concerns already present and potent. But second, and more importantly, the passages I've quoted evidence a lifelong concern to offer a
"sublime suggestion of futurity and a Providence that outlasts time &
connects the finite to infinity; the little and brief concerns of men to
the vast employments & natures of Godhead and Universe" (*JMN3*, 5).
And it is this concern that introduces into the heart of Emersonian
self-culture another law, one that qualifies, even shapes the law of
metamorphosis. Journal VO puts the matter succinctly:

> My philosophy holds to few laws. 1. *Identity*, whence comes the fact
> that *metaphysical faculties & facts are the transcendence of physical.*
> 2. Flowing, or transition, or shooting the gulf, the perpetual striving
> to ascend to a higher platform, the same thing in new & higher
> forms. (*JMN14*, 191–92)

Emersonian self-culture thus embraces at least two laws: one of metamorphosis, the other of compensation. I say that the latter "shapes" the
former because in the VO entry, identity brings ascendancy to metamorphosis, thus opening the possibility that losses might meet their compensations somewhere on down the road. But let's explore this thought
further, attending to the kind of identity Emerson has in mind, the manner of its operation, and the role it plays in Emersonian self-culture.

First, Emerson finds a polarity or balance of forces across nature,
as if each were proportionate to all the others over time. "A perfect
compensation," he announces in an early lecture, "adjusts itself through
all the parts of material and moral nature. Darkness answers to light,
heat to cold, ebb to flow, reaction to action" (*EL2*, 153). The law of identity thus does not reduce everything to an instance of the same, but
admits of differences. Those differences have a point, however. "That
Nature which we all share," he tells an audience one year later, "has not
been vouchsafed to us in like measures. We are only the prophecy of
that we shall be. Here is the great Tragedy, shall I call it, of More and
Less; though robbed of all its bitterness in the great compensations of
the whole" (*EL3*, 44). Compensation thus turns nature into a work of
art that, over the course of its creation, gives everything its due such
that the whole remains a whole unthreatened by its parts. True, at

points it seems as if some corner receives undue emphasis, but over time the appearance of exaggeration gives way to a precise proportionality. "The errors are periodic, as the seasons, as night and day, as sleep and waking, in plant and animal." But do not fear, this late lecture insists, "The eternal equilibrium is restored" (*LL2,* 384).

The analogy of nature with the work of art has limits, however, for it obscures what affects the unity that Emerson finds in nature:

> It was whispered that the globes of the universe were precipitates of something more subtle; nay, somewhat was murmured in our ear that dwindled astronomy into a toy;—*that,* too, was no finality, only a provisional, a makeshift;—under chemistry was power and purpose: Power and purpose ride on matter to the last atom. It was steeped in thought, did everywhere express thought; that, as great conquerors have burned their ships when once they were landed on the wished-for shore, so the noble house of nature we inhabit, has temporary uses, and we can afford to leave it one day. The ends of all are moral, and therefore the beginnings are such. (*LL1,* 299)

Note initially the wild scope of Emerson's vision: globes, that is, planets and stars, the earth and sun. These transformations are enormous with regard to the mass and time frame involved, and in these regards they dwarf the births, migrations, and deaths of a single life, though they also mark the scenes in which such lives are encamped. Moreover, while these movements may elude the reach of efficient causality, ends nevertheless guide them—that is, a final causality reigns over nature, converting change into means for ends.

The results of compensation are thus more than merely aesthetic. If anything, they resemble a series of economic exchanges guaranteed a return. "Things refuse to be mismanaged long," one finds in "Compensation." "Though no checks to a new evil appear, the checks exist and will appear" (*CW2,* 59). Similarly: "Always pay: for, first or last, you must pay your entire debt. Persons and events may stand for a time between you and justice, but it is only a postponement. You must at last own your own debt" (*CW2,* 66). Not that we are the movers and shakers across this scene. Rather, an invisible hand lurks at every turn, preserving goods. "We are escorted on every hand through life by spiritual agents, and a beneficent purpose lies in wait for us" (*CW3,* 112).[5] And this is true in all spheres of social life. Observing the "religious rapture" of Antigone, Demosthenes, Indian ascetics, medieval monks, and New England Calvinists, Emerson pronounces in a late lecture of 1867: "I see that it sprang from the Divine Presence which rushes through all his pragmatic straws" (*LL2*, 382).

And yet this invocation of a kingdom of ends toward which nature seemingly rolls is not based on purported knowledge of either those purposes or the enduring means of their realization. True, Emerson says things like "A lesson which science teaches, unanimous in all her discoveries, is the omnipresence of spirit. Life, creation, and causes meet us everywhere. The world is saturated with law" (*EL2*, 29). But this teaching is not coextensive with demonstration. Rather, Emerson posits the presence of final causes, given the webs of relation that science unveils and the technological power that scientific discoveries often bring. To use terms drawn from the "Humanity of Science," science teaches the lesson of final causes when it is "studied with piety," which is to say, when the "antecedence of spirit is presupposed" by a "soul alive with moral sentiments" (*EL2*, 36). Or, to use later terms: "We believe a great deal which is never or rarely expressed by us. We do not penetrate to our secret conviction so as to be able to define or state it, but it diffuses an odorous atmosphere of tranquility through the days and animates our actions: as the Indian breathes the same air as the chemist, though perhaps he never heard of the air, or thought of it as an element, much less knows its composition" (*LL2*, 185).[6]

This secret conviction, that final causes persist in a universe of metamorphosis, dramatically reconfigures the conditions under which Emersonian self-culture labors. Most notably, it converts what looks like a "natural history of calamity," to use the language of "Compensation," into the "method nature," to use the title phrase of the 1841 lecture we recently engaged (*CW2*, 72). Or, to put the matter in more theological terms, in institutes a theodicy, a philosophy of history that purports to transact the "business of the moralist" in order to show both that the universe is moral and that our strivings overlap to some degree with its own course of development, such that congruence exists between the "brief concerns of men" and the "vast employments & natures of Godhead and Universe."

Toward this twofold end, Emerson at times goes so far as to deny the existence of evil. In his *Philosophy of History* lectures, he proclaims: "What can be more sublime than this doctrine that the soul of the world does impregnate every atom and every spirit with its omnipotent virtue, so that things are tuned and set to good. Evil is merely privative, not absolute" (*EL2*, 154–55). Likewise, in "The Divinity School Address," he says, "Good is positive. Evil is merely privative, not absolute" (*CW1*, 78). Perhaps "Compensation" says it clearest of all: "Justice is not postponed. A perfect equity adjusts its balance in all parts of life" (*CW2*, 60). On this view, every apparent more or less, every instance of unequal treatment at the hands of nature is always already compensated for; its contribution and fate are measured and given their due reward. "It is a doctrine lying at the foundation of natural philosophy & which every new step taken confirms that nature does nothing in vain" (*JMN3*, 22). Moreover, the existence of such a method insures that everything radiates purpose as an *ens creatum,* a created thing. "Things are saturated with the moral law. There is no escape from it. Violets and grass preach it; rain and snow, wind and tides, every change, every cause in Nature is nothing but a disguised missionary" (*CE10*, 86). Turn where you will and the invisible hand of the divine will be at work, for the "self-collected mind piercing to the cause of every mischief sees its origin, its compensation, and its necessary boundaries, and already foresees the good it shall produce" (*EL2*, 184).

Though Emerson often insists that God's justice is everywhere, he presumes that we usually lack the eyes for such fine handiwork. In fact, this kind of equity is only given in the wide shots of history. "A fever, a mutilation, a cruel disappointment, a loss of wealth, a loss of friends seems at the moment unpaid loss, and unpayable. But the sure years reveal the deep remedial force that underlies all facts" (*CW2*, 73). Given the rarity of such insights across the course of a life, and given the indemonstrable acuity of these visions, Emerson returns again and again to a posture of worship before whatever glimmers of compensation he finds. That is, if the law of metamorphosis calls for a life prepared for departure, the law of compensation calls for a life lived in devotional prayer to the justly unfolding powers of nature, and Emerson's theodicy is an integral part of that prayer. Speaking of those who have met with "extraordinary success," Emerson observes: "According to the faith of their times, they have built altars to Fortune or to Destiny, or to St. Julian" (*CW2*, 79). Or, speaking for himself in the later lecture "Natural Religion," he twice states, "Blessed be the inevitabilities," even though: "We affirm and affirm, but neither you nor I know the value of what we say" (*LL2*, 185). Or, to cite yet another, better-known example, "Fate" closes with four similar devotions to "the Beautiful Necessity," a "Law which is not intelligent, but intelligence" which, nevertheless, "disdains words and passes understanding" (*CW6*, 26–27).

It is in this context that Emerson turns prayer away from a practice of spiritual begging toward the practice of worship, and from an isolated activity toward one synonymous with the conduct of life. One can find this turn already in his very first sermon, "Pray without ceasing," and again in "Self-Reliance," where we find: "As soon as the man is one with God, he will not beg. He will then see prayer in all action" (*CS1*, 55–62; *CW2*, 44). We can also read a slight shift at the close of "Fate" in a similar way. After three times asking that we "build altars to the Beautiful Necessity," he says, more economically, "Let us build to the Beautiful Necessity" (*CW6*, 27). I say more economically because on his view, all building establishes an altar upon which we devote ourselves to the divine.[7]

I should note, however, that by "Fate" Emerson no longer believes that evil is merely privative. "No picture of life can have any veracity that does not admit the odious facts" (*CW6*, 11); and: "Fate involves melioration. No statement of the universe can have any soundness, which does not admit of its ascending effort" (*CW6*, 19). Or, as he observes as early as 1849, offering antislavery remarks at Worcester: "This progress of amelioration is very slow" (*EAW*, 49). I find a change here because "melioration" only occurs when problems are present, and that suggests a postponement with regard to justice, a fact that only intensifies the demands placed on Emerson's worshipful posture toward nature. Why? By the time nature comes around to vindicating us, we may be long gone. The long view in which "Compensation" finds comfort may thus only open for those looking back upon our lives.

I think we can characterize Emerson's theodical conception of ameliorative nature along three lines. First, on this view, evil is punished. As he proclaims in a May 3rd address on the Fugitive Slave Law: "It is the law of the world, as much immorality as there is, so much misery" (*LL1*, 263). Second, conversely, good is rewarded. "The magnanimous know very well that they who give time, or money, or shelter, to the stranger—so it be done for love, and not for ostentation—do, as it were, put God under obligation to them, so perfect are the compensations of the universe" (*EL2*, 333). The law of compensation thus punishes and rewards, as this avowal makes plain. "Every secret is told; every crime is punished; every virtue rewarded; every wrong redressed in silence and certainty" (*EL3*, 145). This is not to say that punishments and rewards are meted out according to the rule of worldly success, however. On Emerson's account, riches are neither here nor there. Rather, he takes the health of the soul to mark our paramount concern, thereby locating on its tiers the ledger of compensation, whose standard is proximity to divine life: "Learn that the malignity and lie of the offender are the shadows of death creeping over him; that so far he is deceasing from nature; that in a virtuous action, I properly *am;* in a virtuous act I extend myself into real nature and see the darkness receding on the limits of the horizon" (*EL3*, 149).

A third commitment in Emerson's ameliorative theodicy is that evil, while real, is nevertheless converted into good. Reflecting on the gold rush of 1849, he suggests, in "Considerations by the Way":

> I do not think very respectfully of the designs or the doings of the people who went to California, in 1849. It was a rush . . . a general gaol-delivery of all the rowdies of the river. Some of them went with honest purposes, some with very bad ones, and all of them with the very commonplace wish to find a short way to wealth. But nature watches over all, and turns this malfaisance to good. (*CW6*, 135)

In other words, nature, with Hegelian cunning, converts our narrow ends into broader benefit; for example, "California gets peopled and subdued,—civilized in this immoral way,—and on this fiction, a real prosperity is rooted and grown" (*CW6*, 135–36).

We are tracking the import of Emerson's law of compensation for Emersonian self-culture. On my reading, it funds an ameliorative theodicy that finds a latent moral in every lining and ties our strivings to cosmic dramas. And such results are not innocuous. First, the theodicy combats despair, giving the kind of lift that allows one to persevere when our genius is dull, our fate unkind, our peers abusive, or the scope of nature's stage sufficient to make a mockery of our strivings and laments. It does so because those who live under it can rest assured that things will get better. "When nature has work to be done, she creates a genius to do it," he writes in "Method of Nature," suggesting, I think, in an almost Greek manner, that nature is a self-healing physician (*CW1*, 128).

I find this thought at the close of "Experience," though more as a continuo alongside which the sentences swing:

> We dress in our garden, eat our dinners, discuss the household with our wives, and these things make no impression, are forgotten next week; but in the solitude to which every man is always returning, he has a sanity and revelations, which in his passage into new worlds he will carry with him. Never mind the ridicule, never mind the defeat: up again, old heart!—it seems to say,—there is victory yet for all justice; and the true romance which the world exists to realize, will be the transformation of genius into practical power. (*CW3*, 49)

Thus far, I have emphasized the transformation of genius into practical power as the goal of Emersonian self-culture, and I have tried to detail some of its mechanics, from native and ecstatic genius to a series of reflective acts like aversion to conformity and apology. Here, however, having considered the law of compensation, a return to these closing lines draws out other valences. Faced with the ridicule that nature's fluctuating immensity flings our way, our ventures may derail. As Emerson asks later in *Essays: Second Series*, "Must we not suppose somewhere in the universe a slight treachery and derision? Are we not engaged to a serious resentment of this that is made of us? Are we tickled trout, fools of nature?" (*CW3*, 112). But at that point, in that pitch, revelations concerning the eventual victory for justice would seem to lift the heart and realign its project of ascent. As the passage from "Nature" continues: "One look in at the face of heaven and earth lays all petulance to rest, and soothes us to wiser convictions."

Not that one can be certain that such revelations will arrive. They too, it seems, are moments of ecstatic genius. I say this because, after telling himself, "Never mind the defeat," Emerson pauses, and says, obliquely, "—it seems to say." The vagueness of the "it" is significant, for it leads me to wonder who—or better yet, what—buoys him here. A revelation, no doubt. But from whom or what? The "it" is not exactly a conclusive reply, and it calls me back to "Self-Reliance" and the excessive, incalculable movements of the aboriginal self. Moreover, at the close of "Experience," what this "it" says is less than certain, for Emerson is quite clear that it only *seems* to say such encouraging words, thus underscoring that there are times when the force of such revelations is slim or perhaps even waning. I note this now because if we are to fully gauge the law of compensation in Emersonian self-culture, we not only need to attend to the law but also to the manner in which is given, for that scene may hold prospects in store that are as yet unclear.

Emerson's ameliorative theodicy also quiets despair by assuring us that our strivings matter. Under the law of compensation, genius is not only the work of nature in the sense that we are nature unfolding, something we saw in chapter 2, but also how nature works toward its goal; it is a method of nature. We are thus part of the ameliorative process, and that may prove heartening and ennobling. "A man should know himself for a necessary actor," Emerson states. "A link was wanting between two craving parts of nature, and he was hurled into being as the bridge over that yawning need, the mediator betwixt two else unmarriageable facts" (*CW1*, 128).[8]

Though he marks us as the method of nature, Emerson is not suggesting that our role will be prominent. Given the prodigality or ecstasy of nature, its orientation toward universal as opposed to private ends, we may live a life closer to chaff than wheat. "In short, the spirit and peculiarity of that impression nature makes on us, is this, that it does not exist to any one or any number of particular ends, but to numberless and endless benefit, that there is in it no private will, no rebel leaf or limb, but the whole is oppressed by one superincumbent tendency, obeys that redundancy or excess of life which in conscious beings we call ecstasy" (*CW1*, 126–27). And: "This ecstatical state seems to direct a regard to the whole and not to the parts" (*CW1*, 131). Realizing that one belongs to the method of nature only comforts, therefore, by way of the universal ends that one helps realize. There is no promise of personal glory or achievement.

Almost twenty years later, in "Fate," Emerson terms this regard for universal ends in the face of personal unease or suffering "the double consciousness":

> A man must ride alternately on the horses of his private and his public nature, as the equestrians in the circus throw themselves nimbly from horse to horse, or plant one foot on the back of one, and the other foot on the back of the other. So when a man is the victim of his fate, has sciatica in his loins, and cramp in his mind; a club-foot and a club in his wit; a sour face, and a selfish temper; a strut in his gait, and a conceit in his affection; or is ground to powder by the vice of his race; he is to rally on his relation to the Universe, which his

ruin benefits. Leaving the daemon who suffers, he is to take sides with the Deity who secures universal benefit by his pain. (*CW6*, 25–26)[9]

This is a stark passage, and it recalls the Christian notion of offering up one's suffering to the divine in a posture of worship such that, precisely in that suffering, one affirms the omniscience of God and takes one's fate to also announce God's glory. If this is so, the double consciousness intensely manifests the kind of worship that Emerson believes consummates self-culture.[10]

That worship lies at self-culture's summit is clear from both the early lecture "Private Life" and the later essay "Worship." In 1840 he tells his audience: "Indeed it seems to me that the true culture of the soul has no better measure than the confidence of the man in the compensations of Being" (*EL3*, 252). Then, in *Conduct of Life*, we find: "In the last chapters, we treated some particulars of the question of culture. But the whole state of man is a state of culture; and its flowering and completion may be described as Religion, or Worship" (*CW6*, 108). Moreover, Emerson equates worship with the "public nature" to which the double consciousness would cling in terrible times (*CW6*, 108). For Emersonian self-culture, then, theodical abandonment is its highest moment, though again this "so be it" is predicated, not on discursive knowledge, but on the ungrounded sense (or revelation) that something like a divine, invisible hand husbands nature, that the door to the Creator is not only never closed within our souls but opens on to every point in nature's dynamic web.[11]

Emerson's theodical commitments play yet another role in self-culture: they appear to legitimate self-reliance and involuntary perceptions. As Stephen Whicher puts it, albeit with too great a differentiation: "He could proclaim self-reliance because he could also advocate God-reliance" (1953, 57). Emerson's position is stated rather strongly in Blotting Book III, from 1831: "To think is to receive. . . . To reflect is to receive truth immediately from God without any medium. That is living faith. . . . A trust in yourself is the height not of pride but of piety, an unwillingness to learn of any but God himself" (*JMN3*, 279). Here I am drawn to the thought that self-trust may lay claim to truth because, in the end, self-trust is piety, not egoism. Consider also this even bolder line from "Spiritual Laws": "Place yourself in the middle of the stream of power and wisdom which animates all whom it floats, and you are without effort impelled to truth, to right, and a perfect contentment. *Then you put all gainsayers in the wrong. Then you are the world, the measure of right, truth, of beauty"* (*CW2*, 81). I've italicized the last two sentences because they suggest that a derivation from the purposive strivings of the divine (my reading of the "stream of power and wisdom," what Emerson terms in "Circles" the "flying perfect") provides one with an inter-subjective standard, one that authorizes ignoring one's interlocutors should they propose something contrary (*CW2*, 179). Finally, the 1861 lecture "Natural Religion" repeats the conviction in a scene of discursive debate: "No whiggery, no amount of skeptical statement, makes any impression on high activity, either moral or intellectual. For these faculties owe their life directly to the source of life; are themselves still fresh from eternity, and breathe eternity" (*LL2*, 191).

The invisible hands of God thus not only grant or even assign us a spot on the cosmic stage, but they underwrite to some non-negligible extent the lines we there must learn to utter. In other words, the theodical currents of Emersonian self-culture do more that stave off despair, important as that is to a practice requiring perseverance. They also embolden the affirmations without apology that enable self-culture to have a path of its own; that is, the theodical ecstasies of nature seem to intensify the abandon with which Emerson celebrates self-trust. Moreover, the tug of these divine hands—what amounts to an insistent undertow of final causality—solicits from us a posture of worship that is the crescendo of self-culture's ascent.

In many ways, then, the law of identity underwrites Emersonian self-culture. But what of the law of metamorphosis? "For flowing is the secret of things. . . . *Becoming somewhat else* is the whole game of nature, & death the penalty of standing still" (*JMN10*, 408). Whereas the law of metamorphosis returns me again and again to the movement between primary and secondary experience, Emerson's theodicy appears to exit that flow. Like the "permanent wise man" that he denies exists, it figures nature's endgame with an economy of thorough compensation, a figuration that flies in the face of mortal experience even if helps some put their shoes on. In bringing these two laws together, then, I find myself at a crossroads. And it strikes me, as plain as sunrise, that well before I began this project, I had already taken one path and not the other. I thus need to turn back and specify why the theodical path opens before me as something less than a live option.

In an obvious but nevertheless troubling way, Emerson's theodicy sets history within a sacrificial economy. One can see this rather starkly if one considers the ends and means of the method of nature. Consider these two passages, both of which cast the invisible hands of Divinity into those of an arborist: "The gardener aims to produce a fine peach or pear, but my [nature's—JTL] aim is the health of the whole tree,—root, stem, leaf, flower, and seed,—and by no means the pampering of a monstrous pericarp at the expense of all the other functions" (*CW1*, 126). And: "Pruning: so many of our best youth must die of consumption, so many of despair, & so many be dunces or insane before the one shoot which they all promised to be can force its way upward to a thrifty tree" (*JMN9*, 24–25). The claims are rather precise. As individuals, we are expendable test runs. Moreover, most fail to reach the end of the assembly line. And unfortunate as that is, it is hubris to expect that our singular fate should matter. In fact, such an expectation produces a monstrosity: something out of line with the order of nature and its continual process of converting would-be ends into means.

More than individuals are carved on this bench, however. "Nature and moral laws work in cosmical and secular periods," says the "Natural Religion" lecture, which continues: "They can well wait and work slowly. Races are insignificant, ages are a span, to these long eternal powers. They can well afford to drop a race and an age out of the flowing eternity. We may be sure they will strike" (*LL2*, 186). Recall that Emerson regards race as a collective temperament out of which an individual's native genius is molded, albeit with exceptions. Races are thus not unlike individual experiments, and thus some may prove fit for pruning. "The German and Irish millions, like the Negro, have a great deal of guano in their destiny. They are ferried over the Atlantic, and carted over America, to ditch and to drudge, to make corn cheap, and then to lie down prematurely to make a spot of green grass on the prairie" (*CW6*, 9). True, the latter passage from "Fate" occurs in the essay's first section, what involves a recounting of the *doxa* that the essay as a whole aims to recast toward a humbler though pious regard for fate. And yes, in this paragraph in particular, Emerson is considering the views of Knox, which he had already chastised in *Representative Men*. Nevertheless, he grants to Knox "pungent and unforgettable truths" and begins the following section by announcing that we "cannot trifle with this reality, this cropping-out in our planted gardens of the core of the world" (*CW6*, 9 and 11). This suggests, I think, that for Emerson the method of nature works to just conclusions at the level of racial fates, even in the madness of global racism.

Now, you might recall me to Emerson's suggestion that the "civility of the world has reached that pitch, that their [the slaves—JTL] more moral genius is becoming indispensable, and the quality of this race is to be honored for itself" (*EAW*, 31). But note that should this not be the case, Emerson would find himself, at the level of the philosophy of history, describing the global slave trade as a pruning process and remarking that, in the larger scheme of things, nature can well afford to drop a race out of its production process. To be clear, then, my worry in this context is not Emerson's regard for the native genius of any race in particular, but that his philosophy of history can regard racially perpetrated evil as fair means to a fairer end.

While its sacrificial economy strikes me as barbaric, I do not think that Emerson's theodicy produces indifference, either in him or us. Emerson denies just this, cogently arguing in "Compensation" that the "soul is not a compensation, but a life," and one that we'll lose to the having-lived if we prove indifferent to circumstances we know, in our hearts, must be redressed (*CW2*, 70). In other words, because Emersonian self-culture demands an active soul, his theodicy will not produce fellow travelers. If anything, the invisible hands of history seem to stoke the fire, as evidenced by his March 7th address on the Fugitive Slave Law, which claims, "There is a Divine Providence in the world which will not save us but through our own co-operation" (*EAW*, 89). Not that any lack of cooperation will overturn the method of nature. As he says in "Natural Religion": "Though we fold our hands, these laws will execute themselves." But "we can ill afford to wait such distant avengers. We are not afraid that justice will not be done, but that we shall not live to see it. The laws are of eternity, but we are short-lived" (*LL2*, 186). In other words, because indifference replaces the life of the soul with a life yet to be lived, it promises a fate as distant from self-culture's true romance as conformity.

I should note further that, given our inability to see the ultimate ends of nature, Emerson's theodicy would not produce apologists for widespread programs of violence. In his hands, the double consciousness asks only that we side with universe against our own suffering, not that of others. No, what troubles me beyond the sacrificial economy it institutes is the general bearing that Emerson's theodicy embodies, namely, a kind of asceticism that flees from the mortality of our condition. I say asceticism, given Nietzsche's diagnosis of the ascetic ideal, an economy of valuation that will only affirm life on the basis of its transcendental redemption, one Emerson figures by way of God's invisible hands tending our fates with a final cause well in view.[12] I find this palpably present in Sermon XC: "For the whole value of the soul depends on the fact that it contains a divine principle, that it is a house of God, and the voice of the eternal inhabitant may always be heard within it" (CS2, 267). But it is also apparent many years later, when Emerson confesses that the "Author of Nature has not left himself without a witness in any sane mind" (CE11, 486). The thoughts are congruent because they both banish, from orders of reason and value, lives built around something other than theism. And this is noxious because it renders such lives monstrous, phenomena to be dismissed rather than engaged, let alone essayed, as if, among all things, these alone were mean.

Now, my objection is not that theodical self-effacement produces a world-historical nihilism that threatens to undo us all. I lack the calculator for such predictions, compelling as they sometimes seem. Rather, my unease is Emersonian. This trace of asceticism radiates a kind of shame, one whose life begins in apology. It is as if, unable to either significantly mark the cosmic stage or enduringly bend nature's conversions toward our own ends, we had no right to speak for ourselves, to utter something other than the words of saint or sage, unless, of course, we prove in the end to be *the* saint and sage ventriloquizing. Moreover, insofar as a kind of worship of this divinely strung puppet life consummates Emersonian self-culture, I also find woven into Emerson's theodicy a kind of self-loathing, one that not only flees from the turmoil of our condition but also repudiates it whenever he abandons the "dæmon who suffers" in favor of the "deity who secures universal benefit by his pain," to recall the language of "Fate." I say this because, should we side with our dæmon at such moments, defending Job against the whirlwind, Emerson would be bewildered, at least when he's in the mood that tunes his theodical moments.[13]

George Kateb is also troubled at this point, although his worry is that Emerson is not "content to bless particulars as such" (2002, 64). I see the point. Without the guiding hand of the method of nature apparent, it is unlikely that Emerson would build any altars at all. And yet I'm unhappy with the notion of "particulars as such." Given Emerson's commitment to the relational nature of things, and given the dynamism of those relations, that is, their metamorphoses, I'm not sure what "a particular as such" is; and I fear that it means things as they are in themselves by themselves, which is language that Emerson wisely eschews. I thus prefer locating the vice of Emerson's theodical leanings in a posture of self-apology, one that shows, at its heart, something of a failure of nerve, what can also be termed a lack of self-trust, given the way Emerson sometimes regards that virtue along the lines of courage.

Other worries also leave me wanting to excise the theodical from Emersonian self-culture. Return to the philosophy of history. Emerson's invisible hand continually legitimates the history of the victor. If a race is lost, forgotten, or its remains only thinly apparent, so be it, for as we've seen, the method of nature can sustain the loss of a race. This troubles me in part because it consecrates official histories that erase their victims, thus fueling the fire of ongoing violence. (I think here of the fate of Native Americans in the United States and the way their ongoing suffering walks hand in hand with an obliviousness to the genocidal policies and practices that characterize so much of U.S. history, and this despite landmarks like Dead Indian Road in Ashland, Oregon, or the endless Northeastern towns bearing native names like Chappaqua but housing few or no native peoples.) Looking back, I see just this fate unfolding in Emerson's estimation of the annexation of Texas:

> The question of the annexation of Texas is one of those which look very differently to the centuries and to the years. It is very much certain that the strong British race which have now overrun so much of this continent, must overrun that tract, & Mexico & Oregon also, and it will in the course of ages be of small import by what particular occasions & methods it was done. (*JMN9*, 74)

My point is not that Emerson supported the annexation, but that, given his philosophy of history, one looking back on the event would find and be satisfied with the method of nature at work in its violence and thus fail to consider the methods employed or who, already nameless, was overrun. Like California, "Texas" too would say: "Nature watches over all, and turns this malfaisance to good" (*CW6*, 135).[14]

I suppose that I also find theologically secured final causes a bit too much to countenance, meaning that I experience them as Emerson experienced the attempt to base one's faith on the unique and miraculous incarnation of Jesus: "This claim impairs, to my mind, the soundness of him who makes it, and indisposes us to his communion. . . . It is something not in Nature: it is contrary to that law of Nature which all wise men recognize; namely, never to require a larger cause than is necessary to the effect" (*CE11*, 488). For me, the effect in question is self-trust, and thus the issue concerns what serves as the condition of the possibility of our abandonment to our genius, native and ecstatic. I hope I have shown how dearly Emerson clings to his theodicy in order to achieve this effect and stave off despair, even insanity. And I hope my departure can be seen for what it is. In Emerson's words, to which I haven't added all that much: "Whoever thinks a story gains by the prodigious, by adding something out of nature, robs it more than he adds" (*CE11*, 489).

Set into the larger context of Emersonian self-culture, I suppose one could also say that in attempting to give us a place within the whole, a place that seems to make life worth living, Emerson's theodicy unimaginatively and unimaginably curtails the import of the law of metamorphosis. I say this because although it would check the play of perpetual change, final causality actually seems undone by it. Consider this passage from "The Method of Nature": "We can point to nothing final; but tendency appears on all hands: planet, system, constellation, total nature is growing like a field of maize in July; is becoming somewhat else; is in rapid metamorphosis" (*CW1*, 126). Pictured here is the supersession of any form that could be said to stand as nature's *telos*. But if "*becoming somewhat else* is the whole game of nature, & death the penalty of standing still," how can there be a final cause to which all previous forms ascend? (*JMN13*, 408). In order to have a beginning and an end, one needs the stability of some form over time, like the form of a life that moves from acorn to oak tree. But if every form gives way to other forms, from creatures to planets to systems (and I take the universe to be a system), the identities that could be oriented to something like an end evaporate, and one is left with change, even continuity, but not ascendancy.

For this same reason, I also would hesitate to speak of growth in the face of Emersonian nature, though Emerson does just that in "The

Method of Nature" (*CW1*, 126). Without an identity of form over time, that which can be said to grow proves so diffuse as to fracture the horticultural metaphors Emerson favors in figuring his theodicy. Instead, I prefer "Nature," where we find: "Motion or change, and identity and rest, are the first and second secrets of nature: Motion and Rest" (*CW 3*, 105). I prefer this turn of phrase because "rest" underscores, in a way that teleological trajectories do not, the fleeting nature of those patterns that nature produces, from our own moods, to the emergence and disappearance of species, to the death of stars and whatever gathered around their mass and heat.

I have been charting my departure from Emerson's theodicy, both wary of the prospects it holds in store and less aggrieved than he by those it keeps at bay. I have also been affirming the law of metamorphosis and its import for self-culture, trying to remain true to the observances esteemed at the close of "Experience." In place of a worshipful regard for God's invisible hands, I've been trying to fashion an open and conspiring regard for our incessant movement between primary and secondary experience, heartbreaking and carnivalesque as its casualties may prove.

And yet I fear I've set the table too starkly. You might think at this point that Emerson's theodical commitments exhaust his sense of the divine. You might also think I'm suggesting that we simply excise the divine from Emersonian self-culture. Neither is quite right, but I've no doubt given some reason to think this way. In fact, the matter is far messier than this, and in a way that recalls us to the force and play of quotation in Emersonian self-culture. Moreover, what I have in mind also evidences how wily metamorphosis can prove. Please bear with me, then, as I renew our conversation regarding the divine in Emerson and intensify its stakes.

Throughout his corpus, Emerson's conceives of the divine as immanent, the life of lives, the power of forms. But this is not to say that its immanence is stable, that its movements don't wildly embody the law of metamorphosis, and in ways that offer self-culture some startling prospects. Let me explain by way of a distinction drawn from "The Over-Soul": "Revelation is the disclosure of the soul" (*CW2*, 167). Here the genitive says two things. First, revelation, that which discloses the operations of the divine, is a story regarding the presence of the soul in nature. Let's term this the *theodical divine,* what "Compensation" terms the "in-working of the All, and of its moral aim," that power whose fingers, capable of converting every end into a means toward another end, can be found in every pocket of the cosmos (*CW2*, 62). But second, one can also read the genitive as "to"; that is, revelation occurs *to* the soul. Let's term this the *phenomenological divine*, for it names less the "what" of revelation than how it is given, namely, as a divination—what we have been calling an involuntary perception—whose nature is dæmonic, a "stream whose source is hidden," which is "descending into us from we know not whence," to recall the opening paragraph of "The Over Soul" (*CW2*, 159).

As we've seen, Emerson's theodicy in part secures his self-trust, and thus the theodical divine, to a certain extent, underwrites the phenomenological divine, engenders it. Or to be more precise, the theodical divine tunes Emerson such that he finds divinity and divination in the actions of his soul. But in doing so, the theodical divine elevates the human soul to a site of remarkable authority. Not that it authorizes the human soul to self-consciously legislate the nature of divinity. But it does establish the soul as the principal site of disclosure for the dictates of divinity, and this does establish involuntary perceptions as the arbiters of revealed truths.

I am beginning to sketch a movement within Emerson's own thought, one wherein the figure of the divine, which appears in Emerson's theodicy to ascetically undermine the human, also emboldens and empowers the human.[15] But to what ends? Here's one: "They call it Christianity, I call it Consciousness" (*JMN7*, 28). This is a radical thought, for it characterizes every human being as an incarnation. And yet it reads like the tuition of thoughts we've already encountered. Because Emerson's theodical divine is everywhere, consciousness is a site of revelation in the fact that it apprehends—that is, both in terms of what it apprehends and in its very being.

Now, if everyone is an incarnation, Jesus is just another "divine bard," as Emerson suggests in his Divinity School address: one of the "friends of *my* virtue, of *my* intellect, of *my* strength" (*CW1*, 83).[16] What is startling here is not only the denial of Jesus' unique status as the "son of God" but also the suggestion that his status as revelatory is bound to his reception, hence my added emphases, though Emerson also makes the point: "A true conversion, a true Christ, is now, as always, to be made, by the reception of beautiful sentiments" (CW1, 83).

One end accomplished by this movement of the theodical divine into the phenomenological divine is the Christ-ification of humanity and the humanization of Jesus, though again, this is not to say that humans thereby become the alpha and the omega. The power of the theodical divine lies precisely in its ongoing transformations, for example its ability to be incarnate. What unseats Jesus will therefore unseat us, namely, the fact that the soul becomes, and thus the project of revelation remains unfinished, as Emerson observes in "Uses of Great Men": "With each new mind a new secret of nature transpires, nor can the bible be closed until the last great man is born" (*CW4*, 12). Still, for a time, everyone deserves to be called "gospel-bearer," a title that confers on one a wild authority with regard to what we should take as evidence of the soul's presence in nature, hence Emerson's strong insistence that "we should be so pre-occupied and nailed to the perpetual revelation from within, that we cannot listen to Stoicism, or Buddhism, or Christianity, or only to nod assent and pleasure when these utter somewhat that agrees with our own" (*LL2*, 184).

In question is how far one might push the authority and confidence that the theodical divine brings to the soul in its involuntary perceptions. So far we've seen how Emerson, by way of the phenomenological divine, subdues the claims of tradition and, more particularly, the authority and unique divinity of Jesus. But are there other prospects awaiting those who also champion the phenomenological divine? Note these stark remarks from later lectures. In "The Rule of Life," Emerson acknowledges: "The vast generalizations of science destroy such toy-heavens. In this nineteenth century, everything told us of the Creator must be on the scale in which he is known to us in his Works, and not on the fond legends of some ignorant tribe" (*LL2*, 378). This is noteworthy because it shows Emerson insisting that revelations regarding the "in-working of the All" are subordinate to the divinations of our own minds. "Let us have nothing now which is not its own evidence," he says in "Men of Thought," which I take to mean that one should acknowledge only those claims that have the kind of phenomenological indubitability that characterizes involuntary perceptions or can be shown to belong to their tuition. If so, here the phenomenological divine turns back into the theodical divine as the measure that shall judge the latter's veracity. Said otherwise, it would appear that the phenomenological divine, although it initially grew out of the theodical divine, now has the authority to call the theodical divine into question should a bolder generalization, one born of a more powerful genius, encircle and thereby trump its evidence.

Elsewhere in "Men of Thought," Emerson announces: "Truth is our only armour in all passages of life and death. The words you spoke are forgotten, but the part you took [and thus the effects you add—JTL] is organized into the body of the universe. I will speak the truth in my heart, or think the truth against what is called God" (*LL1*, 187). The final phrase of this passage is ambiguous. On the face of it, Emerson wishes to think on behalf of the true God against what many take God to be, as he does in "The Divinity School Address" when he observes, "Men have come to speak of the revelation as somewhat long ago given and done, as if God were dead" (*CW1*, 84). But what if we read the phrase "what is called God" with greater scope? What if "God," as a figure of revelation, as the fruit of a whole history of ongoing actions of the soul, as a trajectory enduring multiple metamorphoses, were no more than "what is called God"? If so, if we can hear this thought in Emerson's remark, then what is broached here is nothing less than the death of God.

In his *Gay Science*, §125, Nietzsche figures the death of God by way of a madman's confrontation with "those who did not believe in God" (1974, 181–82). Two features strike me as particularly relevant to our discussion. First, the madman presents the event of God's death as "still on its way," as if its significance were apparent only over time, hence the need to declare God's passing to a group of atheists. This is so because the death of God names less the death of some supreme being than the collapse of theistically grounded orders of meaning, from the moral (intuitive conscience) to the metaphysical (a well-ordered because created universe), from the epistemic (the natural light, even Descartes' use of God in his *Meditations*) to the political (natural law and natural right). The slow unfolding of the "divine decomposition" is thus really the slow unraveling of those orders of meaning funded by the notion of an omnipotent, omniscient, omni-benevolent creator. Second, the madman is insistent that we have killed God "All of us are his murderers." I take this to mean that a history of inquiry, imagining, and prospecting has slowly led many to regard the notion of God with incredulity, as the "fond legend of ignorant tribes," to use Emerson's language toward uncertain ends. "But how did we do this?" the madman asks. "How could we drink up the sea? Who gave us the sponge to wipe away the entire horizon?" While the madman doesn't answer these questions, I think we've seen something like an answer in Emerson.

Consider the matter this way. What fueled the strivings that rendered "God" incredible, if not the very notion of God? What pushes the natural light to seek truth or the conscientious to demand justice? Or what raises in one a radical self-trust? In each case, I can imagine that the idea of a God calls us to such ends. For example, an omni-benevolent, omniscient, and omnipotent creator may lead one to expect a just cosmic order. With such an idea in tow, one might then survey creation for indications of a comprehensive justice. But if one finds something quite different, say the inexplicable suffering of innocents, one might then deny the existence of God, given what has come to be called the "problem of evil." In such a scenario, the very idea of God gives birth to notions and practices that in turn assail it. In such a process, I think we can say that we come to kill God by living out lives inspired by God. Or, more generally, one finds in the history of God a history that involves a certain conception of the human, a series of metamorphoses that, though they stem from the idea of God, eventually push past it and toward we know not what.

We are tracing a metamorphosis within Emerson's own thought, one concerning the fate of the idea of God. Our reading, therefore, concerns less what Emerson has to say about metamorphosis than how his texts embody it. But how deeply is Emerson a part of this history of divine decomposition? Do we really find him turning his back on the divine to the point of theocide? I do not think the question admits of a simple answer. As we have seen, the law of metamorphosis and Emerson's theodicy produce movements that are far from stable. In fact, at points they conflict with one another, for example, regarding the notion of transhistorical final causes, a fate that leaves those who would inherit Emerson at something of a crossroads. I think we'll find the same with regard to the question of God's death, though I should stress that my concern in what follows is not what Emerson really thought. No doubt he was a theist. Rather, I'm interested in nascent moments, points at which Emerson ventures a possible future whose prospects might become my own.

In a far from exhaustive way, I've brought together some passages that seem to incline toward theocide. The first is well known. In "Self-

Reliance," Emerson tells an imagined interlocutor who is worried that the involuntary perceptions that Emerson so esteems "may be from below, not from above": "They do not seem to me to be such; but if I am the Devil's child, I will live then from the Devil" (*CW2*, 30). Barbara Packer finds this remark ironic because a "decorous ex-minister in the town of Concord" could in no way live from the devil (1982, 14). Moreover, the remark clearly does not meet the objection to which it is a response. It should thus be read as a kind of ironic subterfuge, she thinks, one that "invites the attack of hostile readers by appearing to offer them exactly the evidence they need to convict him. These passages, like the inkblots of a Rorschach, are less important for what they contain than for the response they invoke. They ask us to imagine a *voice*, and the voice we imagine determines whether we think the author an ironist, a Satanist, or a fool" (19). In other words, if I follow her, the claim is that such ironic flourishes force us to determine whether this is a text we will continue to read, and they make plain that in large measure we shall have to complete the thoughts it initiates.

While I share Packer's sense of Emerson's expectations for his readers, I don't think he envelops them in irony. After all, genuine ventures offered to readers who take them personally will produce a similar relationship between speaker and addressee, as chapter 1 shows. Moreover, irony is a trope of pedagogical or playful self-possession, the evidence of an author fully in control of even those passages that seem missteps. But Emerson also writes in lyric possession, offering essays that *essay*; that is, he venture experiments. One should thus expect lines that risk uncertain futures, and to say so is not to deny that Emerson is a consummate stylist. Rather, it recognizes an aspect of his style.

Of course, it may be that Emerson in no way could venture the devilish identification that "Self-Reliance" seems to offer. But are we so sure that we know what it means to be the "Devil's child"? Are such progeny always of the order of Aleister Crowley?[17] I think Milton might bring something else to our ears. In *Paradise Lost*, Satan's resents Jesus' authority:

> . . . but not so wak'd
> *Satan,* so call him now, his former name
> Is heard no more Heav'n; he of the first,
> If not the first Arch-Angel, great in Power,
> In favour and præeminence, yet fraught

With envy against the Son of God, that day
Honor'd by his great Father, and proclaim'd
Messiah King anointed, could not bear
Through pride that sight, and thought himself impair'd.
(Book V: 654–62)

Finding these lines in this context, I am led to read Emerson's own de-deification of Jesus in a similar light. After all, he takes himself to be, in principle, Jesus' equal, writing, "They call it Christianity, I call it Consciousness," as well as "I shun father and mother and wife and brother, when my genius calls me" (*JMN7,* 28; *CW2,* 30). (The former marks him and every sentient being an incarnation, whereas the latter performatively establishes his genius as a messianic force to which his reflective life stands in discipleship.) But that is not all, for in 1842 he goes so far as to call Jesus the "great Defeat," insisting: "The mind requires a far higher exhibition of character, one which shall make itself good to the senses as well as to the soul; a success to the senses as well as to the soul" (*JMN8,* 227–28). Human beings are thus not only Jesus' peers but also, eventually, his betters. I do not see, therefore, on what grounds Emerson would disagree with the thought, attributed to Satan by Abdiel, that it is "Flatly unjust, to bind with laws the free, / And equal over equals to let Reign," which is what Satan takes the deification of Jesus to entail (Book V: 819–21). Look at what Emerson says in his "Divinity School Address" as he recounts the mischief worked by New England's "noxious exaggeration about the *person* of Jesus":

> You shall not be a man even. You shall not own the world; you shall not dare, and live after the infinite Law that is in you, and in company with the infinite Beauty which heaven and earth reflect to you in all lovely forms; but you must subordinate your nature to Christ's nature. (*CW1,* 82)

It is this refusal to subordinate his genius to the person and insights of Jesus that strikes me as Satanic in Emerson. Not that Emerson champions Satan over Jesus or even God in *Paradise Lost.* If anything, his remarks on Milton ignore Lucifer.[18] But the sentiment of that rebellion percolates in the insistence that "no law is sacred to me but that of my nature" (*CW2,* 30). I thus take the self-trust that Emerson praises to be Satanic in a Miltonic manner, which is to say, that one who lives a life of radical self-trust is a devil's child.[19]

I find Emerson's flirtation with a Satanic lineage provocative because it evidences the depth to which he will remain true to self-trust. I would put it this way: Emerson's commitment to self-trust is so intense that among its prospects one finds an assertion of the right to determine, through receptions of involuntary perceptions, what distinguishes the sacred from the profane, a right that renders one god-like, a source of the sacred. Recall again two lines from "Self-Reliance": "Nothing is at last sacred but the integrity of your own mind"; and: "No law can be sacred to me but that of my nature" (CW2, 30). These are perhaps Emerson's most radical thoughts as far as the history of God is concerned. With them, the phenomenological divine establishes itself as the last court of appeals with regard to what deserves the title "sacred." It is thus difficult to see, in the face of such affirmation, how one can sustain a distinction between a self-revealing God and the demands placed on us by our ecstatic genius. In other words, and to again employ Milton's terms, Emersonian self-trust amounts to "Affecting all equality with God, / In imitation of that mount whereon / Messiah was declar'd in site of Heav'n" (Book V: 760–62).[20]

Now, blurring the distinction between genius and the godhead is not without its effects.[21] Foremost, it renders the idea of God superfluous, at least in this corner of Emersonian self-culture. I say this because if the sacred is always a matter of what is disclosed to the soul, then the idea of God adds nothing by way of authority to the disclosive capacities of our condition. And that, I think, is precisely the kind of subtle murder that Nietzsche's madman witnesses.

Let's now look away from the issue of authority toward one of generation. Here is a remarkable line from "Circles":

> The life of man is a self-evolving circle, which, from a ring imperceptibly small, rushes on all sides outwards to new and larger circles, and that without end. The extent to which this generation of circles, *wheel without wheel* will go, depends on the force or truth of the individual soul. (CW2, 180)

I have italicized the phrase "wheel without wheel" because it invokes Ezekiel 1:15–22, verses that portray the "glory of the Lord" in terms of a world of living creatures circumvented and animated by four wheels—"their construction being as it were a wheel within a wheel." But in describing the life of humans, Emerson finds the interior wheel lacking, a thought that recalls "The Method of Nature," where one only chances upon emanation, or the Journal entry that finds throughout the universe a series of false bottoms. I return to the thought because, in his translation of Ezekiel, Emerson figures our condition without a discernable creator or sustainer, more a mad rush of motion and rest than the handiwork of a supreme craftsman. Or, to recall another line quoted earlier, one that figures Emerson's own quotation, here we see the thought of a translation that precedes the work of a translator—"There was never a time when there was none."

Before us now is less the thought that God is superfluous for the purposes of self-trust than the suggestion, presented in a translation of scripture, that our condition proves the same whether God exists or not. Either way we are wheels without wheels. Either way, "All is riddle, and the key to the riddle is another riddle," to recall "Illusions." In Emerson's philosophy of nature, I thus sense another nail for God's coffin, one driven by the elusiveness of God's presence, a puzzling state of affairs that leads us toward a life that might make do in God's absence. But more than that, Emerson's essay actually begins to indicate the presence of that absence and make do in it. Note how he imagines nature responding to the query "But to what end?" Nature answers: "I grow, I grow. All is nascent, infant" (*CW1,* 126). The reply is remarkable. First, it refuses to answer a request for first or final causes, "grow" replacing *telos* and its finalities, "nascent" replacing some prime motion.[22] Second, it marks that refusal as nature's own, thus delimiting our condition with the terms it does provide—those of perpetual beginnings. Third, the banal tone of the response arrives with a kind of self-satisfaction, as if it were sufficient, as if it were a small matter to make do with whatever proves possible without a final end in view, say a walk, a dinner, or perhaps a life unbounded by either an alpha or omega but nevertheless nascent and flowing, ebbing and waning, that is, continually changing.

At two points, then, Emerson's thought inclines toward theocide. The idea of God is incipiently abandoned in the momentum of self-trust's rising confidence and is found to be expendable when, without melancholy, perhaps even with abandonment, Emerson observes the phenomenological limits of our condition, that behind which analysis cannot go. We have, therefore, within Emerson's own writings, a nascent context of divine decomposition, one that I find thickening in the poem that prefaces "Experience." I have always been struck by the lords of life, the figures that pass us by and that, tomorrow, "will wear another face" (*CW2*, 25). Among "Use and Surprise" and "Surface and Dream," there also walks "the inventor of the game / Omnipresent without name." But how are we to read this? On Emerson's terms, we are not omnipresent, but fragments, and thus the inventor of the game is a theological trope if ever there was one. And yet, here we are told that tomorrow it will wear another face, as if the *theos* too will change. Moreover, the poem concludes with nature whispering words of encouragement, and proclaiming: "The founder thou! these are thy race." In setting the lords of life within our race, our nature, and in underscoring their and our permutations, the poem suggests, I think, that nature addresses us beyond the reach of a theistic creator, thus repeating with even greater boldness the line of thought whose infancy we spied in "The Method of Nature." Furthermore, we, not the inventor, are the ones marked as the founders of the life whose lords daily pass us by, although, as Cavell (2003) has shown, we found such a life by finding and affirming it as our thrown condition, as a race always still to be run, not by grounding it once and for all.

Recall, please, one of the epigraphs to this chapter: "If Christianity cannot look to us as it looked to our fathers, we must thank Christianity for that very enlargement" (*LL2*, 388). Consider also this pronouncement: "Christianity must quickly take a niche that waits for it in the Pantheon of the Past, and figure as Mythology, henceforward and not a kingdom, town, statute, rite, calling, man, woman, or child but is threatened by the new spirit" (*JMN7*, 403). These lines are remarkable, given that they describe quite well the point at which we find ourselves. Surveying Emerson's Christian inheritance, we've found it recoiling against itself to the point of "becoming somewhat else." I say this because at various points—for example, self-trust as well as first and final causes—the hold of theism over Emersonian self-culture perceptibly weakens, even though those points initially belong to lines emanating from the very idea of God. This suggests, I think, that while Emersonian self-culture most certainly sets itself within a theodical universe, it also ventures a future unbound by those limits, thus offering prospects presumably unthinkable in the prose of a once-dedicated minister. Not that Emerson openly declares, let alone celebrates, the death of

God. As we saw in "Fate," he willingly sacrifices the dictates of his dæmon, his genius, to what he regards as the benefit his suffering and confusion secure in God's invisible hands. But Emerson also writes: "The destiny of organized nature is amelioration, and who can tell its limits?" (*CW4*, 20). We should be unsurprised, therefore, we who would inherit Emersonian self-culture, which entails, in part, assuming and conspiring in its prospects, that Emerson's essays might unsettle even the wheel around which it carries out its revolutions.

Let me specify some of what I think awaits those who take up the trajectories of a theocidal Emersonian self-culture. First, our perseverance no longer will find ballast in the thought that "we shall win at the last." Not only does nothing indicate this, but also the teleological figure of the last, the omega, should dissolve from our horizon, thus leaving us to conspire more with the foregrounds of our condition, our mortal steppes. Second, a post-theological self-culture will have to conspire without any expectation that our strivings are congruent with the "vast employments & natures" of the cosmos. Not only is that not our stage, but also there are no forms or agencies that persist long enough to attribute to the cosmos anything like employments. So again, to the foreground, to what addresses us in the movement between what we converse with, in city and country, and whatever the labor of reflection manages to reflect, eloquently or not. Third, the call to an active life that initiates self-culture will lose a few trumpets, the kind that ring out when Emerson announces: "God will not have his work made manifest by cowards" (*CW2*, 28). Instead, we will have to make do with the thought that a cowardly life is liable to manifest nothing—except, perhaps, its cowardice—and I doubt that can be done with any eloquence. "But do your work, and I shall know you," he writes a bit further on. "Do your work, and you shall reinforce yourself" (*CW2*, 32). Fail to, I would add, and our lives will say little to nothing, wind in dry grasses, as Eliot would put it. Fail to, and we shall scatter, an ensemble of quotations chattering past one another.

We were led to the question of the divine by my desire to render more concrete the law of metamorphosis and its place in Emersonian self-culture. I hope this journey has succeeded, if only by showing how Emerson's texts transform when allowed to recoil upon themselves, just as we are transformed when they are read into us as we read into them. I think we might name these transformations "self-overcoming," again finding a prospect in Nietzsche.[23] I find the term felicitous because not only do we find Emerson's texts transforming themselves (and us in the process), but also they occasionally carry forward trajectories immanent to their own quotations. That is, they overcome themselves by abandoning themselves to themselves, if such a phrase can sustain itself. I also am drawn to the thought of self-overcoming because of how it casts the way of abandonment, stressing the leave-taking that is a part of affirmation, underscoring that our casualties are not without casualties. This is an advance because it clarifies how an eloquent life must abandon itself to quoting translations that occur across the relentless movement of our condition, a movement between conversations rooted in our affinities (which includes our genius) as well as reflective engagements with what is found there.

Of course, there is no "self-overcoming" per se, and thus here, as always, one should share Emerson's worry that general rules offer little to self-culture. The cut lies instead with particular transformations. Recall that Emerson's law of identity institutes a theodicy that calls for "such a grasp of the whole, as to preserve it when he is ridiculous and unfortunate," even though this grasp, which Emerson aligns with the soul, flies in the face of our understanding, and to the point that "one prevails now, all buzz & din, & the other prevails then, all infinitude & paradise" (*LL1*, 252; *JMN8*, 10–11).[24] This is the double consciousness that encircles Emerson's theodical self-culture, one whose posture of worship trumps experiences that drive us to ask, "Must we not suppose somewhere in the universe a slight treachery and derision?" (*CW3*, 112). With the death of God, however, this form seems undone. In the least, this kind of worship is no longer possible, deprived, as it is, of its object. But then, this is not simply to champion what Emerson regards as the discourse of the understanding. First, given the fate of the concept of efficient causality, most notably its origins in the casualties of our condition, one needn't worry about a turn to scientism. As Emerson says, even after undermining the pretensions of occult inquiries, "Willingly I too say, Hail! to the unknown awful powers which transcend the ken of the understanding," for example, our ecstatic genius and its involuntary perceptions (*CE10*, 27). Second, the despair of the understanding remains a "shadow of God" insofar as its expectations derive from the promise of a theological agency at the beginning and end of nature.[25] Without such an expectation, however, the supposition regarding treachery fails to arise, thus paving the way for a theologically uncompromised affirmation.

And yet, at this juncture I would still speak of a double consciousness. On the one hand, there is the way of abandonment, a life paved by the involuntary touchstones of our essays and mortared with self-trust. But as "Experience" makes plain, "I know better than to claim any completeness for my picture. I am a fragment, and this is a fragment of me" (*CW3*, 47). The point is that causality is not the only concept born of casualty—such is the life of the mind, and we would do well to live in observance of that fact, that difference between primary experience— our temperamental, moody, and occasionally ecstatic conversation—and whatever reflective life puts into and draws out of it. Thus, while it compels us to affirm our genius, Emersonian self-culture simultaneously compels us to see just past it, to observe the limit that Emerson repeatedly figures as a door through which we and the world enter, intertwined in a host of fickle affinities. But this says little. I will thus use chapter 5 to say more about what this double movement entails.

FIVE

On the Edges of Our Souls

We strangely stand on,—souls do,—on the very edges of their own
spheres, leaning tiptoe towards & into the adjoining sphere.
—*JMN9*, 228

Self-culture labors toward an eloquent life that in part manifests a character we've found ourselves able and willing to live out. And it does so
with an eye on the full range of our being—word and deed, alone and
among others, at home, in the market, wherever our reach runs. Not that
eloquence entails a thorough self-mastery. Given the breadth of our
quoting nature and its ongoing metamorphoses, our lives always manifest more than those possibilities we've found and affirmed. Furthermore, in a manner that confounds analysis, the life we aim to cultivate is
given pre-reflectively in variously mooded events of native and ecstatic
genius. The former is tied to temperament, a determinate affinity with
the world that inclines toward certain corners and thus entails "a determination of character to a peculiar end" (*JMN4*, 378). Moreover, bound
as it is to what it is not, our native manners quote the very world they engage, much like my own work quotes the innumerable conditions that
enable it: the English language, particular authors, trees for paper, tea for
focus, electricity for my computer, and so on, as far as we can see and
then farther. Ecstatic genius involves similar disclosures and alliances,
though these exceed the dictates of our native temperament, thus introducing into Emersonian self-culture a fundamental incalculability, one
Emerson most often aligns with a creator that seems bent on outdoing itself: "To a soul alive to God every moment is a new world. . . . [It] shall

constitute an epoch, a revolution in the minds on whom you act & in your own. The awakened soul, the man of genius makes every day such a day" (*JMN4*, 266).

Together, these two modes of genius form the principal sources of insight and inspiration for an eloquent life. They focus our ongoing conversation with things, allowing us to meet ourselves, coming and going, and to find a place for ourselves among the world that always accompanies those transitions. But they are not self-executing. Instead, they must be translated into practical power, and this requires a series of reflective acts. Some are negative, for example, aversion to conformity and apology; some are positive, for example, abandonment to the ventures our genius proffers. And some of the latter are creative in their own right, for example, prospecting possible futures for what dawns upon us. Self-culture is thus a braid of pre-reflective and reflective events.

Though purposive and thus teleological, self-culture is not the kind of project that concludes, for we are ever subject to motion and rest, a fate that Emerson articulates in terms of a law of metamorphosis. Self-culture is thus an interminable affair; there will always be a chance that our genius will call us to undo the life that we had until then been fashioning. As he writes in *The Present Age* lectures, "The primary question that distinguishes like a Day of Judgment between men is: Are they still advancing? Or are the seals set to their character and [are] they now making a merchandise simply of that which they can do?" (*EL3*, 235). In the previous chapter we underwent just such a redirection in Emerson's own texts, what I termed, following Nietzsche, a "self-overcoming" in order to highlight how certain aspects of a life, even an eloquent life, may turn against the events that enabled them and move toward futures that leave those pasts behind. Concretely, this manifested itself in terms also drawn from Nietzsche: the death of God. Whereas Emerson most often tempers the law of metamorphosis with a law of compensation, one that converts all changes into means for God's theodical ends, his own commitment to self-trust and his acute feel for the phenomenological limits of our condition enable and call for practices that unfold in a manner at times indifferent, at times hostile to God's existence and decrees, thus offering, without either outlining or upbuilding, the prospect of a post-theological self-culture.

Such a transition, such a translation, is not without costs. In fact, I cannot help but wonder whether Emersonian self-culture can even sustain itself, given the changes it undergoes in the wake of divine de-composition. My worry isn't whether Emersonians will be able to bear nascency and the losses that accompany it, if only because I don't see how that could be decided by way of the kinds of tuition I've been as-sembling. At some point, tuition will butt up against what I have been calling "the personal," that arena of events and actions that no one can undergo or pursue for us. "That by which a man conquers in any pas-sage, is a profound secret to every other being in the world," Emerson observes in "Considerations by the Way" (*CW6*, 130–31). So while I want to insist that divine decomposition shouldn't produce the kind of despair that sometimes seeps into Emerson's prose, whether that will prove to be so for you (or even for me, further on down the road), well, that is a personal matter in the sense I've been developing. This is not to say that one may not offer others provocation, ballast, or even cheer (efforts we'll explore in chapter 6), but your "so be it" or your persever-ance through a passage can never be mine, so at this point, I must leave you be.

This thought of leaving another be when personal matters arise brings me partway into Cavell's would-be marriage of Emerson and Wittgenstein. I say this, given Cavell's reading of Wittgenstein and a line from Emerson that I've cited before. In "Philosophy the Day After Tomorrow," Cavell suggests that §217 of Wittgenstein's *Philosophical Investigations* provides something like the following moral: "at some point in teaching the pupil must go on—and want to go on—alone. Another way is to say that the teacher has to know both when, even how, to fall silent and when and how to break her silence" (2005, 114). I think Emerson observes this request when he tells the audience assem-bled to hear about *Human Culture*: "I have as much doubt as any one of the value of general rules. There are heights of character to which a man must ascend alone—not to be foreshown,—that can only exist by the arrival of the man and the crisis" (*EL2*, 239). I note this conjunc-tion not only to make explicit a quotation but also to underscore the force of the personal in self-culture and what, on either side of provo-cation and tuition, it means to respect its irreplaceable singularity.

But what, then, is my worry regarding the ability of Emersonian self-culture to survive divine decomposition? It lies with the following, though I must confess that it will take me this chapter and the next to work through the unease it gives me: "To believe your own thought, to believe that what is true for you in your private heart is true for all men,—that is genius" (*CW2*, 27). For me this fervor has always had an unnerving edge, and with the idea of God "become somewhat else," the edge only sharpens. On Emerson's own terms, the way of abandonment eludes egoism and fanaticism because the call of genius is also the call of a divinely ordained vocation. "No man is quite sane," he writes in "Nature." "Each has a vein of folly in his composition, a slight determination of blood to the head, to make sure of holding him hard to some one point which nature has taken to heart" (*CW3*, 108–109). But if nature writ large takes nothing to heart, what remedy is there for folly? Emerson's theodicy envisions an economy of well-managed forces, and that includes the strivings of humans. As he writes in "Nominalist and Realist": "Each man, too, is a tyrant in tendency [i.e., temperament—JTL], because he would impose his idea on others; and their trick is their natural defense. Jesus would absorb the race; but Tom Paine or the coarsest blasphemer helps humanity by resisting this exuberance of power" (*CW3*, 140–41). But a post-theological self-culture cannot be sure that a Tom Paine will arrive to deflect the excesses of would-be redeemers, or that some Jesus will convert us into incarnations of wonderfully good news. Thus, Emersonians of my bent must find other hands able to temper tyranny.[1]

But fanaticism isn't all that troubles me. I am also concerned with whatever might tame our tyrants. What will the fate of self-culture be, if we dull the edge of Emersonian genius? Might we, in the wake of the death of God, close off the way of abandonment in order to resist the exuberance of our own power? Might we come to regard affirmation in and of the ecstasies of genius as precisely that which must be avoided, or, if that proves impossible, at least interrupted, and incessantly? In trying to curb our enthusiasm at the point of fanaticism, I would not have us be continually embarrassed with second thoughts (to recall "The American Scholar"), dreading waters we yet (or currently) cannot swim. But that is a hope and not equivalent to a concrete feel for how we might continue to feverishly essay our "private hearts" and yet *east* ourselves, to recall the language of chapter 3.

It would take a chapter of its own to demonstrate the mood against which I protest. Nevertheless, it would be unduly coy to refrain from naming it altogether, or indicating extant forms, two of which I find in the pages of Levinas and Adorno. In *Totality and Infinity* (1969, 244–45),

Levinas suggests that *jouissance,* which includes, I think, Emerson's cele-
bration of genius and its disclosive power, is precisely what must be interrupted, and interminably. In a different way, Adorno insists in *Aesthetic Theory* (1997, 32–33) that only a resolutely negative aesthetic, what
presents a "cryptogram of collapse," offers any future. Both postures
trouble me, for they leave us unable to affirm our (or their own) affirmations, and thus they collapse under their own weight, or so I have argued
elsewhere (Lysaker 1996, 533–34; 1998, 233–44). This is not to say that
the kind of orientation being developed here refutes or is an exclusive alternative to such postures. Far from it. It is to say, however, that if, like
me, you find no exit from these positions, and thus, in them, a certain
lack of power with regard to any foreseeable future, then you, again like
me, might take what Emerson has to say regarding affirmation as something of a gulf worth bridging.

I think a few instructive steps toward post-theological, nonfanatic
affirmations lie with Emerson's double consciousness. Recall that on
Emerson's theological terms, we do not know the ultimate ends toward
which our actions move, and thus we suffer. Nevertheless, he would
have us convert that ignorance and pain into a posture of worship, one
wherein we abandon our private discontent and side with the mostly
inscrutable ends and means of God's invisible hands. But isn't this precisely the figure of self-consciousness that I hope to excise from Emersonian self-culture by way of abandoning myself to its own self-overcoming? Yes—and yet the gestalt is not without promise, though we
need to shift the issue if we are to see it. First, set aside the question of
suffering that Emerson answers with the double consciousness. If its
pains only creep when we seek footholds outside the passages that our
condition affords, then a willingness to persevere without faith in inscrutable *teloi* should render the question moot and allow us, in the
wake of divine decomposition, to focus instead on the general contours
of the double consciousness. More particularly, let's focus on how it
combines both an observation of and a venture from the limits of our
condition. On the one hand, the double consciousness remains attuned
to its own limits, namely, the opaque origin and limited perspective of
our interpretive essays. As Emerson observes, "Life is not dialectics"
(*CW3*, 34). And yet, even within the confines of those limits, or rather
at them—which is to say, in part, on the basis of them—or better still,
given their currency, Emersonian self-culture manages a kind of cele-

bration, convinced that: "Every man is an impossibility, until he is born; every thing impossible, until we see a success" (*CW3*, 40). The latter fold of the double consciousness is remarkable because it doesn't allow the former to still its birth but only to transform the conditions under which it understands, or better yet, undergoes, those births. The double consciousness thus seems to offer us Tom Paine's delimitations and Jesus' affirmations within the continuum of a movement.

Let's explore this movement further and see whether it can sustain itself without the intervention of a theological caretaker. I think we find it in miniature at the heart of Emerson's "Experience," a text I cited twice in the paragraph above. Section 4 of the essay, focused on the "middle region" and "mid-world," speaks in the voice of delimitation. Section 5, however, succumbs to "angel-whispering," and thus, though brief, affirms the dæmonic. Moreover, it insists that the "ardors of piety agree with coldest skepticism" (*CW3*, 40). Taken together, the two may evidence something of the gestalt I seek.[2]

The fourth section of "Experience" resonates with an aversion to excess, opening with derision for "fineries" and "pedantries." Instead, it praises the "middle region of our being" as a "temperate zone" and favors the "highway," which entails a rejection of esoteric paths into the "cold realm of pure geometry" as well as a crass empiricism that takes nature to be just as it is given to, or even as, sensation. But what does it mean to respect the "mid-world"? The section offers, I think, two quasi-maxims to that end, though one must stress their "quasi" gleam, for the mood that prevails here is underwhelmed by abstract, generalized reflection. What we are given, therefore, are less maxims that incline toward law, even in a promissory way, than directives, derivative of a certain mood, that aim to help us find our place again.

Consider the first suggestion, what we might record as "Life is not dialectics." Across section 4, Emerson insists: "Intellectual tasting of life will not supersede muscular activity. If a man should consider the nicety of the passage of a piece of bread down his throat, he would starve." And, more generally: "Life is not intellectual or critical but sturdy." The thought is that one shouldn't reduce living to reflection and what it fathoms, that primary experience will never shine transparently in and as our reflections, that thought is always darkened by a degree of *lethe*—as the essay's opening lines observe. The moral, then, is that our best-laid thoughts are, at best, plans that we must act upon if life is to continue.

That is, ventures carry our day. Moreover, given our less-than-perspicacious outlook, no action should ever fulfill our expectations. Rather, surprise awaits the attentive at every turn. As Emerson remarks at the close of section 5: "The individual is always mistaken. . . . It turns out somewhat new, and very unlike what he promised itself" (40).

A second maxim supports the first, one we might transcribe as: "Do not craze yourself with thinking." As I understand it, the suggestion begins with the moral of the former. Reflection only offers gambits on which we might act (and thus there will always be room for "objections to every course of life and action"). We ought not "postpone, refer, and wish," therefore, but make do with "our actual companions and circumstances, however humble or odious," what amounts to, I think, the highway, the public road, the road open to all. In other words, we shouldn't wait until reflection has cleared for us a path that we may essay without fail. That would be a kind of madness, one lost in the question, "Do I dare?" and unable to venture a future in the penumbral light of our condition.

Now, these maxims have varying import. At the dinner table, a plate set with bread, the direction would seem to be clear. But do not forget that Emerson also sets aside a kind of sensualism, one that takes all that is the case, whether in the form of concepts or sensation, to be what is given to self-consciousness. The suggestion is thus not to eschew reflection altogether but to discipline it, to keep it responsive to what its selectivity overlooks. We can begin to see what this would entail if we think the two maxims together, treating the first, "Life is not dialectics," as a ward against another kind of madness, one that claims more on behalf of thought than thought affords. Consider the following parable:

> A political orator wittily compared our party promises to western roads, which opened stately enough, with planted trees on either side, to tempt the traveler, but soon became narrow and narrower, and ended in a squirrel-track, and ran up a tree. So does culture with us; it ends in a headache. Unspeakably sad and barren does life look to those, who a few months ago were dazzled with the splendor of the promise of the times.

The vice indicated involves mistaking a prospect for the journey, which, the arboreal images suggest, eventually shuts whatever passage had opened, and which may, over time, lead to despair. For example, one might take the fury of an initial crush to indicate what an intimate relation should always afford and thus abandon fine partners in favor of an impossible dream. Or one might denigrate contemporary music because it fails to replicate the tunes of one's youth, never pausing to determine whether the stakes had changed, and on both sides—that is, for those now making music, and for one's own ears. In either case, a step along a way is mistaken for a consummation, so reflection chains itself to ends it cannot realize, perhaps to the point of despair.

Of course, despair might not result. Instead, one might simply steamroll experience with presumptions. One can find an obvious example of this in totalitarian outlooks that regard the word as immanent to their own economies of meaning and treat difference as deviation. And this is precisely the problem of fanaticism: it reifies temporary powers, proves unresponsive to the fluxing web of life, and thus its limbs curl up until growth ceases. Not that "fanaticism" is Emerson's term for this phenomenon. He instead attacks the mystic who "makes now the stereotype turn & return," who "beholds the flux and yet becomes pragmatic on some one particular of faith," who "nails a symbol to one sense, which was a true sense for a moment, but soon becomes old and false" (*JMN9*, 172 and 383; *CW3*, 20). But the two are analogous.

In reply to these maladies, section 4 asks us to focus on the present, to keep to a mid-world between bloodless abstraction and false concreteness. "Since our office is with moments, let us husband them," Emerson says. The suggestion is that we should wed ourselves to our moments (as opposed to clinging to ebbing successes or overly speculative futures). Moreover, we should cultivate our moments; even raise them (as opposed to preparing for "five minutes in the next millennium," i.e., the heaven of Christianity's three-millennia eschatology). In other words, "Experience" confronts fanaticism with an ethos of the moment, in terms of both what our condition in its metamorphoses does and does not offer, what Emerson terms the "potluck of the day."

Permit me a word or two about *ethos*. I invoke the term because the issue at stake concerns character, or ηθος, and those ways of acting that indicate its virtue, what for Aristotle falls under the concern of ethics, or εθος. In directing us to avoid confusing life and dialectics, in warning us about the madness that imprudent paths of reflection risk, and in charging us to husband moments, Emerson is marking out a

[126]

kind of conduct that purports to be virtuous, that indicates a kind of excellence, given the exigencies of our condition. (Or, we could say that conduct of this sort is both eloquent and able to facilitate eloquence for a metamorphic being and is thus exemplary, i.e., worthy of being ventured.) I also invoke the term because, in the form of εθος, understood as custom or even ethical habit, the English *ethos* connotes a dispositional or habitual way of being. And this resonates with Emerson's observation in "The American Scholar": "Character is higher than intellect. Thinking is the function. Living is the functionary" (*CW1*, 61). The point merits underscoring because, as I've already noted, what Emerson offers is less a matter of rules than provocations that set for us the task of realizing their prospects in the course of our lives. My reliance on "ethos" thus aims to exploit meanings current in two Greek words that the English lumps together, albeit now, if I've been circumspect, more eloquently.[3]

That said, the heart of this ethos might still be somewhat vague, even platitudinous. My claim is that the maxims of section 4 are less inclined to negate reflection than to keep it closer to life than it often remains. Let me thicken the thought with a meta-theoretical observation. "Mood" is a term of Emerson's genius, one that focuses his self-culture (and possibly ours) on the fragility *and* affective power of insights that might remake a life. But what precisely does such a term offer, and how should we employ it; that is, how should we undergo its emergence in the course of our lives? How might we inherit it, moment by moment, without mistaking life for dialectics and crazing ourselves with its terms?

Let's begin with a contrast. If we set mood alongside involuntary perceptions and quotation in order to chart our condition, what have we accomplished? We haven't really provided a clear and distinct set of determinations, certainly none that would unveil, to invoke the Heidegger of *Being and Time*, something like a fundamental ontology of our condition, one that exhaustively lays out conditions of possibility for pursuing self-culture. Nor should we press on to do so. That is, in pursuit of self-culture I don't feel obliged to inventory the full range of our moods and the disclosures they facilitate. Nor am I ill at ease with the odd usages I've ventured (like my combination of "mood" and "maxim," or "virtue" and "maxim"), at least not to the point that I wish to render the concept of "mood" precise enough to square Smith and

Kant, or Aristotle and Kant. I would rather pursue, as I have been, the prospects that terms like *mood, temperament, involuntary perception,* and *genius* provide. Of course, those futures may require clarification, as *genius* did (hence, my distinction between its native and ecstatic forms), but the need for those refinements arose as the disclosive power of these terms waned or muddled, not because I was or am beholden to categorical exactitude.

I think the last section of "Experience" exemplifies the orientation I'm describing, as one might expect, given what I say at the outset of chapter 4. Section 8 begins by recalling the "lords of life," what might mark the beginnings of a fundamental ontology, only to confess: "I dare not assume to give their order, but I name them as I find them in my way" (*CW3*, 47). This says quite a bit. First, it acknowledges an inability to order and render transparent those forces that govern life, what amounts to recognizing that life is not dialectics. Second, it nevertheless does not cease the effort of ordering, but names, "in my way," the forces that govern life, that is, according to what insights one has, those a temperament affords. And third, it names those forces that are "in my way," that render life problematic. Thus, rather than crazing oneself with thinking, one should, the line suggests, address impediments that arise in the conduct of life rather than lose sleep over possible worlds.

For some, even me at times (for example, when I'm in moods that find a fundamental ontology just the thing), this lack of systematic rigor is a source of frustration. For others, however, what first stands as vagueness can assume the aura of a studied restraint, or so I've come to come think, given Stanley Cavell's readings of Emerson. It is a virtue, Cavell thinks, to work within the poverty of one's condition, thereby acknowledging one's condition—and thereby, I would add, standing a better chance at transfiguring it. The virtue, in Aristotelian language, involves a kind of philosophical reticence, that is, a silence born of insight, a refusal to seek greater precision than one can convincingly achieve. "This would not be a matter of keeping your mouth shut," Cavell writes, "but of understanding when, and how, not to yield to the temptation to say what you do not or cannot exactly mean" (2003, 23). But this may say too much, for I am dubious, as I was in chapter 1 with regard to the language of "method," that one can know precisely just how imprecise one can be, as if the lines between orders of knowledge (the exact, the almost exact, the not very exact, etc.) could be so clearly drawn and toed. Moreover, at times one should speak beyond what one can mean exactly, when one is taken to the quick by an involuntary perception, or when one is mapping one's condition for the sake of self-culture. That is, how much imprecision one can bear varies with the stakes of the matter. I take this to be a lesson learned in the wake of verificationist theories of meaning. What counts as meaningful, even well formed, hangs a great deal on what the various interlocutors regard (or better yet, experience) as the degree of rigor needed to accomplish the task at hand, say, passing the salt, proposing marriage, publishing an essay in a professional journal, deciding to write on Emerson.

One could ask here whether Emerson "evades" philosophy when he rests content with a kind of terminological vagueness. For the reasons I'm assuming from Cavell, I think not. I would thus amend Cornel West's claim that Emerson evades philosophy (1989). Emerson evades a certain kind of philosophy, call it the search for categorical exactness and truth criteria, but his refusal is philosophical; that is, it evidences a desire to philosophize in a different way, and it offers reasons for doing so, albeit not the kind of reasons one expects if one is still hungry for criteria that will alert everyone that one has kept one's apples and oranges distinct.

In accounting for the virtue of philosophical reticence, we thus should regard it, as Cavell himself seems to do in "An Emersonian Mood" (2003), less as an act of understanding and more as a mood that gives one a feel for the point when multiplying distinctions becomes silly and bequeaths more difficulties than it meliorates.[4] Here is Cavell's example: Whereas Kant insists that we exhaustively inventory the pure concepts of the understanding, Wittgenstein refrains from producing a rigorous taxonomy of the forms his central terms might take, for example, rule, language game, form of life. "But in the *Investigations* there is no such system of the understanding, nor a consequent such system of the world, and the demand for unity in our judgments, that is, our deployment of concepts, is not the expression of the conditionedness or limitations on our humanness but of the human effort to escape our humanness" (Cavell 1989, 87). It's as if Wittgenstein takes to heart the close of section 4: "The wise through excess of wisdom is made a fool."[5]

I think we might also cast Emerson's refusal in a Heideggerian idiom, though we should note that Heidegger's own thought has roots in a Kantian distinction dear to Emerson himself, namely, that between reason and the understanding. The worry being advanced is that a certain demand for terminological precision leads us astray. The fault lies in the obscuring logic of discursive judgment, what German Idealism regarded as the labor of the understanding, the application of concepts to states of affairs, for example, "mood" to certain brain states or "quotation" to certain linguistic operations. In rendering the necessary and sufficient conditions for what counts as an Emersonian "mood" or "involuntary perception," one abandons reflexive access to whatever enables that rendering, what may itself be a "mood" of one kind or another. What I have been calling philosophical reticence is thus part of an effort to preserve the possibility of disclosive dividends that will enable us to run our fingers through the sediment that flows beneath the activities of discursive judgment, thus better attuning us to our condition, take us where it will. To return again to the language of "Experience," philosophical reticence claims us when we realize, as Emerson does in section 8, and right after confessing that he cannot order the lords of life, "I cannot claim any completeness for my picture. I am a fragment, and this is a fragment of me" (*CW3*, 47). But this is not to acquiesce to any given fragment. Rather, it is to begin the labor of observing limits so that we are poised for enlargements.

In the midst of these philosophical examples, you might be wondering whether I haven't mistaken life for dialectics. I appreciate the concern, but I resist the presumption that the concerns of philosophy and the concerns of life are necessarily distinct. At its core, philosophical reticence is a virtue for the conduct of any belief. One could thus replace Kant with a school administrator in step with an educational program that measures intelligence and learning within the parameters that govern standardized tests. Now, such tests are attractive because large groups of students take the same test. And to some minds, that is sufficient to render the tests objective. But here one would profit from a bit of reticence. First, if the tests do not address a univocal audience, they run the risk of favoring populations culturally tutored in the kinds of questions posed, and disadvantaging those for whom the examples are foreign and the vocabulary esoteric. Second, what evidence do we have that performance on standardized tests correlates with performance in other intellectual endeavors? Perhaps they only test how well one takes standardized tests. If so, then schools that teach to standard tests actually leave students ill-prepared for the kind of intellectual challenges life will throw their way.

Now, you might find this call for reticence little more than a call for commonsensical caution. But is that kind of caution, as well as what it calls for, namely, continual returns to the world with which we converse, apparent in appeals to common sense? I think we have to answer both yes and no; that is, it depends on who one asks, on their character, and precisely with regard to how they undergo their own commitments. Yes, there are those who, as a matter of course, wouldn't cling dogmatically to practices that seem potentially ill-suited to achieve their stated aims. But for others, appeals to common sense are conversation stoppers, little more than appeals to beliefs regarded as self-evidently true. (I take it as a given that one finds both kinds of folk in debates concerning the educational value of standardized tests.) And in these latter cases, common sense tends toward madness, for it leaves us unresponsive to new information as well as to those addressing us with objections.

Here is another phenomenon to which the ethos of Emersonian self-culture offers a corrective. While debating the prudence and justice of his decision to invade Iraq, George W. Bush often appeals to his certainty that he made the right choice. This is problematic, for it suggests that a feeling that accompanies a belief warrants that belief beyond question, and even when evidence is produced that calls that belief into question. But I don't want to identify the problem as an epistemological one. Instead, I take this to be a matter of character, of how one lives in the difference between the world we think and the one with which we converse. Bush's vice is that he willfully takes life to conform to the dialectics, or even the raw assertions, of his mind. It is not that he believes this on the basis of some theory, but only that he conducts himself in this way, and to the point that he offers his intractableness as a virtue. But this is perverse; it presents an unwillingness to respond to others and to the disclosures of one's own primary experience as exemplary. One might as well expect others to acknowledge and even praise one's solipsism.

There is more to say, but this must suffice. Faced with the demands of exactness, Emerson becomes reticent (as opposed to tenaciously laying claim to certainty). But this is not just a matter of humility; in that reticence, dividends are paid. I speak of dividends in this context for pragmatic reasons. Emerson's restraint not only avoids certain activities, but it also funds others. For all their imprecision, terms like "mood" and "involuntary perception," provided we let them, lay rough grounds, even steps, from which the essays of self-culture can proceed. I would thus say that Emerson's reticence involves a functional appreciation for the prospects that a given determination offers. If we expect too much from the designator "mood," we'll forget self-culture and bicker over its proper extension. So crazed with thinking, we'll waste the day in explanation as we evidence what is more a matter of self-avoidance than self-discovery. Or, fired in the confidence that insights often instill, we might become overly confident that our concepts capture our condition and thus invoke them without taking up the real work their invocation sets before us, thus confusing life for dialectics.

My suggestion, then, is that section 4 of "Experience" proposes a kind of philosophical reticence with regard to what our condition affords, a reticence that sets us in a mid-world between pure abstraction and the faux concreteness of sensation. And I am inclined to regard this reticence, which follows from a few choice maxims, as an ethos of the moment, one that will not say too much on its own behalf or mistake its footholds as final.

What, though, of section 5? In a way, we've already traveled a good distance toward its wisdom. After celebrating the present hours of the mid-world in section 4, Emerson rattles its equanimity:

> How easily, if fate would suffer it, we might keep forever these beautiful limits. . . . But ah! *Presently* comes a day—or is it only a half-hour with its angel whispering—which discomfits the conclusions of nations and of years! . . . Power keeps quite another road than the *turnpikes* of choice and will, namely, the subterranean and invisible tunnels of and channels of life.

I've highlighted two terms because they clearly recall section 4. "Turnpikes," recalls the highways of the mid-world, but from a pose of negation. The highway, we are now told, cannot always be ours. At times, the path of power sets us at a crossroads. But this is not to negate wholesale what section 4 offers. The departure in question is no less a possible occurrence in the present hour (or half-hour) that Emerson's philosophical reticence would husband. Section 5 thus displaces some of the confidences of section 4 while affirming its ethos. But let me elaborate.

Section 5 offers us a third maxim, what we might phrase as "Thrive by casualties." I say this, given:

> All good conversation, manners, and action come from a spontane-
> ity which forgets usages, and makes the moment great. Nature hates
> calculators; her methods are saltatory and impulsive. Man lives by
> pulses; our organic movements are such; and the chemical and ethe-
> real agents are undulatory and alternate; and the mind goes antago-
> nizing on, and never prospers but by fits. We thrive by casualties.
> Our chief experiences have been casual.

I hope this passage recalls a good deal of thought already considered, so I'll read it quickly. Here Emerson returns to genius and its involuntary perceptions, what he terms a few lines later "the kingdom that cometh without observation." As we've seen, "genius" names an event of meta-morphosing nature that arrives in the form of self-authorizing, sponta-neous insights, events that begin a conversion of sorts that we must then further pursue, translating it into practical power. In turning to genius, in succumbing to angel whispering—or rather, in affirming its intima-tions, both explicitly and performatively—Emerson forsakes the high-way of common usage for a kind of dancing that forsakes gradual transi-tions—deductions, inferences from representative samples, modest gambles, and so forth—in favor of leaps (or so I read, rather literally, "sa-lutatory"). The maxim, then, articulated and obeyed, directs us to aban-don ourselves to our genius when it claims us. "Thrive by casualties!" we are told, amid an observance of the fact that genius is fathomless, its prospects full of departures, even loss.[6]

Now, you might think that by taking sections 4 and 5 together in the gestalt of an ethos, I have simply embraced an antinomy of practi-cal reason, something like, "Avoid extremes" and "Venture extremes." I don't think so. Take the last line of section 4: "The wise through ex-cess of wisdom is made a fool." In closing section 4, the line also recoils upon it and asks us to pause before the wisdom we have just been of-fered. But this does not simply aim at performative consistency, though it accomplishes that. In closing section 4, the line also serves as the hinge on which section 5 opens. I thus take its force to be prospective as well as retrospective. By delimiting the confidence of section 4's moderation, the warning opens us to what might lie outside the mid-world, to what might lead off the highway. The warning thus inclines toward that which section 5 would have us take to heart. In other words, I take philosophical reticence to also involve an openness to whatever an hour or half-hour might offer, whether it be a shaken confidence or a spontaneity that "makes the moment great." This ethos of the moment isn't riddled with an antinomy after all, therefore. Instead, sections 4 and 5 meet and move into one another in an open, attendant responsiveness, what I've termed an ethos of the moment, an observant regard for the fact that life is not dialectics and that too much reflection might craze us, perhaps leaving us unable to venture our moments, or perhaps dulling us to their emergence, which, most emphatically, we should greet with abandonment, a So be it! that curves into prospecting perseverance.

I think we now have the makings of a figure of double consciousness that addresses the threat of fanaticism in Emersonian self-culture and that does so without vitiating the way of abandonment on which it is incalculably and opaquely predicated. At hand is a figure of self-consciousness, one that aims to "detect and watch that gleam of light which flashes across [our—JTL] mind from within," to cite the first paragraph of "Self-Reliance" and return us to the heart of self-culture. This figure is doubled in that, from a shared moment of incalculability, it awaits both the surging, disclosive powers of those gleams—while remaining observant of the limits impressed on us by their casual origins—and the impending surprises that are their (and thus our) futures.

In a way, then, the double consciousness I've been elaborating combines, without fusing, something we earlier found Emerson terming "Jesus" and "Tom Paine," namely, a kind of pious affirmation as well as a studied irreverence. On the side of Jesus, it lies in wait for genius, poised to venture prospects that open with the arrival of involuntary perceptions. Not that it wields some criterion like certainty that allows it to distinguish real genius from faux inspiration. Emersonian self-culture, derived as it is from native and ecstatic genius, can never be sure it isn't becoming the devil's child. Involuntary perceptions are self-authorizing, arriving as, and offering us, a "last fact behind which analysis cannot go." If anything, then, affirmation in this context is more a shooting venture than discrimination between the real-deal and yet another naked would-be king. But recall as well that what arrives with genius is a prospect, and here, in the ethos of the moment, it is ventured as such. Something of Tom Paine is thus already part of Emersonian divination, for affirmation here acknowledges what "Experience" terms the "fall of man," namely, the realization that we exist, that our life is "ours" in both a theoretical and practical sense, that is, schematized by our temperament and mood, and very much, though far from exclusively, up to us.

Tom Paine informs the ethos of the moment in another way as well. Because the observances of this double consciousness are primarily practical, that is, oriented toward the conduct of life, they let go of what is waning without regret, without melancholy. Again, release is not accomplished because one has mastered the applications of a concept like "form of life grown old." Rather, in the creep of a kind of dimness, in idle hours without prospects, when inertia carries the day, one proceeds, in the ethos of a moment, without bluster, that is, reticently, keeping to the highway of convention and common usage. But that is not all, and precisely because of the inertia of habit. Recall "Circles": "It is the inert effort of each thought having formed itself into a circular wave of circumstance . . . to heap itself on that ridge, and to solidify, and hem in the life" (CW2, 181). In husbanding a moment, then, this double consciousness picks through what had once seemed so full of promise. I note this latter move, call it "easting ourselves" or "keeping a foolish consistency at bay," because the ethos of the moment holds together in a poise of receptivity. It thus labors toward reception by loosening sclerotic habits so that we might rush into a breach should genius arrive. In Emerson's hands the figure of Tom Paine does not principally name Pyrrhonian efforts to undermine whatever would orient an eloquent life. Instead, it calls to mind the labor of preparation, one convinced by, even charged with, the thought offered in section 5— "Life is a series of surprises, and would not be worth taking or keeping, if it were not." In still other words, Tom Paine is not unconcerned with quasi-messianic arrivals, and thus the ethos of the moment maintains a kind of open movement within its gestalt.

We can readily concretize these preparatory efforts. One might seek out new thoughts by reading or in conversation. Or one might take a walk and see what the landscape solicits, and across multiple landscapes, presuming different locales jar us differently. In this context, I also think of Walter Benjamin's practice of rewriting what he had already written.

Somehow the repetition always proves to become more than repetition. Or one might take up a new activity, less a hobby to distract than a new way to meet and greet a self and world we thought we knew. Perhaps pottery will awaken our fingers, or cycling expand a sense for our region, for who and what live along alleys and outskirts. Or we might pursue something at the limits of our talents, like singing in public, in order to strengthen our humility while thickening our courage.

We might say this all in a different way, employing language quoted in the epigraph for this chapter. "We strangely stand on—souls do,—on the very edges of their own spheres, leaning tiptoe towards and into the adjoining sphere" (*JMN9*, 228). Here the soul is doubled, at once within and without itself, and so too the ethos of the moment. On the one hand, it remains attentive to "my way"; and as "my way," that is, it observes the fact that "it is the eye which makes the horizon, and the rounding mind's eye which makes this or that man a type or representative of humanity" (*CW3*, 44). And yet it remains poised to receive from an adjoining sphere whatever might surge up and reconfigure that horizon, say, an event of genius or, less dramatically, some exposure of a facet of nature that we had been unconsciously quoting.

Doubled in this way, the ethos of the moment, even as it exemplifies it, is a boon for self-culture. If eloquence entails a life that manifests a character we have found ourselves able and willing to conduct (i.e., harness and express), then receptiveness at the limits of our soul is a path toward grander eloquence. As we metamorphose, it enables us to continue to track ourselves and thus, perhaps, fashion a character that does not announce one whom life has left behind. Or, perhaps more concretely, if I begin to see how my life is bound to the lives of others in my practices of consumption, then an attentiveness to how my soul engages other spheres could enable me to ask after and influence the kind of character that announces itself when it sits down to dinner, ties two shoes, starts a car. If entombed, however, if subject to thoughts that hem us in, confusing life and dialectics, I lose opportunities for eloquence and announce instead, wherever I go, the inertia of what once had dawned on me.

Of course, Emerson requires the canopy of a theodical universe to embrace this kind of double consciousness. He casts the surprises of life in terms of "God's delight in isolating us every day from past and future" (*CW3*, 40). Likewise, we can keep to our solitudes, he thinks, because even there we remain "God's darling" (*CW3*, 38). And finally, most forcefully, he finds that the "ardors of piety agree at last with the coldest skepticism" because "all is God. Nature will not spare us the smallest leaf of laurel" (*CW3*, 40). But an ethos of the moment need not have recourse to divine circumspection in order to tie its ends together, or rather, keep them open to one another. In fact, it won't, for it eschews what a theodicy presumes—a more than momentary historical vision, one wherein the fluctuations of an hour or moment are borne as "distractions," as the "coetaneous growth of the parts" that "will one day be *members*, and obey one will" (*CW3*, 41). Such a view abandons the moment in favor of what Emerson later describes as "periods in which mortal lifetime is lost" (*CW3*, 48). But an ethos of the moment does not recognize such periods, except in the moment of their birth, and it holds to such moments, seeking only to be true to those currents, to husband what is found there.

Emerson remarks in the essay's final section: "All I know is reception; I am and I have: but I do not get, and when I fancied I had gotten anything, I found I did not. I worship with wonder the great Fortune" (*CW3*, 48). But for that final capitalization, which deifies "Fortune," the line just quoted would begin to say the vitality of a post-theological affirmation. Note the restraint in its emphasis on reception, which is intensified at that paragraph's end—"The benefit overran the merit the first day, and has overran the merit ever since. The merit itself, so-called, I reckon part of the receiving" (*CW3*, 48). Our genius, while ours, is also not ours, so its arrivals and destinies exceed our ken, offering ventures that we, finding them in our way, might take up in the labor of self-culture, might come to call our own, perhaps by way of something like a "fortune" to which we abandon ourselves.

Is this post-theological ethos of the moment a kind of stoicism, then, even an *amor fati*? I don't think so. In those cases, what is accepted or even loved has been won through the labor of the concept: the not-me that the stoic ignores, the destiny that a lover of fate embraces. In either case, a judgment foregrounds the affirmation, securing terms that make the affirmation bearable. But here, in the ethos of a moment, reception marks the first step on which we find ourselves, which is to say, that even our ability to receive experience was itself, initially, received—a gift—or so I read the suggestion that our so-called merits are also part of the receiving. Broached here, therefore, is an affirmation—worship, even—without concept or measure.

Now wait, you might say. To speak of "fortune" is to employ a concept and even a measure insofar as it connotes the arrival of something fortunate. Fair enough. But let's not be too sure we quite understand what we are doing when we name the lords of life "fortune." On the reading unfolding here, in the ethos of the moment, the language of "fortune" designates neither a realm beyond what arrives in and as my way nor something affirmed as "fortunate" on the basis of a discovery that is in fact so. Instead, "fortune" performs affirmation; that is, it is an affirmation, another way to say "so be it."

One sees something like this in the first edition of *Leaves of Grass*:

> I have perceived that to be with those I like is enough,
> To stop in company with the rest at evening is enough,
> To be surrounded by beautiful curious breathing laughing
> flesh is enough
> To pass among them . . . to touch any one . . . to rest my
> arm ever so lightly round his or her neck for a moment
> . . . what is this then?
> I do not ask any more delight . . . I swim in it as a sea.[7]

I cite this passage from what later came to be known as "I Sing the Body Electric" for two moments. First, the lines interrupt their own turn to reflexivity. The speaker asks, ". . . what is this then?" but refuses to pursue the question. Instead, and this is the second moment, s/he *swims*. Without instantiating an action/reflection dichotomy—one undone by the discussions of abandonment in chapter 3—I regard the poem's turn from interrogation toward swimming as a performative embrace of movement, as an occurrence that, at base, is not the action of a subject but a receiving (and thus quoting) of the interaction of multiple forces: limbs, lungs, a brain, cells, synapses, our last meal, muscle memory, and then salt, kelp, other creatures making way or not, the tide and thus the moon and thus the sun and so on, until, both within and without, the figure of swimming becomes sublime and leaves us at sea.

Now, one might caution me here, noting that the speaker of Whitman's lines swims only in a sea of delight. But how does delight swim? In allowing a reflexive question to rise and dissipate like breath, the speaker takes the measure of "delight" into a pre-reflexive interplay of self and sea, an interplay in which "delight" no longer measures but swims. In other words, "delight," in this poem, is evidence of affirmation, even worship, not its precondition. Still, the worry is a good one, and thus I would inflect Whitman's song with "The Heavens," a poem from Denis Johnson, one I keep finding in my way, wherever I go.

> From mind to mind
> I am acquainted with the struggles
> of these stars. The very same
> chemistry wages itself minutely
> in my person.
> It is all one intolerable war.
> I don't care if we're fugitives,
> we are ceaselessly exalted, rising
> like the drowned out of our shirts . . .[8]

Without any pastoral gloss, this poem fiercely casts the sea in which Whitman's speaker swims. This sea is a battlefield: creatures eating other creatures, rocks worn to sand, swimmers lost, and all without the invisible hands of God's theodical arms below or above—just a sidereal unfolding in subjects, objects, and the weave of their nested lives. Nevertheless, and here is the post-theological affirmation, therein and thereby we are exalted: we rise, intensify, and take place as praise (to recall three meanings of exalt).

But what of fanaticism? you might ask. Well, insofar as fanaticism entails reification, even enthusiastic reification, a kind of compulsive insistence on the credibility, even invulnerability of one's footholds (i. e., one's inspirations, orientation, beliefs, values, even mood), then an Emersonian double consciousness formed in an ethos of the moment begins in, and persistently undermines, fanaticism—able, as it is, to keep life and dialectics distinct and to remain open to the former even while essaying the latter. Likewise, it seems to alleviate the headache that self-culture hurtles toward when it fails to observe the difference between the life one thinks and the one we converse with in farms and cities. In fact, the double consciousness of the ethos of the moment enables precisely what Emerson expects of self-culture. "As soon as he sides, with his critic, against himself, with joy, he is a cultivated man," that is, one able to husband moments, even if they prove idle or undermine the arc of a life.

But back to fanaticism, for Emerson has more to teach us on this score. If by fanaticism one means essaying what may only prove to be a passing fancy (and thus offer only a passing future), if fanaticism means staking one's eloquence on an incomplete picture of who one is and where one stands, well, those are simply the terms of our condition. And as we essay them, Emerson would not have us spend the day in expiation, as I noted in chapter 2. In fact, in the ethos of the moment, that would be a kind of madness. But given its slanderous intension, I would resist using the term *fanaticism* in this way. That would reek too strongly of malcontent with what we have in our way, with what our fortune seems to hold in store. But this is not the lesson I had in mind. Rather, I want to add that Emerson's ethos of the moment, in opening its seat to succession, is not merely a figure of self-consciousness, but also one of conversation with cities and farms. That is, in observing the difference between the world we think and the one with which we converse, moment by moment—for we are always quoting—our ways and days open onto multiple paths that might heave rather hem.

> Culture is the suggestion from certain best thoughts, that a man has a range of affinities, through which he can modulate the violence of any mastertones that have a droning preponderance in his scale, and succor him against himself. Culture redresses his balance, puts him among his equals and superiors, revives the delicious sense of sympathy, and warns him of the dangers of solitude. (*CW6*, 72)

But how exactly does this work? How might others succor us against ourselves, and what does this introduce into self-culture? Let that be our next concern.

SIX

Commended Strangers,
Beautiful Enemies

He defrauds himself of half his life who can & does not ally himself to
his companion by stricter bonds than mere acquaintance.
—*JMN2*, 198

If we, dear friends, shall arrive at speaking the truth to each other, we
shall not come away as we went.
—*JMN7*, 513

Since chapter 4, I have been trying to elaborate a post-theological self-culture. Its goal is an eloquent life that presents, wherever possible, a character it both husbands and affirms, and without forsaking momentary occurrences for "periods in which mortal lifetime is lost." More specifically, we have just considered how an ethos of the moment, a double consciousness freed from the shadow of God, might present and further Emersonian self-culture. On the one hand, it poises us for our metamorphoses and exhorts us to take up what begins in and as reception: genius. On the other hand, it remains observant of the fragmentary horizons that our futures always are, attuned and ready for surprise and succession, and willing to struggle with the inertia of habitual life.

The ethos of the moment not only indicates how Emersonian self-culture weathers divine decomposition, however. It also exemplifies, from idleness to ecstasy, a series of postures or bearings that preserve the way of abandonment and resist our devolution into fanaticism. But we would be mistaken to presume that this newly ever-doubling consciousness does justice to the depth of Emerson's response to what he sometimes terms egoism, those times when a "man runs around a ring formed by his own talent, falls into admiration of it, and loses relation to the world. It is a tendency in all minds" (*CW6*, 70). That Emerson has more to say on this score is unsurprising. Self-culture is, in part, an attempt to enlarge oneself beyond the reach of yesterday. As we've noted:

> Culture is the suggestion from certain best thoughts, that a man has a range of affinities, through which he can modulate the violence of any mastertones that have a droning preponderance in his scale, and succor him against himself. Culture redresses his balance, puts him among his equals and superiors, revives the delicious sense of sympathy, and warns him of the dangers of solitude. (*CW6*, 72)

I would thus be remiss if I did not try to articulate how we might succor one another against ourselves. Not that we should excise what temperament affords. Far from it—"The primary point for the conduct of intellect is to have control of the thoughts, without losing their natural attitudes and action" (*LL2*, 207). Or, more precisely:

> He is only a well-made man who has a good determination. And the end of culture is not to destroy this, God forbid! but to train away all impediment and mixture, and leave nothing but pure power. Our student must have a style and determination, and be master in his own speciality. But, having this, he must put it behind him. He must have a catholicity, a power to see with a free and disengaged look every object. (*CW6*, 71)

An ethos of the moment can begin this process by attuning us to our personal styles, evolving as they are, and by undergoing them in the difference between what "we think" and the conversations that arise wherever we go, thus contesting our inertia. But it remains fixed on the sallies of our own mind, on what others cannot undergo for us, namely, the personal disclosures of experience. What can be said about the address of others, however? On my reading, friendship opens a site where answers might be found. Everything hinges, of course, on addressing and receiving our friends appropriately, on conspiring with and in the conversation that friendship is. In this chapter, therefore, I'd like to trace the warp of friendship's place in Emersonian self-culture by fingering the weft of those less-apparent registers where friends keep "company with the sallies of wit and the trances of religion" (*CW2*, 121).

In order to focus my discussion, I'll concentrate on the essay "Friendship," engaging letters and journals where they complement it. Viewed as a whole, the essay, including its opening poem, is not of one mind. First, the inaugurating poem grants friendship extraordinary power. Lines 3 and 4 suggest that friends root one in an uncertain world, whereas 18 and 19 announce that a friend's nobility helps "master despair." In fact, the "worth" of a friend can turn the "mill-round of my fate" into a "sun path." In the essay proper, similar enthusiasms surge. The second paragraph tells us: "From the highest degree of passionate love, to the lowest degree of good will, [friends] make the sweetness of life" (CW2, 113). And in paragraph 18: "Should not the society of my friend be to me poetic, pure, universal, and great as nature itself?" (CW2, 123). In paragraph 7, however, Emerson declares: "Friendship, like the immortality of the soul, is too good to be believed" (CW2, 116). And then, in paragraph 21 (out of 24): "Friends, such as we desire, are dreams and fables" (CW2, 125).

"Friendship" perplexes because it addresses us with both ecstatic affirmation and despair. In fact, if read as a synchronous assemblage of propositions, the essay appears riddled with contradiction—for example, friends make the sweetness of life, but they don't exist. The contradiction also seems performative when Emerson confesses in paragraph 7: "I cannot deny it, O friend, that the vast shadow of the Phenomenal includes thee also" (CW2, 116).[1] And yet, I find the essay's tensions phenomenological. After all, friendships ebb and flow—initial enthusiasm, then disappointment, and later, perhaps, renewal. And won't this be a continual process for vibrant friendships, for those in search of more than retrospective affirmations? If so, then the essay's tendency to tack manifests an almost mimetic acuity, one that less defines friendship than unfolds the task it entails and the prospects that await those who assume it. I'll thus stick close to its lines because they show, in their movements, more than they tell.

Let's begin with the first six paragraphs, a set flush with promise and focused by the confession: "A new person is to me a great event" (CW2, 115). Several observations provoke the remark. First, the occurrence of reciprocal sympathies stirred by mutual affection is a source of great pleasure. "What is so pleasant," Emerson writes, "as these jets of affection which make a young world for me again?" (CW2, 114). I hope the sensation is a familiar one. Time passed with those dear is thick and fixating. What would otherwise be a mere chore, say a trip to the store, can become an occasion for witty banter and the sharing of observations that had been lying in wait. "Oh, I've been meaning to tell you . . ." Or shared sensibilities can make a film with a plot that unfolds slowly all the more absorbing, our focus proportionate with our excitement to compare notes.

But pleasure is not the half of it. Emerson claims that the event of a friend renews the world. I understand this in two ways. First, the discovery of a friend evidences that the world is less barren than we had thought. I recall my first month in West Haven, Connecticut, a small, smelly town on the New Haven harbor where I'd lodged myself for a year. Initially alone, waiting for my brother to join me, I felt the town grow increasingly hostile as I made do with cans of tuna and beer. But then, when I found a job at a bookstore and got on well with its manager, Bruce, and owners, Henry and Susan, a kind of possibility became evident, one wherein sociality could be more than grunts and bumps in grocery aisles. And how much more was this the case when, in Nashville, fussing with my dissertation, I pestered my pal Joe with the latest version of the same old thought, night after night? I know well what Emerson tells Margaret Fuller: "Yet every assurance that magnanimity walks & works around us we need" (*CL2*, 44).[2]

Friendship renews in another way. Emerson writes: "Our intellectual and active powers increase with our affection." I used to conjure awful jokes on my bus ride to work, just to have something with which to punish Bruce, jokes on the order of: "Why do rows of corn make such good choirs? By nature they sing in hominy." Or later, both in graduate school, Alex and I would study late into the evening, sipping free refills at a bar frequented by cocaine-fueled country music stars. Left to my own devices, I might have closed the bar, but I doubt I would have brought along Arnauld's objections to Descartes, let alone observed aloud their nuances, or listened as intently to anyone's reflections on the intricacies and implications of visual perception. But I did, and as I did, I grew in and through the orbit of another, as I did again and again, reading, jawing, and reflecting with Mike on the ways and days of global capitalism and its indifference, even hostility to reflection. I'm thus persuaded by Emerson's early letter, which suggests that without friends our inspirations tend to fizzle. "A thousand smart things I have to say which born in silence die in silence for lack of his ear" (*CL1*, 224). Or, in words that Emerson recorded in Topical Note-book XO: "'Thou learnest no secret,' says Hafiz, 'until thou knowest friendship, since to the unsound no heavenly knowledge comes in'" (*ETN2*, 224).[3]

Already we should see the force of friendship in Emersonian self-culture. A friend can stir our genius, whether by observations, exem-plary behavior, thoughtful questions, or a simple presence that we do not wish to disappoint, as if proximity could also be a mother of inven-tion. As Emerson says of Margaret Fuller: "Whoever conversed with her felt challenged by the strongest personal influence to a bold and generous life" (*MMF1*, 282). It seems, then, that friendship is a site where we are given back to ourselves, and in ways we might miss if left alone. Friendship thus broadens our conversation with nature, attun-ing us to more of what we are and might be, thereby extending the range of our eloquence, if we can affirm what is found there and trans-late it into practical power. But before we say more, let's consider why a friend might have this power.

In the presence of one we admire, we want to shine. Recalling how he tried to dazzle Alice, his wife, Calvin Trillin says: "But I never stopped trying to match that [first] evening—not just trying to enter-tain her but trying to impress her. Decades later—after we had been married for more than thirty-five years, after our girls were grown—I still wanted to impress her."[4] It isn't that we wish to win favor. Rather, another's judgment can matter, and deeply, for with some, it is also our judgment; that is, we praise what we esteem. I thus sweat a bit when I test drive a thought by Michael Sullivan, for I'm confident he'll scruti-nize it with the care I aim to show in advancing matters. This suggests, I think, that when the one we admire is impressed (or not), we meet with a kind of conscience peering out of other eyes.

Set within this scene of mutual recognition, friendship finds a core that binds even when the players are apart. It thus can buoy our perse-verance when the way of abandonment rises too steeply. Or, when a worn path beckons in a moment of crisis, the internalized gaze or voice of a friend might help us pass it by. But Emerson reaches further than this, suggesting that friends reach strangers through the friends they've (in part) made. "Will these too separate themselves from me again, or some of them?" Emerson asks. "I know not," he continues, "but I fear it not; for my relation to them is so pure, that we hold by simple affinity, and the

Genius of my life being thus social, the same affinity will exert its energy on whomsoever is as noble as these men and women, wherever I may be" (*CW2*, 115). Three thoughts catch my attention. The first I've anticipated. Emersonian friendship weaves itself into character. Second, also anticipated, in terming genius "social," Emerson suggests that its self-authorizing, disclosive power can leap from one to another. Perhaps another's enthusiasm for yoga opens a new relation to my body, while another's vegetarianism might lead me to see how eating habits enmesh us in practices I normally condemn. Or a friend's care for the dignity of others in asymmetrical power relations, say, while shopping for food or eating out, might expose me to a kind of comportment I too would have. Or, and let this be the last example for now, another's praise of film might convert cinema into something more than a site for entertainment, say, one wherein a language of gesture is continually refined, such that our facial ticks and quirks come into relief. In all these cases, the genius of another, whether native or ecstatic, bathes more than one in its gleam. Finally, what I receive from you, or you from me, might leap to a third, and so on. Emersonian friendship is thus tinged with hopes for a community of friends, some of whom have yet to meet, even though each is compatibly tempered and tuned. In the plays of self-culture, friends stimulate our genius and share their own, leaning into our spheres. Yes, they will have to catch us up as well; that is, we will have to recognize and feel the pull of their genius, but when they do, our orbit will extend and our eloquence broaden by a part.

In appreciating the great event that a new friend is, Emerson tends toward what Aristotle regards as a friendship of ηθος, what we translated as "character," and in a way that underscores its orientation toward the good life, hence, the term's cognate, ηθικος, or "ethics." Whereas friendships of use and pleasure share temporary ends or satisfactions, ethical friendships share a vision of flourishing, thereby convening characters that are oriented toward a mutual good. I find this connection in a line offered near the essay's end: "In the last analysis, love is only the reflection of a man's own worthiness from other men. Men have sometimes exchanged names with their friends, as if they would signify that in their friend each loved his own soul" (*CW2*, 125). This is a remarkable thought. Love for friends acknowledges their worthiness (i.e., nobility) and tends to their flourishing insofar as they are noble. For example, we may help them develop talents, overcome vices, or explore new vistas. In doing so, we aren't simply respecting nobility, however; we are being noble as well, addressing a worthy peer in a worthy manner. Now, if s/he is truly noble, s/he will return the favor, turning friendship into a mimetic praxis that eventuates in characters analogous to one another. Finally, friendships like these are their own reward. As Emerson says: "The only reward of virtue is virtue: the only way to have a friend is to be a friend" (*CW2*, 124).[5]

In conceiving of friendship's reward through the terms of ethos, Emerson actualizes an early inclination, contra those he calls the "Hobbists," namely, that we genuinely "promote the very good fortune of my friend" (*JMN3*, 25). In an ethical friendship, we seek another's flourishing because we hold that virtue should be rewarded, and our own virtuous response is that reward. Such a response is neither altruistic nor egoistic, however. First, friends aren't setting their own interests aside in tending to one another. Seeing one another flourish is precisely their reciprocal interest. But this isn't a matter of egoism. Friendship rewards virtue with virtue because that is what nobility entails, not because it furthers one's strategic goals. In fact, we regard those who are only interested in their own well-being as ignoble and undeserving of a friend's love.

I note the ethical cast of Emersonian friendship for several reasons. First, it makes plain how distant this kind of friendship is from prevailing conceptions. Unlike those of pleasure and use, ethical friendships set terms that do not admit of compartmentalization. Instead, they claim us at every point along the rim of our being and by way of ends they both articulate and actualize: virtue. Ethical terms also dramatically present the initial promise of friendship—another self, and should the fever spread, something approaching an actualized humanity, a concrete universal. As Emerson says to Caroline Sturgis: "A true and *native* friend is only the extension of our own being and perceiving into other skies and societies, there learning wisdom, there discerning spirits, and attracting our own for us, as truly as we had done hitherto in our strait enclosure" (*CL2*, 326). No wonder, then, that Emerson finds in friendship the power not only to please and stir but also to cheer and sustain: "Let the soul be assured that somewhere in the universe it should rejoin its friend, and it would be content and cheerful alone for a thousand years" (*CW2*, 114).

The ethical cast of Emersonian friendship evidences something else.

In the face of a friend, the relative virtue of our affirmations comes to the fore, and we are led to ask—Are these affirmations worthy? In "Spiritual Laws," Emerson writes: "Human character evermore publishes itself. The most fugitive deed and word, the mere doing of a thing, the intimated purpose, expresses character. If you act, you show character, if you sit still, if you sleep, you show it" (*CW2*, 90). In the crossings of an ethical friendship, where ethos is character, we could say that our relative nobility "evermore publishes itself." This is noteworthy because it makes plain that the eloquence sought by self-culture isn't antithetical to concern for others (as if it were egoistic instead of altruistic). Moreover, in the great event of friendship, how one conducts oneself among others is as much an issue for self-culture as any other characteristic publication. Not that Emersonian self-culture offers or requires a comprehensive doctrine regarding the good life. Its ethos of the moment should make that plain. Rather, the focal question is whether, in our shared lives, our character expresses who it is that we would be, say, generous rather than stingy, cheering versus disheartening, responsive instead of oblivious.

In a present like ours, bound to an altruism/egoism binary, it is essential to grasp how unwillingly Emersonian self-culture inhabits the ranges that distinction affords. A very late journal reads: "Culture is one thing, & varnish another. There can be no high culture without pure morals. With the truly cultivated man—the maiden, the orphan, the poor man, & the hunted slave feel safe" (*JMN16*, 140). Self-culture is never an exercise on moral holiday.[6] Rather, it unfolds through questions concerning the nobility of the life to which one has abandoned oneself. For all their greatness in his eyes, Goethe and Shakespeare fail Emerson with regard to this particular concern. He finds Goethe "incapable of a self-surrender to the moral sentiment," and Shakespeare unwilling to "explore the virtue which resides in these [Shakespeare's own—JTL] symbols" (*CW4*, 163 and 124). Not that they were wrong to seek self-culture at the expense of virtue. Rather, their self-culture proved less than exemplary with regard to virtue. This indicates rather clearly, I think, that Emersonian self-culture doesn't compete with an ethical life. Instead, virtue's cultivation is an integral part of the eloquence that orients its every essay.

Just six paragraphs in, Emerson's essay leaves us flush with the promise of newly found friends whose charge propels us toward an expanding eloquence that aims, with their help, to right its wheels. Do not forget, however, that no one ever remains so new. Under the law of metamorphosis, our event subsides. And in that ebb another's promise tarnishes until, in the "golden hour of friendship, we are surprised by suspicion and unbelief," and eventually we are forced to acknowledge that friendship, "like the immortality of the soul is too good to be believed" (*CW2*, 116). This is the despair of paragraph 7 (*CW2*, 116–17), one that reverses the essay's ascent with the observation that "I cannot make your consciousness tantamount to mine." In the knowledge that we are distinct, in what Emerson elsewhere terms our "fall," enthusiasms wane, and the weave of an actualized ethos begins to fray in the suspicion that "all persons underlie the same condition of infinite remoteness."

The notion that our friends are not what we take them to be troubles because it undermines the reliability of whatever stimulus and recognition a friend provides. Are we regarding them rightly? Will they read us well? Once we have these thoughts, our friends transform into something like the "commended stranger" that Emerson introduces in paragraph 3:

> A commended stranger is expected and announced, and an uneasiness betwixt pleasure and pain invades all the hearts of a household. His arrival almost brings fear to good hearts that would welcome him. The house is dusted, all things fly into their places. . . . Of a commended stranger, only the good report is told. . . . He stands to us for humanity. . . . But as soon as the stranger begins to intrude his partialities, his definitions, his defects, into the conversation, it is all over. He has heard the first, the last and best, he will ever hear from us. (*CW2*, 114)

And so too with friends who prove less than ideal. We may still hang out together, but we'll travel less venturesome orbits.

The breaches that Emerson visits in paragraph 7 are also common. If a friend shows a consistent toleration for schlock, or an overly patient demeanor among those who speak first and think later, one might come to doubt those points where affinities are evident. ("Maybe she's just indulging me as well," we might think. Or: "I hope he knows I'm genuinely funny.") Not that Emerson suggests our desire for friendship halts whenever this fault line shakes. Rather, it recasts our longings as moments in a continual movement between solitude and a communion that pleases, but only as another flicker in the "vast shadow of the Phenomenal." And that, in turn, renders friendship a "delicious torment" of longings for what will never come to pass. In its first seven paragraphs, then, "Friendship" swings from a bursting confidence to a dispirited lament.

But the beat goes on, as do friendships. In fact, paragraphs 8 through 10 deny that we should accept terms that lead us to regard friendship as a "delicious torment" (*CW2*, 117–18). Such "uneasy pleasures and fine pains are for curiosity, not for life." This distinction between curiosity and life forecasts the move that opens "Fate," wherein a question concerning the *Zeitgeist* resolves into one concerning the conduct of life. That is, here, as in "Fate," Emerson retreats from speculation into primary experience, into the conversations that are conducted there.

To my mind, we are at a principal pivot, one where a turn in how to think the friend begins to teach us how to *be* a friend, and where the ethos of friendship finds its way into an ethos of the moment. First, we are chastised in paragraph 8: "We seek our friend not sacredly, but with an adulterate passion which would appropriate him to ourselves." I take this to say that the divergences of the friend, his or her so-called partialities, shouldn't be read as cracks in the character of our friendship. Or, said otherwise, ethical friendship, in seeking another self, should seek enlargement, not agreement. As Emerson will say later, trapped in masculine metaphorics: "Let him not cease an instant to be himself. The only joy I have in his being mine, is that the *not mine is mine*. I hate, where I looked for a manly furtherance, or at least a manly resistance, to find a mush of concession. Better be a nettle in the side of your friend than his echo" (*CW2*, 122–23). Or, in the words of paragraph 9: "I ought to be equal to every relation," a line that adds provocation to paragraph 8's chastisement, one that indicates an open conversation where paragraph 7 found a fissure.

One certainly could read this third set of paragraphs as a retraction of paragraph 7, as if despair were an epistemic error. But note how paragraph 10 begins: "Our impatience is thus sharply rebuked"; that is, in its initial hopes and despair, the essay proved overhasty. I find this language instructive. It suggests less a conceptual error than one of conduct; that is, it is impatient to expect that the actualization of our ethos could be coincident with a friend's arrival. Emerson's point isn't simply negative, however; it sets patience within the constellation of virtues that make up ethical friendship. "Respect the *naturlangsamkeit*," Emerson stresses, that is, the natural slowness "which hardens the ruby in a million years," and "let us approach the friend with an audacious trust in the truth of his heart." What emerges from paragraph 7's despair is thus less a repudiation of earlier affirmations than an intensification of the demands facing those who would affirm ethical friendships.

But why call for patience? (We'll return to trust.) I think the answer lies in appreciating Emerson's reasons for redirecting our inquiry toward life and away from curiosity, reasons we found at the close of "Experience": "I know that the world I converse with in the city and in the farms, is not the world *I think*. I observe that difference, and shall observe it" (*CW3*, 48). Curiosity moves in the world of the "I think," which takes its leave from the realm of life, the realm where I converse, a realm wherein I might think the friend phenomenal but nevertheless address her or him, as Emerson twice does in paragraph 7. Among friends, therefore, we should proceed in observance of that difference, which is to say, we should return again and again to those scenes where life is conducted and strive to prove equal to what is found there, say, the fact that we've addressed another as friend or been hailed as one. If so, we might conclude, as Emerson does in his "Wide World" journal, that: "Friendship is the practical triumph over all forms of malignant philosophy" (*JMN2*, 193).

Exploring the eddies of friendship, we've found our way back into the ethos of the moment, a double consciousness whose observations are kept fluid in an ongoing observance of the difference between primary and secondary experience. Here, among friends, it pulls us back from the expectation that another's consciousness could ever be ours, thus returning us to what I have called the personal, the folds in our unfolding lives that another cannot undergo or accomplish for us. Though a buoy, a friend cannot persevere for us, and her genius will never light us up if we do not also catch hold of her fire and feel its heat. In leaving behind the despair of paragraph 7, Emerson's essay thus allows friendship to season with the thought that: "We must be our own, before we can be another's" (*CW2*, 124). Not that the essay ends here, as if the ethos of the moment exhausted the ethos that orients Emersonian friendship. But in some ways, the essay does begin here, or rather—and this is the point—it begins again, turning to identify, almost by way of philosophical definition, some of friendship's essential traits. It's as if, in the reorienting powers of the ethos of the moment, which direct us toward conversations where life is conducted and which keep us observant of the differences that mark out that region, one can better essay the demands of friendship.

The discussion that runs from paragraphs 11 through 13 (*CW2*, 118–21) is striking in several ways. First, as if to remind us of the stakes, Emerson explicitly eschews consideration of friendship's social benefits. Second, one has to wonder whether the proposed "elements that go into the composition of friendship," namely, sincerity and tenderness, aren't offered as a test. (I say this, given the resistance to curiosity.) Not that they are offered ironically. Rather, the previous discussion should prepare us to receive these elements in a particular way, more as friendly maxims than as components of a categorical definition, as aids to being and having friends, not as criteria for identifying the real McCoy. In other words, I read these elements under the aegis of Emerson's own observation that a "friend is a sane man who exercises not my ingenuity but me."

Other provocations also grace these paragraphs. One arrives at its close: "It should never fall into something usual and settled, but should be alert and inventive, and add rhyme and reason to what was drudgery." I find it helpful to read this through the opening poem's suggestion that in the worth of a friend, "The mill-round of our fate appears / A sun path" (lines 15–16). The thoughts come together in what they avoid—foolish repetitions, even consistencies—as well as in what they affirm—the unexpected and its occlusion, or a sun path, what is a matter of dawns and twilights, night and noon. Friendship is thus not merely seasoned by invention but kept lively. Moreover, if we are to be equal to every relation, particularly among friends, we must be patient and alert, poised to "detect and watch that gleam of light which flashes across [another's—JTL] mind," to translate a line from "Self-Reliance." I recall this line because being equal to every relation means being able to rise to its occasion, and that may prove surprising, even strange, given that the soul becomes. Moreover, in ethical friendships "the Genius of my life" proves social; that is, the ethical affinity of friends can "exert its energy on whomsoever is as noble as these men and women," and so we must remain alert for such exertions, uncertain of the quarter from which they'll seize us. When they do arrive, however, we must seize them, that is, thrive by the casualties they introduce. In fact, Emerson later commands, "Worship his superiorities: wish him not less not a thought, but hoard and tell them all. Guard him as thy counterpart" (*CW2*, 124).

Recall that the ethos of the moment keeps us ever ready for the sparks of genius. Here, in friendship, genius can hail and assail us from many sides, thus offering an even greater range of resistance to our mastertones or sheer inertia. Of course, if friendship is to prove such a lively affair, it must be sincere, which is to say, more or less naked.

> Before him, I may think aloud. I am arrived at last in the presence of a man so real and equal, that I may drop even those undermost garments of dissimulation, courtesy, and second thought, which men never put off, and may deal with him with the simplicity and wholeness, with which one chemical atom meets another.

This exuberance has the heat of genius, the claim of disclosures that overwhelm and form the vantage point from which other thoughts flow like tuition. In allowing our genius to be social by taking on the sallies of another or risking our own in their presence, we are exposed, possibly embarrassed. I stress this because the images say more than "Always be frank with your friends." Fair enough, sincerity may require that. But let's not think this reduces to telling our pals how much we dislike their decor. The charge instead, drawing upon the opening poem's penultimate line, is to broach contact in the "fountains of my hidden life," which is a charge to be true to what unfolds, risky as that may be, which helps me think of Emerson's earlier claim that friendship requires a total trust. At the point of genius, we must be willing to revel in involuntary combustions, and that requires a trust that exceeds the reach and performativity of inductive foresight.

It's apparent that the ethos of Emersonian friendship leans toward and into an agon, though one less concerned with disputation than dæmonic flurries. I was thus cheered by Emerson's later command to receive the friend in ways that subvert the taxonomic force of the category: "Let him be to thee forever a sort of beautiful enemy, untamable, devoutly revered, and not a trivial conveniency to be soon outgrown and cast aside" (*CW2*, 124). If, in our love, we are open to a friend's noble bearing such that it might become our own (and I take it that such openness is part of the ethos of Emersonian friendship), then she or he might arrive as the enemy of who we have been, and, like any bit of genius, call us down paths we hadn't expected to travel. I appreciate this rhetorical inversion because it keeps us alert to the potential strangeness with which our friends might reward our virtue, and to how those who aren't yet our friends might prove rewarding. In other words, if the ethos of Emersonian friendship requires us to be equal to every relation, its claim extends us beyond any circle of extant friends and into an open regard for the full breadth of our conversations.

At this juncture, surrounded by a sea of fellow beings who might, at any turn, prove friend or enemy, or friend *and* enemy, given our transitioning nature, I think we finally can come to terms with Emerson's proclamation at the outset of "Self-Reliance": "To believe your own thought, to believe that what is true for you in your private heart, is true for all men,—that is genius" (*CW2*, 27). The insistence startles because it rings with the kind of fanaticism I've been trying to check. In the sociality of our genius, however, and schooled in ethical friendship and the ethos of the moment, I find its sense coming into focus. Recall that in the sociality of genius, we ceaselessly publish ourselves before an ever-expanding audience. Recall also that ethical friendships leave us considering the worthiness of our affirmations; that is, the arrival of the friend should lead us to renew (or not) our commitment to what has claimed us (and that includes our regard for this very friend). But if anyone might prove a friend in his or her arrival, then any addressee of our ceaseless publications merits a revisited if not revised edition.

I recall these three thoughts because they suggest that our lives, eloquent or otherwise, are offered to all, whether we like it or not; that is, their scope is universal. Not that they involve categories hell-bent on universal extension. In fact, the issue here is less about predication than about second-person relations. That is, our lives face a universal audience, one expanding through time. To put it another way, the publications of our character, that is, our lives, address any and all potential friends (or "unknown friends") as potentially exemplary. Emerson's call for a universalization of our heats thus amounts to an insistence that we should feel the claim of genius in what and whenever we model, or respect its absence.

Set within the ethos of the moment, I could imagine translating Emerson's proclamation into a maxim that says, "Be true whenever you essay," recalling, as I do, this thought from the *Human Culture* lectures: "I acknowledge that the mind is also a distorting medium so long as its aims are not pure. But the moment the individual declares his independence, takes his life into his own hand, and sets forth in quest of Culture, the love of truth is a sufficient gauge. It is very clear that he can have no other" (*EL2*, 227). Given that genius names that behind which analysis cannot go, Emersonian self-culture abandons the search for truth-criteria in favor of cultivating a character that is true to itself and others in its presentation of what has claimed the life it cannot help but publish. Not that "being true to oneself" functions like truth criteria (as Descartes seemed to think "being certain" did). Emersonian self-culture remains a practice of essays, of ventures and experiments that might "unsettle all things" even though, eventually, they too will be unsettled. "Nothing is secure but life, transition, the energizing spirit," one finds in "Circles." "No love can be bound by oath or covenant to secure it against a higher love. No truth so sublime but it may be trivial tomorrow in the light of new thoughts" (*CW2*, 189).

In inheriting Emerson's thought of universalization, I want "essay" to carry a good deal of weight because it casts how we should take the sense of what it means to regard one's thought as "true" for all. In its ethos of the moment, Emersonian self-culture remains observant of how the world we think differs from the one with which we converse. Genius isn't proven, therefore, through perpetual conformity to what fired us once upon time. In fact, a desire for such a resting place evidences a lack of self-reliance to the point of treason for one living under the law of metamorphosis. Rather, to take something as true for all is to take it as worthy of orienting a noble life, and to offer it as such to yet-to-be-known friends, with one's own life as evidence on its behalf. Not that we can be certain that others will agree, as long as we remain true to ourselves. Only a theodicy could affect such harmonies, and I abandoned that ship in chapter 4. But seasoned in friendships, Emersonian self-culture strives to offer its affirmations with the kind of restlessly good conscience that gives one hope that another will also find passage there.

As you can see, friendship looms larger in Emersonian self-culture than one might have thought. It not only offers checks against myopia, but in rendering unstable our ability to determine, once and for all, friend from foe, and in its demand for sincerity, friendship inflects the very way in which we share the life that we would render eloquent. Sincerity is not the only virtue that characterizes Emersonian friendship, however. Another element bears notice, and precisely as an element, that is, as a point where atoms meet. According to Emerson, venturesome friendships also require "tenderness" (*CW2*, 120):

> The end of friendship is a commerce the most strict and homely that can be joined; . . . It is for aid and comfort through all the relations and passages of life and death. It is fit for serene days, and graceful gifts, and country rambles, but also for rough roads and hard fare, shipwreck, poverty, and persecution. (*CW2*, 121)

This is a hardy companionship, as loyal as it is tender, and it observes two insights already apparent in an early journal entry: "It is good for a man to feel that he is cared for, that anxious eyes are cast upon the course of his fortunes as they are tossed on Time's waters. He will not distrust the powers/faculties that another does not distrust" (*JMN2*, 198–99).

Ethical friendships sustain because, as we have seen, the high regard of one that we find noble is itself ennobling, so tenderness not only tends to wounds but also to the future. When I was young, "ethnic jokes" were still common, and I offered and enjoyed them like many others. Were they more than informal rehearsals of racism? I don't think so, but regardless, I was oblivious to the fact that they were even that. At some point before high school, however, Peter, already a long-standing friend, admitted unease in our use of such jokes, as if to say, "This isn't the kind of person I think we should be." I hadn't thought of it, but once noted, it struck me as a right reorientation of our actions and pleasures. Not that I was instantly converted. I recall his later reminding me of the reach of some ill-chosen words, which all the better evidences Emerson's point. Peter was tending to my future self, weaning me of a vice I now recall with a sense of shame he helped instill, even though it became a genuine force only insofar as I acknowledged its claim upon me.

Tenderness not only buoys the other, however. "Every man who aspires to high things is more or less suspicious and suspected of being more exquisitely self-loving. The best way to parry this charge, is to be deeply interested in another's welfare" (*JMN3*, 198–99). The only way to have a friend is to be one, you might recall, and this we do, in part, by proactively tending to each other. In other words, reciprocal tenderness rewards both parties, rendering each the more deserving of the other.

When paragraph 13 closes, so does the essay's fourth part, one that recasts ethical friendships in terms that respect the irreducibly personal dimension of our loves and thicken the virtues that orient it. At this point, then, I would say that "Friendship" essays an ethos that eschews self-preservation in favor of far-flung ventures of self and other, what appears to be a reciprocal feat of ongoing self-culture. But how often is that possible, and for how long? This is the precise question that opens the essay's final section, paragraphs 14 through 24 (*CW2*, 121–27). "Friendship may be said to require natures so rare and costly . . . that its satisfaction can very seldom be assured." I find this wording precise. Given its demands, its elemental characters, friendship's terms are rarely satisfied, and we, in striving to meet them, rarely meet with satisfaction. Because this observation concerns assurances, I do not hear the despair of paragraph 7 in its turn, but instead a kind of humility before a daunting task, perhaps even a caution. I also say this because paragraphs 14 through 16 thicken the terms that friendship must satisfy. For instance, a "rare mean betwixt likeness and unlikeness" must meet, for in its absence, folk "will never suspect the latent powers in each." And while Emerson doesn't limit friendship to two, he does suggest that naked, dæmonic conversation, which consummates friendship, is a two-person affair, and a fleeting one at that, an "evanescent relation—no more." Finally, whether we encounter others fit for our features, well—"My friends have come to me unsought" (*CW2*, 115). Some measure of luck lies at the root of profound meetings, friendship being the "uprise of nature in us to the same degree it is in them," a matter that is beyond our control. Moreover, because these are relations, we cannot manufacture friendships through dint of will. "We talk of choosing our friends, but friends are self-elected" (*CW2*, 123).

Emerson's feel for the fragility of friendship is particularly refined at this point in the essay. Thoroughly amicable relations are born of accidental beginnings, and its consummations do not linger. This is not what truly keys this final section, however; rather, it's Emerson's response to it in paragraph 17: "Friendship demands a religious treatment. . . . Reverence is a great part." Deep in friendship's rising, Emerson again invokes a bearing, what Heidegger, quoting praxis, terms a

Haltung, a determinate regard for what we undergo and how we undergo it. In this case of friendship, Emerson's favored regard has phantasmic implications.

> Treat your friend as spectacle. Of course he has merits that are not yours, and that you cannot honor, if you must needs hold him close to your person. Stand aside; give those merits room; let them mount and expand. . . . To a great heart he will still be a stranger in a thousand particulars, that he may come near in the holiest ground.

This adds to the patience of paragraph 10 by acknowledging that friendship draws us near enough to discover divergences, even traits that we cannot praise (though not because they are vicious, but simply because they are too like or unlike to fuel the fire). But rather than have them threaten our satisfactions, Emerson asks that we step aside to better witness, enjoy, even facilitate our friends' unfolding. In our fellows' surfeit, one must keep in part to one's own patch, thus leaving space for their evanescence. Without that reserve, delicious torments await, and breaches open where extraordinary sights might otherwise be. Or, one meets with suffocation—"All human pleasures have their dregs & even Friendship itself hath bitter lees," writes Emerson. "Who is he that thought he might clasp his friend in embraces so tight, in daily intercourse so familiar that they two should be one?" (*JMN2*, 227). Not that one should turn one's friend into an entertainment. Rather, in leaving room for their abundance, their spectacle will also prove a spectacle for our visions, "something that aids the intellectual sight," as Webster's tells us in 1828. Said more directly, finding space for another's particular flurries facilitates his or her enlargement as well as ours.

Patience, alertness, sincerity, humility, tenderness, and worship, these are some of the terms of the ethos convening Emersonian friendship, terms offered to keep us close—though not too close—to hidden fountains that sometimes jet into one another, mixing like and unlike, remaking each. And as we've seen, these terms overlap with the ethos of the moment insofar as the former comes into its own only when it remains observant of the differences between primary and secondary experience, differences that evidence that no one is reducible to the other, while disclosing how one can be enlarged, even ennobled, by whatever genius another solicits or imparts. The ethos moving through

Emersonian self-culture thus affirms what provoked despair in paragraph 7, namely, difference and departures:

> Seest thou not, O brother, that thus we part only to meet again on a higher platform, and only because we are more our own? A friend is Janus-faced: he looks to the past and the future. He is the child of all my foregoing hours, the prophet of those to come, and the harbinger of a greater friend. (*CW2*, 126)

This passage thrills me because a Janus-faced friend is one of ebb and flow, one whose departure may later prove a homecoming to an enlarged "I" and "we." What once seemed strange may return in the glare of genius, fixing us with insight, provocation, and prospect. It also thrills because it suggests that in each instance we should receive the friend like the "commended stranger" introduced in paragraph 3. A reverent regard receives the friend as a "stranger in a thousand particulars," commended by foregoing hours. In order to be equal to her or his occasion, we must eschew, therefore, what is usual and settled, alert to the possibility that one of these thousand strange particulars may prove the prophet of future hours.[7]

At such points, friendship and self-culture converge, meeting in what is really a double consciousness, one wherein we side with our emerging selves against the inertia of our foregoing hours, alert to the prophecy of one another and loyal to our prospects. A friend thus not only helps us stay true to ourselves but enables us to venture and travel wider orbits than we might otherwise have found, our tether both lengthened and held fast by his conduct. From the perspective of self-culture, then, we can speak of friends as Emerson speaks of history's great figures: "Yet within the limits of human education and agency, we may say, great men exist that there may be greater men" (*CW4*, 20).

But note also how our own double consciousness must be itself doubled when the ethos of the moment is woven through friendship. Ethical friendship tends to more than one life; that is, we owe our friends all that we too hope to gain. We must also remain alert to their comings and goings, therefore, if we are to tend to their well-being. In fact, in owing them a noble bearing, less as debt than gift, less as evidence of our love than as the very substance of our love, we should seek to be as eloquently noble as possible. This is how we reward (and deserve) their virtue, and we should do so wherever we can manage it, whether in word or deed, at home, at work, or before the state, and wherever these sites flow into others. Or to put it another way, presuming complacency is a vice, something akin to hubris, as if we had come into our own once and for all; we owe our friends a life of proactive self-culture, one capable of proving a prophet of hours to come. It would appear, then, that friendship thrives in the wake of self-culture even as self-culture expands among and through friends, much as Emerson suggests of those friendships celebrated in Judeo-Christian scriptures: "They [scriptures—JTL] have sanctioned these alliances inasmuch as they have raised and refined the soul, and whatever refines the soul increases its capacity and its relish for friendship" (CS4, 49).

Once again, we have traveled some distance with Emerson, welcoming his essay in the hopes of seizing on the prospects that Emersonian friendship offers self-culture. In much of what Emerson presents, a kind of humble restraint has proven key, which is not all that surprising, given what we articulated in the last chapter as his ethos of the moment. Like all activities that would be virtues, however, it risks excess, and in this instance, Emerson's own essay, at least toward its close, teeters and falls in the direction of what I consider impersonality, a word drawn from "Love."[8]

> But this dream of love, though beautiful, is only one scene in our play. In this procession of the soul from within outward, it enlarges its circles ever. . . . Neighborhood, size, numbers, habits, persons, lose by degrees their power over us. . . . Thus even love, which is the deification of persons, must become more impersonal every day. (CW2, 107)

If the fountains of hidden lives commence in an upsurge of nature, we'll eventually prove sublime as vaster relations arrive in and as our spectacle. But how far might we follow out our expansions and credibly remain friends? The worry isn't lost on Emerson, who sees quite well that "the higher style we demand of friendship, of course, the less easy to establish it with flesh and blood" (CW2, 125). But how well does he negotiate what might prove a gulf between two?

In the essay's penultimate paragraph, Emerson announces: "I do then with my friends as I do with my books. I would have them where I can find them, but I seldom use them. We must have society on our own terms, and admit or exclude it on the slightest cause" (CW2, 126).[9]

This line potentially clashes with the promise of paragraph 13, which insists that friendship is "fit for serene days, and graceful gifts . . . but also for rough roads and hard fare, shipwreck, poverty, and persecution." The clamor rings in the analogy with books. They may impoverish, but they will not suffer a poverty we ought to remedy, at least not with as much urgency or in the same manner. But then, "tenderness" is precisely one of Emerson's own terms, and thus the inconvenience of another's malady shouldn't offer him sufficient cause for exclusion. Nevertheless, he also confesses:

> I cannot afford to speak much with my friend. If he is great, he makes me so great that I cannot descend to converse. . . . It would indeed give me a certain household joy to quit this lofty seeking . . . and come down to warm sympathies with you; but then I know well that I shall mourn always the vanishing of my gods. (CW2, 126)

What trips me up is the contrast between "household joys" and the earlier statement that the "end of friendship is a commerce the most strict and homely that can be joined." "Homely" says much: that the demands of friendship are sometimes unattractive, but also that home is where we live, and friendship should prove equal to whatever arises there. I'm also struck by the fate of conversation in this passage. Not only does conversation mark the consummation of Emersonian friendship, but it is also that site to which the ethos of the moment continually returns us.[10] If one cannot descend to such a site, however, I fear our friendships will meet with a curious fate and little more. I'm thus compelled to return this lofty seeker to a previous passage in "Friendship": "We cannot forgive the poet if he spins his thread too fine, and does not substantiate his romance by the municipal virtues of justice, punctuality, fidelity, and pity" (CW2, 121).

At stake in my grievance are tone and bearings, not categorical missteps. But so too in friendship, where the how of what we do can misalign orbits. For example, if we do not visit one another, I may come to wonder whether our intercourse is less evanescent than brief. "To my friend I write a letter," Emerson writes, "and from him I receive a letter. That seems to you a little. It suffices me. It is a spiritual gift. . . . It profanes nobody" (CW2, 124). Or imagine receiving this declaration: "So I will owe to my friends this evanescent intercourse. I will receive from them not what they have, but what they are. They shall give me that which properly they cannot give, but which emanates from them. But they shall not hold me by any relation less subtle and pure. We will meet as though we met not, and part as though we parted not" (*CW2*, 126). Of course, the line between sacred and profane, emanation and accident is decisive, determining where, in our evanescence, "flesh and blood" evaporates. But I expect that you share my intuition about friends who never meet, namely, that one of the two has gone missing in a rising monologue.[11]

At this point, Emerson's own struggles with Margaret Fuller are instructive. I say this because Margaret Fuller reproached Emerson for not facilitating her unfolding, for not "offering me the clue of the labyrinth of my own being."[12] In Emerson's own words: "She stigmatized our friendship as commercial. It seemed, her magnanimity was not met, but I prized her only for the thoughts and pictures she brought me" (*MMF1*, 288). And in reference to a slightly later time, Emerson notes a period in which Fuller found thoughts that he didn't favor, thus irking her. He writes: "She was vexed at the want of sympathy on my part, and I again felt that this craving for sympathy did not prove the inspiration" (*MMF1*, 308–309). Looking back, and without probing whatever psycho-sexual complexities may have been at work, it seems that Emerson lacked what he attributed to Fuller herself:[13] "Her mood applied itself to the mood of her companion, point to point, in the most limber, sinuous, vital way, and drew out the most extraordinary narratives" (*MMF1*, 312).

Now, perhaps Fuller asked too much. Who, after all, can unlock our being for us? Particularly in moments of crisis, the personal envelops us, and gulfs appear that we alone can cross. As Emerson suggests:

> He soon comes to feel a deep interest in the prosperity of certain persons; he returns daily and hourly to their society. He needs it as he needs bread. Their aversion would make him unhappy.
>
> But he cannot be long in discovering another fact no less certain, that, notwithstanding all this dependence, each man is, by his consciousness, separated wholly from all other men; that, dearly bound to others as he is, he is yet wholly alone. (*CS4*, 218)

Moreover, sincerity remains a constitutive virtue of Emersonian friendship, so one must be open to criticism as well as praise. Still, Emerson himself confesses to Fuller a lack of tenderness in his relation with her:

Can one be glad of an affection which he knows not how to return? I am. Humbly grateful for every expression of tenderness—which makes the day sweet and inspires unlimited hopes. I say this not to you only, but to the four persons who seemed to offer me love at the same time and draw to me & draw me to them. Yet I did not deceive myself with thinking that the old bars would suddenly fall. No, I knew that if I would cherish my dear romance, I must treat it gently, forbear it long,—worship, not use it,—and so at last by piety I might be tempered & annealed to bear contact & conversation as well mixed natures should. (*CL2*, 351)

And in Journal C, he laments that he has trouble giving aid to others beyond that which thoughts provide. "The Newspapers persecute Alcott. I have never more regretted my inefficiency to practical ends. I was born a seeing eye not a helping hand. I can only comfort my friends by thought, & not by love or aid" (*JMN5*, 298).

I find fascinating the history of Emerson's friendship with Fuller because it appears to manifest two vices that undermine the kind of reciprocal self-culture that ethical friendship affords. First, if we ask another to resolve our being for us, then we ask too much and abandon self-reliance in order to conform to another's arc. But so too we fail our friends if we refuse to tend to their growth when they falter and stutter or need cheer and affirmation. But not only that, for as I've noted, tenderness is a proactive as well as a palliative art. Unsolicited invitations and provocations are also the right of friends, and they do much to assure us that we are welcome beyond the foyer of our companions' lives. It seems, however, that Emerson was at times unable to prove equal to such occasions. In the least, this is how Fuller viewed matters, comparing him to a palm that promises shade and nourishment to a weary traveler but proves too tall and unresponsive when one finally reaches the oasis (Hudspeth 1983, 290–91).

But perhaps I'm simply resisting the consummation of Emersonian friendship. Paragraph 21 insists: "We walk alone in the world. Friends, such as we desire, are dreams and fables" (*CW2*, 125). And isn't a monologue the voice of the solitary walker? But from what I've found thus far, the point of Emersonian friendship has been both to respect the irreplaceably singular nature of the self and to lead and encourage one to venture and find oneself reflected in the character and love of another, hence the claim: "A friend, therefore, is a paradox in nature" (*CW2*,

120). Moreover, Emersonian friendship is prophetically en route. What we desire in such a friend, therefore, is very much someone who keeps open the dream of a better future. In fact, noble friends should provide, by example, even fabulistically, steps toward that horizon, like Socrates does for Crito. As Emerson notes in *Platonia*: "Crito bribed the jailor, but Socrates would not go out by treachery. Whatever inconvenience ensue, nothing is to be preferred before Justice. These things I hear like pipes & drums whose sound makes me deaf to everything you say" (*JMN10*, 483).

And yet, Emerson seems to be hushing precisely my fret over indifference when he says: "It is foolish to be afraid of making our ties too spiritual, as if we could lose any genuine love," adding in the essay's final paragraph: "But the great will see that true love cannot be unrequited" (*CW2*, 125 and 127). But from where are such assurances made? An early line holds a partial answer: "The laws of friendship are austere and eternal, of one web with laws of nature and morals" (*CW2*, 117). A second occurs in "Compensation": "All things are moral. That soul which within us is a sentiment, outside of us is a law. We feel its inspiration; out there in history we can see its fatal strength. . . . A perfect equity adjusts its balance in all parts of life" (*CW2*, 60). I'm drawn back to "Compensation" because only that degree of strength, the kind wielded by divine invisible hands could assure that love doesn't dissipate in its own evanescence.

This invocation of the doctrine of compensation may seem invasive, but paragraph 11 already announces what I'm only now marking. It terms friendship a "sacred relation which is a kind of absolute" compared to which "nothing is so divine." And look at how paragraph 10 grounds its trust of the friend—"Love, which is the essence of God, is not for levity, but for the total worth of man. . . . [L]et us approach our friend with an audacious trust in the truth of his heart, in the breadth, impossible to be overturned, of his foundations." And as he tells George Adams Sampson: "But never do I despair that by truth we shall merit truth; by resolute searching for truth ourselves we shall deserve & obtain wisdom from others. If not now, yet in God's time & the souls, which is ages & ages" (*CL1*, 378). With "God's time," we have once again ventured into "periods in which mortal lifetime is lost." That is, a theological suture binds the ethos of Emersonian friendship, from its foundations to its audacious trust. And the weave of a theodicy holds together "flesh and blood" at points where others, say, those writing in the wake of divine decomposition, find only traces of a foregone great event.

Because I find myself writing in just that aftermath, I would pull back from the theological heights and depths that bookend Emersonian friendship. As before, my problem is not simply incredulity in the face of compensation. Nor do I think the doctrine calls for too much one-on-one time with the Divine. I take Emerson at his word when he professes a "sublime hope . . . that elsewhere, in other regions of universal power, souls are now acting, enduring, and daring, which can love us and which we can love" (*CW2*, 125). But his reliance on the reconciliations that "God's time" affects leads him to imagine friendship's consummation in terms that leave little room for "flesh and blood": "We may congratulate ourselves that the period of nonage, of follies, of blunders, and of shame, is passed in solitude," he writes, "and when we are finished men, we shall grasp heroic hands in heroic hands" (*CW2*, 125). To my ear, this sensibility offers friendship few prospects. First, if the period of nonage persists until compensation works its magic—and like Emerson himself, both in "Circles" and "Experience," I take "nonage" to name a state into which we fall again and again—then mortal life may prove friendless. Second, if friendship, in its provocations and tenderness, is essential to the ongoing task of coming into one's own, then gratefulness for solitude prior to maturity is a self-undermining disposition. Third, if folly and blunders are to be borne in solitude, what is the role of tenderness in Emersonian friendship? When wedded to the eternal, heroic hands have little need for tenderness, nor should they expect it if we are obliged to bear our infirmities in silence.

If what I foresee is right, I'll preserve the homely and strict commerce of paragraph 13, one rich in loyalty, sincerity, patience, alertness, and humility. Poised for the arrival of commended strangers who might prove beautiful enemies in the sociality of genius, I'll do without guaranteed compensations. Instead, I'll address my friends, without melancholy, in the spirit and letter that Emerson offers Margaret Fuller in 1839: "Let us in the one golden hour allowed us to be great & true, be shined upon by the sun & moon, & feel in our pulse circulations from the heart of nature. We shall be more content to be superseded some day, if we have once been clean & permeable channels. I should indeed be happy tonight to be excited by your eloquence & sympathy up to the point of vision,—and what more can friendship avail?" (*CL2*, 246).

But what about the essay's closing lines? you might ask.

> Yet these [impersonal—JTL] things may hardly be said without a sort of treachery to the relation. The essence of friendship is entireness, a total magnanimity and trust. It must not surmise or provide for infirmity. It treats its object as a god, that it might deify both. (*CW2*, 127)

I agree that this mucks things up. At times, though less frequently of late, I find this passage to mark one more tack in the essay's mimetic fidelity, a pull back from a language whose elevation provides for infirmity, thereby profaning friendship. If so, this ending might complement what I've been arguing, that is, that Emerson's doctrine of compensation leads him to favor a kingdom of heroic friends over mortal companions, thereby cooling, if not rendering unnecessary, the loyal tenderness he earlier celebrates. But at his essay's close, Emerson is chiefly concerned with whoever catches wind of his solace amid asymmetrical relations, so he calls himself back to a more magnanimous pose, lest his observations prove too nettlesome. My worry, though, is with the bearing of one who receives others without meeting or parting. There, beyond mortal hours, Emersonian friendship is forced to trust in that which impersonally secures the fountains of its hidden life. But this is to say that neither social genius nor the self-culture it both rides and drives are genius enough to make the sweetness of life, to convert the mill-round of our fate into a sun path. And to that I can only say, "No thanks."

Lest I prove ungrateful, let me close by recalling all that I have accepted from Emersonian friendship in my effort to elaborate and advance Emersonian self-culture. I turned to friendship in order to further check the surges of fanaticism that Emersonian self-culture faces once it undergoes divine decomposition. What I found was a site of enlargement that evidenced the sociality of genius, thereby broadening the influx of what we might eloquently quote and be. Alongside, or rather in the ethos of moment, Emersonian friendship very much resists whatever chokeholds our temperament might have on us, particularly since its excitement is bound to encountering and being exercised by the "not-mine."

Emersonian friendship also evidenced something unexpected. It broadened the ethos of the moment into an ethos that also orients how we receive and present ourselves to others. I say "broadened" because, in Emersonian friendship, the ethos of the moment continues to play a crucial role—for example, in reorienting us in the face of a friend's differences. Lying atop its various maxims, therefore, one also finds a series of questions that lead us to continually reassess and renew the character that we cannot help but publish with every action. Does my behavior embody the virtue(s) to which we, as friends, are devoted? Am I sincere and patient? Am I seizing moments of enlargement wherever and by whomever they are offered? Am I tending to my friends' enlargement as well, say, with comfort, cheer, or the kind of prophetic provocations that an advancing character always presents? Not that such questions strike only in company. Since this is a friendship of character, these questions persist even when my friends are absent, as Emerson notes in Sermon CXL: "We hardly consider how much we live with our friends, how much we are indebted to them for this insensible influence. It is present when they are absent. In the silence of night, in solitary thought, in the gloom of discontent, in the stress of temptation they talk with, they exhort, they succor us" (*CS4,* 50). Friendship thus weaves itself into the heart of self-culture, calling us toward eloquence even as it empowers our pursuit of it.

More remarkably still, because it destabilizes the distinction between friend and enemy, leaving us uncertain who will prove which, Emersonian friendship also reorients us toward whomever we meet. In that undecidability, it's as if everyone becomes a "commended stranger" who might prove a friend. In Emerson's hands, this thought leads to an insistence that we strive to prove exemplary wherever we go, equal to whatever might present itself, that is, receptive to moments of social genius and equally provocative in our own efforts, laying out what is true in our hearts for all, albeit in a manner observant of the difference between primary and secondary experience, for that is what exemplary provocation entails.

SEVEN

Tending to Reform

Cannot I too descend a Redeemer into nature?

—*CW1*, 199

What fairer renown can an epoch ask with all following ages, than
that it did not sleep on the errors it inherited, but put every usage on
trial, and exploded every abuse?

—*EL3*, 257

An eloquent life orients the labors of Emersonian self-culture. Our
genius, in native and ecstatic flurries, each a mooded disclosure, gives
us prospects that we might essay. The result should be a character
whose contours and course we have both affirmed and, to a certain extent, shaped. And not just once and for all. Living out mortal hours, re-
curringly thrown into and as some outcropping of nature, we find renewal and redirection lurk at every bend. Now, if we are true, keeping
to an ethos of the moment, our bearings should evidence a keen feel for
what a moment's time might both erase and enable. If not, we will tell
the part we've quoted, but not how we conspired in the saying. But if
we do conspire, and well, we may transform what there is to say on the
matter.

Not that we proceed alone. Friends, those sufficiently like and unlike us, offer provocations toward a more eloquent range of characteristic expressions. Emersonian friendship requires a particular ethos,
however, one that complements and keeps pace with the ethos of the
moment. Shaped by virtues like patience, sincerity, and tenderness,
our lives expand as they wind through ethical friendships oriented to-

ward noble ends where virtue is its own reward. Moreover, in what proves to be a sociality of genius, ethical friends, by example and expectation, provoke one another to greater eloquence, living out a mimetic praxis of self-culture, one character a prophet for the other, both sign and enabler of what could be.

Emersonian friendship is thus an integral part of Emersonian self-culture, both fruit and trunk of an eloquent life, though even in the deepest friendships, what I've been calling "the personal" persists, a range of events and efforts that no one can carry out for us. So conditioned, our being unfolds as a kind of bearing, that is, an enduring, a carrying (which entails a conspiring), and an orientation. "Considerations by the Way" is to the point: "All revelations, whether of mechanical or intellectual or moral science, are made not to communities but to single persons" (*CW6*, 133). That said, Emersonian friendship does succor. Moreover, it evidences how porous we prove, and thus how influential we are. And it does so in a context of responsibility. Friends tend to how they influence one another, avoiding harms, addressing hurts, and proactively pursuing well-being. But what of those who aren't our friends? How should we tend to them? On my reading, "reform" names the fold in Emersonian self-culture to which we should bring this concern.

In order to address Emersonian reform, I must delimit the scope of my reflections. As I think it, "reform" names a more general bearing than "politics" (which I take to be bound to statecraft and the writing of positive law), so one shouldn't take what follows to be an exposition of Emerson's politics, though it touches on his estimation of state-based reform. Also, I will neither settle whether Emerson was an apologist of capitalism, nor determine whether his efforts on behalf of abolition were sufficiently aggressive, nor investigate his relative silence on Native American genocide.[1] More generally, my concern is not whether Emerson's life was sufficiently virtuous to retain the mantle of cultural hero. Rather, my concern is how reform, an activity he sometimes celebrates, relates to the labors of self-culture. To what degree, and in what ways, does an eloquent life tend toward reform?[2]

At the outset, I should state that reform is less an option for Emersonian self-culture than the effect, even the direction of our bearings. According to Emerson, reformation marks our very presence in and as nature. In the "Reforms" lecture from 1840, Emerson proclaims: "It is the eternal testimony of the soul in man to a fairer possibility of life and manner than he has attained that agitates society every day with the offer of some new amendment" (*EL3,* 259). Here is the claim. Intellect is prospective, and prospects are potential reforms. By taking them up, we remake our lives and the world on which those lives (quotefully) depend. The thought is elaborated in an 1860 "Reform" lecture:

> Reform is a vital function. It is not an old impulse by which we move, like a stone thrown into the air, but by an incessant impulse like that of gravitation. We are not potted and buried in our bodies, but everybody is newly created from day to day, and every moment. Just as much life, so much is the power it exerts,—a strong race, a victorious civilization. What we call the preservation of the body is re-creation. (*LL2,* 151)[3]

I find this view compelling. Human bodies do not simply persist in a state of rest. Cells regenerate, replacing one another, and we organize our environment in order to provide ourselves with the energy this regeneration requires. As organisms, many of our metamorphoses are thus reconstructions of self and world, and in daily ways. We thus do live according to an "incessant impulse" (as opposed to a single throw from a primal mover), which rounds us out and organizes our orbits. I would thus say that an Emersonian conception of reform begins with the tendency of human lives to recreate the world in their fashion as they venture lives of more or less daring.

Given Emerson's theodicy, this initial sense of reform may prove unsurprising. If some god is husbanding the garden, we'll have the best of all possible parts to play, each pulse another brick for the city of god. But even without the specter of such a heavy hand in our affairs, reform remains a part of our eating, sleeping, walking life. And this weave only thickens when we recall the nature of genius. "Genius is the activity," Emerson says, "which repairs the decay of things" (*EL3,* 74). True, this can also be read by way of Emerson's theodicy, but it also states, rather bluntly, that genius finds possibility where others find stasis, perhaps even necessity. Classicism grows stale, and Beethoven finds paths into romanticism. Carver finds hundreds of uses for the peanut. Disputes seem irresolvable, yet a combination of good listening, imagination, and a will to believe locates and clears a few spots for joint ventures. I thus consider Emerson quite astute when he writes,

"Genius is the power to labor better and more availably [i.e., power-fully—JTL] than others" (*CW1*, 211).

As the emergence of possibility, genius is thus, at its inception, initial reform. Not that discovering this facet of involuntary perceptions is sufficient to gauge the play of reform in Emersonian self-culture. But it does mark a starting point. Insofar as Emersonian self-culture is centered (and recurrently de-centered) by genius, and insofar as genius tends toward reform, reform seems bound to every step with which we conspire.

I think a quick review of Emerson's admiration for John Brown might make an inverse point.[4] Brown strikes Emerson as remarkable, given a "singleness of purpose" that stems from an oath purportedly "made to heaven and earth forty-seven years before [in 1813—JTL]" (*EAW*, 121 and 122). Emerson found in Brown's character radiating ideals to which the latter had abandoned himself. "I said John Brown was an idealist. He believed in his ideas to the extent, that he existed to put them all into action" (*EAW*, 119). This language of ideals recalls the figure of genius, Emerson's source for the kind of involuntary perceptions that call for oaths. As he writes in "The Progress of Culture": "The miracles of genius always rest on profound convictions which refuse to be analyzed" (*CE8*, 229). Brown merits this kind of language because, in Emerson's eyes, he is a "romantic character," "living to ideal ends, without any mixture of self-indulgence [i.e., egoism—JTL]" (*EAW*, 122). In its own way, then, Brown's life signifies, eloquently, the "true romance which the world exists to realize," to recall the language of "Experience," namely, the "transformation of genius into practical power" (*CW3*, 49). My claim, then, is that for Emerson, Brown is a genius of the sort he celebrated in his remarks on the Emancipation Proclamation: "Every step in the history of political liberty is a sally of the human mind into the untried future, and has the interest of genius" (*EAW*, 129). More generally, though, my claim is that Emersonian reform roots itself in genius. "Every project in the history of reform, no matter how violent and surprising, is good when it is the dictate of a man's genius and constitution, but very dull and suspicious when adopted from another" (*CW3*, 151). Like all of Emerson's ventures, therefore, reform commences along the way of abandonment.

If Emersonian genius tends toward reform, and if Emersonian reform derives from genius, self-culture and reform share a common if unpredictable root. How, though, should we think the place of reform in an eloquent life? The question is crucial, for an answer may offer a compelling way out of the dead end opposition between self-cultivation and concern for others. Let us begin by noting that in our reflections on friendship, we've already indicated a site of Emersonian reform. Because genius is social, self-culture folds into other-culture, and irrespective of whether we are among friends. By way of example, let me repeat why I regard this as a powerful insight. In carrying out a job, one cannot help but offer co-workers a portrait of how one might go about one's business, say, conscientiously, with gentle humor, or divisively, even selfishly. And such examples can breed. Or take another example. In teaching a class, one models how to respond to language, ill and good will, controversy and frustration. And students take note, observing passions, authoritarian insistences, as well as how generous or mean one is with half-developed thoughts. From this I conclude that an eloquent life is simultaneously an influential life. "Who shall set a limit to the influence of a human being?" Emerson writes in "Power." "There are men, who, by their sympathetic attractions, carry nations with them, and lead the activity of the human race" (CW6, 28). Or, with self-culture explicitly at issue: "For, it is not what talents or genius a man has, but how he is to his talents, that constitutes friendship and character. The man that stands by himself [i.e., eloquently—JTL], the universe stands by him also" (CW6, 102). Of course, the persuasive power of our exemplifications exists along a continuum, but that is sufficient to warrant the following: In our pursuit of an eloquent life, we should take responsibility for our influences as best we can. And wherever we are most influential, we should strive to be most eloquent.

Let me concretize the charge, and in a way that makes plain its implications for you and me. Given the inevitability of our influences, self-culture asks us to be role models. In "The Young American," Emerson makes plain that he expects the proponent of self-culture to lead by example: "I think I see place and duties for a nobleman in every society; but it is not to drink wine and ride in a fine coach, but to guide and adorn life for the multitude by forethought, by elegant studies, by perseverance, by self-devotion, and the remembrance of the humble old friend [by tenderness—JTL], by making his life secretly beautiful" (CW1, 238–39). In this context, I take "secretly" to run counter to didacticism. At stake is the manner of our pursuits—how we conduct our lives is what will serve as a guide for others. One finds in Journal E: "The reform that is ripening in your mind for the amelioration of the human race, I shall find already in miniature in every direction to the domestics, in every conversation with the assessor, with your creditor, & with your debtor" (*JMN7*, 394). Actions speak like words, it seems, and behavior conducts our aims. In every course of action, therefore, Emersonian self-culture asks, What is it you would say to those who'll see and hear of what (and how) you do?[5]

In focusing on the manner in which we pursue our abandonment, it may seem that Emerson's feel for reform is substanceless. But consider what he also tells those gathered to hear "The Young American": "That is his nobility, his oath of knighthood, to succor the helpless and oppressed; always to throw himself on the side of weakness, of youth, of hope, on the liberal, on the expansive side, never on the defensive, the conserving, the timorous, the lock and bolt system" (*CW1*, 240–41). And note how he eulogizes John Brown: "All gentlemen, of course, are on his side. I do not mean by 'gentlemen,' people of scented hair and perfumed handkerchiefs, but men of gentle blood and generosity, 'fulfilled with all nobleness.' . . . For what is the oath of gentle blood and knighthood? What but to protect the weak and lowly against the strong oppressor?" (*EAW*, 123). This language of protection and liberality recalls, strikingly, the kind of tenderness that friendship exacts from friends, in their relations both with one another and with those commended strangers ever arriving. In fact, these words from 1844 and 1860 lead me to regard an eloquent life as one oriented toward a reactive and proactive melioration. When hurts are apparent, they should be remedied. In their absence, our behavior should still bear witness to expansion and growth. Our conduct should thus not only cheer, but evidence possibility where others had only found impasses. It is thus unsurprising that Emerson should announce in "Culture": "Incapacity of melioration is the only mortal distemper" (*CW6*, 74).[6] Melioration is a fruit of self-culture, and in an eloquent life, it should be evident wherever we are. We might thus rewrite the entry from Journal E in the form of a maxim: The reform that is ripening in your mind for the amelioration of the human race should appear, in miniature, in every direction to the domestics, in every conversation with the assessor, with your creditor, & with your debtor.

It is perhaps worth reiterating why Emersonian self-culture orients itself toward tenderness. Tenderness is a characteristic virtue of ethical friendship, to which Emersonian self-culture abandons itself. Recall also that lives carried out under a law of metamorphosis are unable to know in advance who will prove friend or foe, a fact that renders everyone a commended stranger, one who may prove a prophet of future hours. In that undecidability, Emersonian self-culture tends to the arrival of commended strangers, seeking the expansion of its conception of the good life (via what the arriving stranger offers and/or takes) as well as the rewards that come from an overall increase in noble characters. Emersonian self-culture thus throws itself on the side of youth and hope, on the "expansive side." By why tender to the weak and the poor in particular? Why single them out if everyone stands before us as a commended stranger? To appreciate this commitment, we need to draw tuition from a point first ventured in chapter 2.

In "Self-Reliance," Emerson construes his principal virtue with the image of nonchalant boys certain of dinner, finding there the "healthy attitude of human nature" (*CW2*, 29). Likewise, in "Wealth," he insists that living out the calls of genius requires a good deal of underwriting. "Nor can he do justice to his genius, without making some larger demand on the world than a bare subsistence. He is by constitution expensive, and needs to be rich" (*CW6*, 45). Finally, in "Society and Solitude" we are told: "Society cannot do without cultivated men. As soon as the first wants are satisfied, the higher wants become imperative" (*CE7*, 11). These thoughts, offered across some thirty years, evidence Emerson's awareness that those without sufficient means, who haven't satisfied the first wants, have little chance to follow their genius and thus are unlikely to live eloquently. One could say, then, that a certain degree of material security is a precondition of self-culture. In the context of reform, this suggests that one should try to tender goods that self-culture requires, knowing that the ends one affirms will not prosper if one's peers are unable to meet subsistence needs. Or, to use words from "Man the Reformer": "Every man ought to have this opportunity to conquer the world for himself" (*CW1*, 152). And thus: "The state must consider the poor man, and all voices must speak for him. Every child that is born must have a chance for his bread" (*CW1*, 159).

This focus on material needs should not obscure the fact that self-culture has a wide appetite. "A man is entitled to pure air and to the air of good conversation in his bringing up, & not, as we or so many of us, to the poor-smell & musty chambers, cats, and paddies" (*JMN9*, 433). While the images are obscure, the suggestion is less so. Recall that conversation is an event of ignition for Emerson. One needs it, therefore, both in order to come into one's own and to hear arrangements of an order outside the range of one's "mastertones," that is, the predilections of one's temperament.

> Our conversation once and again has apprised us that we belong to better circles than we have yet beheld; that a mental power invites us whose generalizations are more worth for joy and for effect than anything that is now called philosophy or literature. In excited conversations, we have glimpses of the Universe, hints of power . . . such as we can hardly attain in lone meditation. (*CW6*, 144)

Emersonian self-culture thus faces the demand both to generally distribute this good and to enable it with one's own conduct, say, through public education and, should you be a scholar, through generous responses to queries raised in bars, on busses, or wherever one happens to meet another seeking expansion. Why? Emersonian self-culture affirms itself, takes self-culture to be fit for a noble life; and thus it should facilitate its emergence among the full set of those it would see noble.[7]

In seeking to broadly enable self-culture, Emerson is driven to meliorate those conditions that prove relevant to its emergence. His commitment to melioration is thus very much a commitment to establishing conditions that facilitate the upbuilding of humanity here and now as well as in the future. Here is a confession from 1841: "I will not dissemble my hope, that each person whom I address has felt his own call to cast aside all evil customs, timidities, and limitations, and to be in his place a free and helpful man, a reformer, a benefactor, not content to slip along through the world like a footman or a spy, escaping by his nimbleness and apologies as many knocks as he can, but a brave and upright man, who must find or cut a straight road to everything excellent in the earth, and not only go honorably himself, but make it easier for all who follow him, to go in honor, and with benefit" (*CW1*, 145–46). This captures, I think, the heart of Emersonian reform and the kind of bearing it brings to Emersonian self-culture. Wherever one's foot falls, it should widen the path for another, and we are eloquent to the degree to which our life takes steps in that direction. Or, in much sterner language from *Conduct of Life*: "A man should make life and nature happier to us; or he had better never been born" (*CW6*, 141). I add this line because it complements the pathos of the first, giving us something of the mood in which reform is sought. On the one hand, reform requires high spirits, a feel for the possible, and confidence in immanent transitions. On the other, it is hounded by an imminent shame that rises whenever we fail to properly love the world, that is, when we prove either unable to "see to it that the world is the better *for me*," or unable to take that doubled result as a sufficient reward (*CW1*, 159; emphases added).

Presuming that the basic contours of reform in Emersonian self-culture are sufficiently articulated, let's survey some sites that eloquent lives should meliorate and indicate some means. The basic principle is this: Wherever my life becomes part of another's, I should aim to enable those ends to which I wish my life to bear witness, including those ends whose realization underwrites the pursuit of self-culture. This requires, then, that I take the political personally. In Sermon CL, Emerson writes:

> And this too is a perpetual duty. We ought to be always sad and ashamed of our national sins. We ought never to lose sight of the truth that national offences are private offences carried out and represented at length, so that men shudder at the vice when seen at full length which they tolerate and indulge in miniature, as the traveler in mountain countries is sometimes terrified by the apparition of his own shadow magnified on the mist. (*CS4*, 114)[8]

I find this manifold thought compelling. First, insofar as my quotations and affirmations carry me into the authorship, execution, and enforcement of laws, to that degree they are mine, thus rendering public offences private. So if one's government is a source of shame, its machinery at odds with one's way of abandonment, then one's eloquence is curtailed, one's nobility compromised. One should resist such complicities, and not simply by stating that one didn't vote for so and so. First, in affirming the voting process, one is affirming the victor, even if one voted for someone else. Second, and more significantly, our complicity is not limited to persons or policies we directly endorse, but stems from the reach and entanglement of our quoting nature. With this in mind, and turning toward my present, I find that U.S. oil policy is my policy whenever I drive, and regardless of how I cast my ballot.

Now, in response to such entanglements, one can march, write letters, donate money to alleviate so-called collateral damages, and so forth, and these are meliorating efforts. But also note how Emerson responds to his shame. He turns back toward local haunts and wonders whether our local engagements aren't also part of the problem. Here's an obvious example. No doubt many bemoan world hunger. And many are outraged by the indifference of governments to the fate of those suffering from drought, famine, hunger, and, in many cases, the wars that initiate such conditions. But how many of us also tolerate hunger in our local communities? Or even among those who support local projects, how many would strenuously resist hosting such services a block or two away from their homes? Though rhetorical, the questions suggest that Emersonian reform not only protests national crimes, but it uses them as mirrors with which to examine analogous local failings.

Now, Emerson may overly individuate national offences, as if they were hypertrophic extensions of local vices. This would mark a problem, for it might obscure the full range of factors in need of melioration. For example, we compromise our ameliorative power if we primarily regard U.S. militarism as a simple extension of individual patterns of aggression and avarice, though it surely is that. At the very least, we must also address it as a manifestation of an ideology that measures human well-being in terms of capital expansion, colonial conceptions of self and other, and the structural susceptibility of U.S. federalism to influence derived from wealth and social power. Still, one can find a history of domestic invasion in the United States, and thus Emerson may be right to inquire at home for patterns witnessed abroad, thus multiplying areas where melioration is required. For example, when I think of U.S. militarism, I also think of how large real estate deals are brokered, and of who is often displaced in the process, whether by rezoning, eminent domain rulings, or outright harassment and police intervention. Think of the sordid history surrounding Chavez Ravine and what is now Dodger Stadium in Los Angeles. Between 1950 and 1959, a poor, predominantly Latino community was slowly displaced by eminent domain decisions, entailing eviction with varying degrees of compensation. Initially, these evictions were accompanied by the promise of a new housing development underwritten by federal funds, what was to be called Elysian Park Heights. For multiple reasons, including Red scare lunacy, that project never got off the ground. But rather than make good on initial promises, the land was eventually sold at a loss to the L.A. Dodgers for their new stadium. Moreover, the stadium was built even though several families remained who had refused to leave during the initial phase of acquisition. In fact, on May 8, 1959, they were forcibly evicted by the sheriff's office, which then bulldozed the remaining homes.[9]

The ties between local and national action are also apparent in ways that more directly render the political personal. I presume that the second U.S. invasion of Iraq reflected a desire for greater U.S. influence in oil markets. Given this, I wonder whether local reliance on fossil fuel didn't help sponsor the invasion through the economic opportunity those habits represent, call it leading some thugs into temptation. Just think of how many of us drive to work, drive to stores, and buy goods delivered by boats and trucks. Our behavior is an aggregate market share ready for the taking. Or so I think when I count the dead while accelerating among thousands of cars on an interstate highway.

The thought before us is that because more than charity begins in the home, anyone seeking an eloquent life must confront that fact. To put it more directly, our eloquence withers when relations we enable conform to paths we'd rather not follow. Moreover, in enabling those relations, we, to the degree they are ignoble, undermine the very world we took ourselves to be upbuilding. Now, I have turned to Emerson's personal feel for politics less to prepare us for a discussion of civil disobedience than to suggest, more generally, that one should follow out one's quotations and determine whether the life that grows there, in part through one's participation, merits renewal or melioration. And not just with regard to the state. Domestic spaces are also sites where eloquence is tested. One sees this in Emerson's poignant image that, under conditions of slavery, those with sufficiently keen tongues should taste blood in their sugar (*EAW*, 20). Similarly, in "The Method of Nature," he recalls the origins of cotton, proclaiming: "I would not have the laborer sacrificed to the splendid result,—I would not have the laborer sacrificed to my convenience and pride, nor to that of a great class such as me. Let there be worse cotton and better men" (*CW1*, 121). I think the claim is twofold. First, as with laws, those who are party to shameful practices should cease and desist.[10] Second, no educated class (or self-cultivated class) should regard its emergence as sufficient justification for practices that erode the lives of others. Rather than conducting such conversations, they should be reformed, or meliorated, until the practices in question prove beneficent influences on the lives they touch, even require.

We are exploring tendencies toward reform that are characteristic of Emersonian self-culture. Driven by genius, self-culture pursues reformation, whether it wishes to or not. In conspiring with such projects, one thus should prove a meliorating force along lines of influence, affiliation, and dependency. Interestingly, if we see reform in this way, we can read a famous, possibly infamous line from "Self-Reliance" more sympathetically. Somewhat petulantly, Emerson writes:

> Then, again, do not tell me, as a good man did to-day, of my obligation to put all poor men in good situations. Are they *my* poor? I tell thee, thou foolish philanthropist, that I grudge the dollar, the dime, the cent I give to such men as do not belong to me and to whom I do not belong. (*CW2*, 30–31; emphasis in the original)

The passage shocks because it seems so callous. But I take the italicization of *my* to render the question more than rhetorical. Is this a fate to which I am bound? Is this what nobility demands of me? If so, I should meliorate the situation. If not, say, because our lives only overlap at the point of superstring theory and I can do little to help, or if I could offer help only at great cost to others who are mine, then we might conclude that in such instances they are not sufficiently mine to warrant meliorating attention. Thus, rather than negating the project of reform, this passage from "Self-Reliance" helps figure it, marking reform as the appropriate response to those who have some claim on us, given the interweaving of our lives.

That said, I should add that Emerson seems acutely aware, and helpfully so, of how often we hide our entanglements from ourselves:

> It does very well for the English and American towns to exchange peace-tracts. . . . But war has not ceased in either country for a moment. If France, and England, and America are forced, by a keener self-interest, to keep the peace with each other, that does not hinder that some poor Algerines, Sikhs, Seminoles, or Mexicans, should be devoured by these peace-loving States at the same moment. (*EAW*, 43)[11]

I cite this passage to underscore how complicated it may prove to determine whether another belongs to the class of *my* poor or *my* victim. Given our quoting nature, our fingers are in many pockets. But knowing that is precisely one of the strengths of Emersonian self-culture. Not that it has answers to every particular question we might ask. How could it, if the soul becomes? Rather, its strength lies in being constitutionally haunted by the question, and as self-culture; for an eloquent life will strive to determine to whom it belongs. It will want to be known among its friends as one who seeks such. And it will pursue reactive and proactive melioration wherever it answers in the affirmative.

While exploring the various sites in which our lives are disclosed as more than ours—for example, in the state and across the exchanges of home economies—we should also remember that each locale is personal in another way. Lecturing on the evils of slavery, Emerson announces: "It is not to societies that the secrets of nature are revealed, but to private persons, to each man in his organization, in his thoughts" (*EAW*, 102). I take this to say two things. First, in speaking of the secrets of nature, Emerson reminds us that our roots, including our genius, are events of nature. As he says later in 1863, "Committees don't manage revolutions. A revolution is a volcano, and from under everybody's feet flings its sheet of fire into the sky" (*EAW*, 153). That said, recalling the tongues of Pentecost, even revolutionary fires must light on each revolutionary, both in their organization (I read character) and thought (I read genius). Returning to 1855: "My political economy is very short, a man's capital must be in him" (*EAW*, 103). I take this to mean that how we conspire with reforms has a say in their fortune, and no one else can conspire for us. "There is no help but in the head and heart and hamstring of a man," Emerson says, responding to the Fugitive Slave Law. "Covenants are of no use without honest men to keep them. Laws are of no use, but with loyal citizens to obey them" (*EAW*, 83) But this is just to say, Emersonian self-culture won't leave reform to the auto-administration of a state apparatus.[12] To take such matters personally is not only to believe that one is implicated in affairs of state but that, in some measure, no doubt incalculable for a paltry empiricism, their success is contingent on how we conspire with our condition.

Let us turn to a question of means, noting that, as Buell (2003, 269) observes, quoting Cadava (1997): "There is no single form of political engagement in Emerson." First, Emerson prefers affirmative actions to condemnations:

> Yet for the most part there is a liberal monotony in the history of our young men of the Liberal or reforming class. They have only got so far as rejection, not as far as affirmation. They seem therefore angry

& railers: they have nothing new or memorable to offer; & that is the vice of their writings,—profuse declamation but no new matter. (*JMN7*, 431)

Emerson's point, I take it, is that relentless negation exhausts rather than inspires, perhaps to the point of breeding cynicism. I am not sure how one could prove such a thing, but I am more than familiar with those who vehemently condemn a status quo they lack the wit to reconstruct. And so they content themselves with denunciations. Moreover, I've witnessed how denunciation rallies emotions that dissipate when the shouting ceases. But this is an unsurprising result. Melioration requires a feel for how our prospects might be realized, and thus a dearth of imagination promises a dearth of reform. More surprising are cases where denunciation becomes the principal means of reform, and to the point that reconstructive efforts are rejected as insufficiently radical. At such moments, I have the feeling that condemnation has become the point, not melioration. And it is precisely at such moments that I think of the following. "Not by hate of death but by new & larger life is death to be vanquished: in thy heart is life. Obey that it is inventive, creative, prodigal of life & beauty. Thence heroism, virtue, redemption, succor, opportunity, come to thee & to all" (*CL2*, 375).[13]

And yet, though Emerson favors affirmative efforts, he regards certain withdrawals and refusals as necessary. A case in point is his refusal to address the New Bedford lyceum in 1845 after it had voted to deny membership to a person of color. In declining the invitation, he writes: "Besides, in its direct counteraction to the obvious duty and sentiment of New England, and of all freemen in regard to the colored people, the vote appears so unkind, and so unlooked for, that I could not come with any pleasure before the Society" (*EAW*, 39).[14] Rarely is the question of unjust entanglements so easily resolved, however. It is more likely that one's allegiances result in good and bad, thus complicating the calculus. Emerson thus warns against an excessive fear of moral contamination. "I do not wish to be absurd and pedantic in reform. I do not wish to push my criticism on the state of things around me to that extravagant mark, that shall compel me to suicide, or to an absolute isolation from the advantages of civil society" (*CW1*, 155). I find this significant because it suggests that Emerson's focus is less the purity of his own life than the ameliorative consequences of his actions. Emersonian reform isn't undone, therefore, by the thought of allegiances with somewhat compromising means, as long as one's prospects are good. In fact, a noble character will suffer certain indignities for a greater benefit.

> There is a sublime prudence which is the very highest that we know of man, which, believing in a vast future,—sure of more to come than is yet seen, . . . As the merchant gladly takes money from his income to add to his capital, so is the great man very willing to lose particular powers and talents [or suffer ineloquent moments—JTL], so that he gain in the elevation of his life. (*CW1*, 160)[15]

Of course, one needs to choose well, as the language of "prudence" conveys. And by definition, choosing well is something no rule can specify. Still, one can offer examples, as Emerson does when thinking of the state and its multiple projects, some of which no doubt offend. He counsels: "You cannot fight heartily for a fraction. But wait until you have a good difference to join issue upon" (*JMN9*, 446). Not that the ends sanctify the means. Given the terms of Emersonian self-culture, one needs to follow up one's compromises, that is, "we must not cease to *tend* to the correction of these flagrant wrongs, by laying one stone aright every day" (*CW1*, 155; emphasis in the original).

Virtues of omission aside, what of proactive reform? Emerson ranks his means while raising money for John Brown's Kansas agitations. "First, the private citizen, then the primary assembly, and the government last" (*EAW*, 113). Let's begin with the first, or rather, return to it. In large measure, Emerson has exemplary living in mind when he looks to private citizens as reformers, with the how and what of their conduct. He sets his foot here because, as we've seen, self-culture obliges one toward reform, and Emerson regards the character of self-culture as a precondition for enduring and praiseworthy collective transformation. But he also has great faith in what Gougeon terms "moral suasion," and what I've termed, more broadly, the fingers and sociality of genius. One finds this faith at its possible height in 1840:

> And herein is my hope for all reform in our vicious modes of living. Let a man direct his inquiry on details in attempting amelioration, & he will be met at every step by unanswerable objections, insoluble difficulties. But let him propose to himself a grand Aim, to live a Prophet, a Helper, a member of Morning and Nature . . . a pure Power, a calm & happy Genius through whom as through a lens the

rays of the Universe converge to the joy of the eye that seeth,—and I
think he shall be floated into his place of activity & happiness by
might and mind sublime over all these rocks & shoals that now look
insuperable. Fix his heart on magnificent life & he need not know
the economical methods: he shall be himself astonished at the great
solution of the problem of means. (*JMN7*, 350)

This is a wild passage, at once thick with Emerson's theodicy—the capitals announce divinity—while gently subverting it, proclaiming a
kind of heaven on earth in that, with genius, we have more than dark
glass for magnification. Moreover, in characteristic Emersonian fashion, it elevates the power of genius above the calculations of cause and
effect, that upon which an "inquiry on details" focuses. But what particularly intrigues is the thought that a "magnificent life" can affect
solidarity (i.e., reform dissent and/or indifference), by addressing "unanswerable objections" and bringing joy to the "eye that seeth."

In this context, the point is not only, once again, that our essays
begin with genius and that its provocations resist analysis, but also that
genius-inspired reformations are intersubjectively intelligible, even
persuasive. "These laws refuse to be adequately stated," he observes in
"The Divinity School Address." "They will not by us or for us be written out on paper, or spoken by the tongue. They elude, evade our persevering thought, and yet we read them hourly in each other's faces, in
each other's actions, in our own remorse" (*CW1*, 77). This passage is instructive because it not only evidences Emerson's faith in moral suasion, but it grounds suasion in character and thus in self-culture. What
compels solidarity among private citizens, then, is really the eloquent
life. As Emerson writes of Luther: "He was like them [Ezekiel, Isaiah—
JTL] the Prophet, the Poet of his times and country. Out of a religious
enthusiasm he acted on the minds of his contemporaries" (*EL1*, 132).

According to Cavell, Emersonian solidarity relies on the character
of the agent more than on any discursive standard of evaluation that
s/he presents in the agon of debate. In his words, judgment is "backed
not by a standard (a moral law, a principle of justice) but fronted by the
character of the judger" (Cavell 1990, xxx). I like this line of thought.
Emersonian reform, at its heart, underwrites its sallies with the life
that self-culture enables, and in multiple ways. First, character announces the sincerity of the proposal, evidencing the commitment in
works and days. Second, a noble character stands behind its ventures

such that his or her bearing communicates a promise to meliorate unforeseen and untoward consequences. Third, one's character can commend the reform itself. Recall that Emersonian self-culture offers its ventures as those befitting a noble life. Insofar as one's character radiates nobility, one's ventures do as well, at least initially, thus acquiring a kind of plausibility, even attractiveness.

But what does this kind of underwriting have to do with solidarity? In proving sincere and in being a stand-up character, even a tender one, the kind of person who doesn't leave co-conspirators in the lurch, one proves trustworthy, thus giving others reasons to join the venture. Moreover, one's affirmation will prove more persuasive if previous affirmations have been worthy, as if the attractiveness of one's bearings improves when former choices bear witness to a noble manner. And this affects, I think, what Emerson says of the English in Journal IO: "Solidarity in the sense of that they believe and rely on each other" (*JMN13*, 317). Of course, none of this "proves" that others should agree, and no appeal to character will resolve disputes in an endgame of incommensurability. Moreover, no amount of "fronting" will erase the fact that our actions are only as deep as our genius, that they occur under a law of metamorphosis and thus they remain ventures that might confound our expectations of one another and the world. Nevertheless, noble character is for Emerson the most salutary starting point for cooperative ventures, and that includes, I think, the venture of cooperative inquiry and argument.

In considering Emersonian reform, we have dipped below proposals into a kind of proto-reform that enables cooperative ventures. My claim, quoting Cavell, is that Emersonian self-culture, particularly when it does the work of private citizens, is particularly suited for ventures that meliorate conversations. Of course, reform of this sort is also a venture, an invitation to conduct life with another, an invitation fronted by a character who promises to conduct him- or herself along certain lines, come what may—say, sincerely and tenderly, with perseverance, aversion to conformity, and abandonment (to recall some of the virtues of Emersonian self-culture). Not that such invitations offer to assume full responsibility for another's life. Quite the opposite. Emersonian reform begins from and remains respectful of the personal, knowing full well that "truly speaking, it is not instruction, but provocation, that I can receive from another soul. What he announces, I must find true in me, or wholly reject; and on his word, or as his second, be he who he may, I can accept nothing" (*CW1*, 80).

I've paused over the issue of moral suasion (which thickens, I think, our conception of the sociality of genius), because it accentuates the "democracy of the intellect" that Kateb (2000, 5) finds so characteristic of Emerson's *oeuvre*. In its respect for the incalculable sociality of genius *and* the inelinimable personal dimension of our condition, Emersonian reform refuses to replace another's pledge of allegiance with solidarity wrought for any and all rational agents. I think Emerson's faith in the sociality of genius also does justice to the incalculable power of genuine conversation: "genuine" naming those who come together as commended strangers formed in part by an ethos of the moment; "conversation" naming both discursive exchanges and the conversation that all conduct entails. As we've seen in our considerations of friendship, such meetings may burst into spectacles that prove prophets of future hours. With a prospective faith in the sociality of genius (if not in the theodical guarantees of divinity), I am inclined to agree, therefore, when Emerson writes: "The mind is one, and the best minds who love truth for its own sake, think much less of property in truth. They accept it thankfully everywhere, and do not label or stamp it with any man's name" (*CW2*, 165). Or rather, I would have that disposition when seeking solidarity among commended strangers, what amounts to a promise to abandon oneself to whatever claims us in the now of an address, to converse beyond the spell of self-preservation or consistency.

Of course, means other than character and conversation lie at the disposal of private citizens bent on reform. Among them, writing stands out. On the one hand, Emerson's essays, lectures, and speeches extend the lessons he expects from any noble character. Beginning in their performative stance toward their addressees, they embody the ethos of self-culture in a manner that instructs the attentive eye and ear (as I have tried to show throughout). They treat their addressees as "unknown friends" or "commended strangers" and eschew finished thoughts, thus provoking self-reliance even as they offer notions another might essay. The writings also embody the ethos of the moment, changing course when lessons are learned, doubling back on their ventures so that most thoughts (and figures) are affirmed *and* delimited as well as open for further review.[16]

In the ethos of the moment, Emerson's prose thus pursues reform without embracing an overall polemical tone. "The Conservative" and "The Transcendentalist" are cases in point. To each, some measure of respect is accorded, and while Emerson clearly inclines toward the latter, he recognizes that while the "boldness of the hope men entertain transcends all former experience," one must admit, it was not "imported from the stock of some celestial plant, but grew here on the wild crab of conservatism," a thought unsettling to either camp, insofar as they proceed like camps. This is instructive, for it embodies an approach to reform even as it advocates for particular courses of action. Now, Cavell suggests that Emersonian "philosophical" writing eschews polemics on the whole (2003, 206 and 210). There are grounds for this, including the request in "Fate" that one sound out all of the "leading topics which belong to our scheme of human life" in order that the "true limitations will appear" (*CW6*, 2). I see no reason to hold the two so far apart, however. Philosophy and polemics, like philosophy and literature and philosophy and rhetoric, slide into one another. Polemics arise, I think, whenever one denies that something is worthy of a noble life, for example, slavery or conformity. All writing has polemical moments, therefore, whether explicit or not. (Think of Emerson's denigration of friendships of use and pleasure.) The key is to remain alert for enlarged spectacles, which might redeem the excluded, and to meliorate the effects of one's exclusions, should they prove hurtful.

Emerson's writing also tends to reform by way of figuration. In Journal F2, Emerson writes:

> I retrace my old steps and do not believe in remedial force, in the power of change and reform; but some Petrarch or Beaumont & Fletcher filled with new wine of their imagination write me a tale or a dialogue in which are the sallies & recoveries of the soul: they smite & arouse me with the sharp fife, & I open my eye on new possibilities. They clap wings to the side of all the solid old lumber of the world & I see the old Proteus is not dead. (*JMN7*, 523–24)

Here we find the precise terms of melioration: a renewed soul, possibility, and transformation. For such effects, Emerson seems to valorize poets, those who, in unfolding their own experience, appraise us of the commonwealth and give an age a new confession by re-attaching things to the whole. "Poets are thus liberating gods. Men have really got a new sense, and found within their world, another world, or nest of worlds; for, the metamorphosis once seen, we divine that it does not stop" (*CW3*, 17).[17] While I would fold all figuration under this banner, including the law of metamorphosis and the terms of ethical friendship (thus blurring poem and essay, and essay, lecture, and speech), the key is that one's figurations offer unknown friends points from which to essay their own lives, thus meliorating movements trapped in their own inertia.

One could continue at great length about the reforming force of Emerson's writings, but I'll only note two more facets. The first concerns an image that arises in "An Address on the Emancipation of the Negroes in the British West Indies," that of "raking" language, which Emerson pursues because the "secrets of slaughter-houses and infamous holes that cannot front the day, must be ransacked, to tell what negro-slavery has been" (*EAW*, 9). Now, outside of the particular context of slavery, this might mean exposing unseen crimes, such as the truth of the treaties brokered with Native Americans; or contesting various reports, say, about the conditions of workers under global labor; or objecting to particularly ideological words and phrases employed to justify practices that seem prima facie indefensible, like "terrorism." An example from Emerson occurs in a speech on behalf of John Brown's efforts in Kansas:

> Language has lost its meaning in the universal cant. *Representative Government* is really misrepresentative; *Union* is a conspiracy against the Northern States . . . ; *the adding of Cuba and Central America* to the slave marts is *enlarging the area of Freedom. Manifest Destiny, Democracy, Freedom,* fine names for an ugly thing. (*EAW*, 113–14)

I find this salutary because it frustrates the ease with which such terms establish solidarity, and thus it reforms our associations by reforming the words that help bind them. Now, language requires reform of this order because it too is a site of affiliation and influence, and its persistence depends, in part, on how we conspire with it. Emerson writes: "The very language we speak thinks for us by subtle distinctions which already are marked for us by its words, and every one of these is the contribution of the wit of one and another sagacious man in all the centuries of time" (*CE11*, 502). It seems, then, that Emersonian self-culture must rake language whenever its designating and expressive tendencies leave us less eloquent than we had hoped.

This scouring and gathering of language is not altogether unpoetic, however, if the poetic names, as it does for Emerson, a symbolic rendering of some fact that reattaches it to the whole.[18] In reminding his audience that the slaves were "producer of corn and wine, of coffee, of tobacco, of cotton, of sugar, of rum, and brandy," Emerson not only draws near the apparently distant West Indian slave, but also inflects those commodities with traces of slave labor, thereby turning a pantry into a plantation. But not just the commodities, for in the hands of one raking language, the words also become symbols of slavery, each an echo of whips and chains. A raking style thus retunes our language, leaving it haunted by what it had effaced, even defended, thus paring us away from what previously seemed wholesome.

Raking language might also enable another to see that various alliances need not persist. Emerson says in Blotting Book PSI:

> This is the merit of every reformer. One talks about the abolition of Slavery with perfect conviction/coolness whilst all around him sneer or roar at his ludicrous benevolence. They with their sinful eyes can not see society without slaves. He sees distinctly that difference & knows that the crime is unnecessary. And this is the progress of every soul. What it joined before it now severs & sin & error are perpetually falling away from the eternal soul. (*JMN3,* 209)

For example, one might rake "family" in order to free it from the snares of compulsive heterosexuality, or "sex" in order to show how genital intercourse isn't the sole avenue for eroticism. The cases are instructive because they show how raking language can serve an expansive as well as an interruptive function, thus unifying as well as parsing a community. In other words, reform (whether in writing or not), is analogous to ethical friendship. "Thus each reformer carries about him a piece of Me, and as soon as I know it, I am perforce his kinsman & brother. I must feel that he is pleading my cause & shall account myself serving myself in giving him what he lacketh" (*JMN7,* 109–10).

Alongside the rake of a reformed and reforming language, Emerson would have writers cheer (*CW1,* 62). As with most of Emerson, cheer is a thematic and performative venture. In wildly praising self-reliance and its promise of power, in calling scholars to the task of their present, Emerson fires a wide range of souls, for example Nietzsche, and Amal Equiq, a doctoral student in one of my Emerson seminars, who confessed, upon reading and discussing "The American Scholar," that she came to think that she could and should be the next Edward Said, albeit in her own manner. By raising spirits and inspiring as well as demanding a genuine response, cheer can meliorate conditions of doubt and despair, or just plain indifference.

No doubt much more could be said. But let me leave matters here in order to discuss Emerson's two other means of reform, namely, the primary assembly and the state. I agree with Gougeon's assessment that "Emerson never eschewed the political process itself" (1990, 338). As I have shown, Emersonian self-culture is threatened when the state waxes ineloquent, and voting is certainly a way to address the matter, as a letter of 1851 makes plain: "I make a point of conscience of casting my vote on all second Mondays of November" (cited in Gougeon 1990, 171).

Not that one's conscience should be ruled by a sense of purity when voting. As we saw, Emerson's relation to the state is oriented toward long-range consequences, and this holds true for voting as well. "The Purist who refuses to vote, because the govt does not content him in all points, should refuse to feed a starving beggar, lest he should feed his vice" (*JMN13*, 20; cited by Gougeon 1990, 171). I consider this stance admirable because, in tenderness, it observes that ours is never a solitary project. As Emerson tells his Boston audience: "A man is a little thing whilst he works by and for himself" (*EAW*, 101). My suggestion, then, is that those who, when voting, prioritize the purity of their conscience, prove selfish when they transform an ameliorative venture into an exercise of self-presentation. Not that all commitments can be forfeited in the interest of some set of long-range gains. But when one takes such stands, it should be on the basis of the worthiness of that commitment, not in order to maintain a pure conscience.

Viewed from within the orbit of Emersonian self-culture, voting should tend to lines of dependency that underwrite and enable lives of potential eloquence. That said, Emerson's faith in the power of voting is not great, and thus, in the order of influences, he ranks it below the sociality of genius. True, as Gougeon notes, Emerson writes: "Those who stay away from the election think that one vote will do no good: 'tis but one step more to think one vote will do no harm" (*JMN13*, 304). But this is tame praise. Moreover, Emerson also writes, in the same journal entry: "I have already written once my belief that the American votes rashly & immorally with his party on the question of slavery, . . . & does not entertain the possibility of being seriously caught in meshes of legislation. But one may run a risk once too often" (*JMN13*, 303–304). When the ballot hits the road, therefore, Emerson does regard voting as a risky enterprise, particularly if one conforms to party politics or shortsighted ventures. So, while voting remains a viable practice, Emersonian reform prefers more intimate, probing, and provocative exchanges.

When Emersonian self-culture confronts the state head on, there isn't much to specify beyond activities already mentioned: giving speeches, writing letters, lobbying, and so forth. Like all of social life, the state becomes a concern because it implicates us: "The state of me makes Massachusetts & the United States, out there" (*JMN9*, 85). Furthermore, the state extends our reach into those conditions that enable self-culture. "What are governments," Emerson suggests, "but awkward scaffoldings by which the noble temple of individual genius is reared" (*JMN10*, 156). That said (which simply reiterates points that arose in the context of voting), Emerson regards the state as even more of a snarl than general assemblies. "I own I have little esteem for governments," he writes. "I esteem them only good in the moments when they are established" (*EAW*, 113). The fear, I take it, is that state apparatuses run on inertia until, over time, they prove mechanical. They thus not only come to lack the proactive spark of genius, but they often frustrate it, as Emerson notes in his journal: "The teaching of politics is that the Government which was set for protection & comfort of all good citizens, becomes the principal obstruction & nuisance, with which we have to contend" (*JMN14*, 350). Moreover, given the reach of positive law, they also, of necessity, proceed with an instrument unable to take seriously the difference between persons. Emerson could thus, in a letter to Elizabeth Hoar, say of statesmen what he says of political figures more generally: "I do not wish to know the opinions of celebrated reformers or celebrated conservers, or indeed of celebrated leaders of either sex. They are all officers & through their lips I hear always Mr Million speak" (*CL2*, 237). Finally, in their lack of nuance, governments force one to side with parties, and that blunts one's judgment. "The relation of men of genius/thought to society is always the same. They abhor whiggism, they abhor rebellion. They refuse the necessity of mediocre men, that is, to take sides. They keep to their own equilibrium/self-poise, and the Ecliptic is never parallel with the earth's equator" (*JMN11*, 263). One might say, then, that governments are among the least eloquent of human ventures, if only because their clumsiness rarely resolves into power, and thus they rarely advance our condition into wider and more wondrous orbits.

And yet, Emerson will not abandon statecraft: "I will not cripple but exalt the social action. Patriotism, public opinion, have a real meaning, though there is so much counterfeit rag money abroad under it, that the name is apt to disgust. A wise man delights in the powers of many people" (*EAW*, 103). Not that this commends much. But again, how could one, outside the confines of a particular conversation? Statecraft concerns determinate situations. Policy calculates with a specific network of causes and effects, and it must respond to the variety of interests that seek representation therein. Once outside such contexts, and most of the Emersonian corpus moves among those reaches, a respect for the limits of the world of "I think" calls for a kind of reticence once one's provocations have been played.

Before the reach of the state, particularly given its current scope (e.g., controlled interest rates, "acceptable" pollution levels, tariffs, tax breaks for homeowners and "esteemed" enterprises, school curricula, zoning, the very principal of incorporation, the commodification of the airwaves, etc.), one has to ask whether Emersonian self-culture requires one to assume office at some point, or at least to pursue state-centered activism. According to Emerson, this is more a matter of temperament (and thus vocation) than anything else, as Gougeon rightly notes (1990, 52). While delivering an address on the Fugitive Slave Law, Emerson confesses, "I do not often speak to public questions" (*EAW*, 73). By way of explanation, he continues:

> The one thing not to be forgiven to intellectual persons is not to know their own task, or to take their ideas from others and believe in the ideas of others. From this want of manly rest in their own, and foolish acceptance of other people's watchwords, comes the imbecility and fatigue of their conversation. For they cannot affirm these from any original experience. (*EAW*, 73)

One's task is a matter of the prospects opened by native and ecstatic genius. For many, Emerson among them, the collisions of statecraft fail to animate either. And in the absence of the dæmonic, one is vulnerable to the terms of the day, forced to conform to their usage, particularly in situations circumscribed by extant parties. Now, one might view such a concern as a vice, a kind of vanity, a desire to be a strong poet where something other is needed. I don't see it this way. Locked in the terms of the day, one's efforts are bound to the realm of "I think," where one lacks access to the kind of "original experience" that provides, in the ethos of the moment, the means by which we measure ourselves. There is reason, therefore, to keep to one's compass when pursuing melioration.

Now, I must stress that in forgoing offices, lobbying, and the like, one is not withdrawing from reform. Nor is one simply abandoning the state. (Emerson's stance on voting should make this clear.) Rather, one is opting to seek enlargement and melioration from vantage points of greater (personal) power, picking one's spots. In Journal U, 1844, Emerson notes:

> I think substantial justice can be done maugre [i.e., in spite of—JTL] or through the money of society, and though it is an imperfect system & noxious, yet I do not know how to attack it directly, & am assured that the directest attack which I can make on it, is to lose no time in fumbling & striking about in all directions, but to mind the work that is mine, and accept the facilities & openings which my constitution affords me. (*JMN9*, 85)

This says well, I think, the principle of selection that guides Emersonian reform. The issue is not *whether* one should seek melioration but *how*, and answers to that question are tied to what claims us and infuses us with power: the ability to strike blows that open up prospects and paths to their realization. "You must elect your work; you shall take what your brain can, and drop all the rest. Only so, can that amount of vital force accumulate, which can make the step from knowing to doing" (*CW6*, 39).

Though Emersonian reform follows the lead of temperament, it can be trumped by ecstatic genius, and thus one may find oneself called to take up tasks that feel alien. In a Journal entry from 1861, Emerson writes: "Do the duty of the day. Just now, the supreme public duty of all thinking men is to assert freedom. Go where it is threatened, & say, 'I am for it, & do not wish to live in the world a moment longer than it exists" (*JMN15*, 111). I speak of ecstatic genius here because the duty that Emerson invokes has the force of an involuntary perception, something like the one we noted in chapter 2, namely, "Slavery is an abomination."[19] In other words, temperament can prove tyrannical, as we saw in chapters 5 and 6, and thus one must be open to demands that ask us to except ourselves from our more native orbits. As Emerson tells his Boston audience just after confessing to his unease in addressing the topic: "Still there is somewhat exceptional in this question [of slavery—JTL], which seems to require of every citizen at one time or other, to show his hand, and to cast his suffrage in such manner as he uses" (*EAW*, 91).[20]

Given the need to sometimes leave temperament behind, it would seem that reform not only flows from Emersonian self-culture but feeds on it. First, reform needs to be an egoless occasion. "To be sure, the reformer's a poor creature, as bad as you or I: —egotist, tyrant . . . What of that? What have you to do with his nonsense? only with his sense" (*LL2*, 156). In such contexts, Emersonian self-culture secures us. Ever attendant to genius and to its anonymity, it focuses us on the substance of what claims us, not on the prophetic persona. (After all, it isn't as if we could ever claim to be the authors of our genius.) Second, the ethos of the moment, in its double consciousness, enables us to withstand the severity of reforms that would remake even cherished affirmations. Journal E suggests: "The terror of reform, that is, of true obedience [or abandonment—JTL], lies in the discovery that we must cast our virtues also, or what we have always esteemed such, into the same flame that has consumed our grosser sins" (*JMN7*, 352). Because the ethos of the moment enables one to resist the draw of a foolish consistency, it allows us to let go of what previously gripped us, fiercely, and to abandon ourselves to what now compels obedience. Finally, radically attuned to the becoming soul, the ethos of the moment keeps us alert to how reforms undo themselves over time. With precisely this feel for the temporality of genius and of nature writ large, Emerson observes: "But the Committee on Reform should be made of new persons every day: of those just arrived at the power of comparing the state of society with their own daily expanding spirit. Fatal to discuss reform weekly" (*JMN8*, 371).

We are nearly ready to conclude our discussion of the place and character of reform in Emersonian self-culture, whose reach is wide. "The scope of man is to advance," Emerson says, "to stand always for the Better, not himself, his property, his grandmother's spoons, his corner lot, and shop-till . . . but to stand for his neighbors, and mankind; for the making of others as good as he is; for largest liberty; for enriching, enlightening, and enkindling others, and making life great and happy to nations" (*LL2*, 157). I take the breadth of this enkindling project in two directions. First, Emersonian reform, bound to genius, addresses everyone, not just some segment of society. Not that one shouldn't try to reform certain institutions or offices, but one reforms them for all who engage them. (As I suggested earlier, this restates the commitments of ethical friendship. One offers one's sallies to all commended strangers as worthy of essay, and one tends to those conditions that such essays require.) Second, the object of one's reform is principally the whole of a life (i.e., character), not simply a facet of it. Concretely, this means that Emersonian reform prefers changes that reorient lives in general: "But the genius of the soul can only be appeased & gratified not by a deed but by a tendency. . . . You shall love rectitude & not the disuse of money or avoidance of trade; an unimpeded soul & not a monkish diet; sympathy & usefulness & not hoeing or coopering" (*JMN8*, 12). In other words, the conversion of a tendency broadens the scope of the transformation. Rectitude, for example, is not limited to conduct in trade, but to every case wherein another can expect us to remain true to a norm or to explain our deviation.

Emersonian reform begins and ends with character. It concerns itself with the life that ascends or proves mean, that expands or preserves itself in the face of change. Of course, character building is an expensive project and subject to the sociality of genius, so this focus on broad reform does not entail a negation of institutional melioration. But an Emersonian will always focus on the character pursuing and emerging from every reformation. And the hope will be, across each gulf, that eloquence marks every dart and aim.

No doubt some, in the hopes for more radical transformations, will find this kind of meliorism insufficient. Independent of particular initiatives, I cannot comment for or against. Moreover, the point of this chapter was not to present Emersonian reform as a politics sufficient unto itself. Rather, it was to show how self-culture not only doesn't eschew activism and state-based initiatives, but directs us toward them, and precisely in order to fulfill its goal of an eloquent life. We would be mistaken, therefore, if we found an antinomy between self-culture and politics, or self-culture and social reconstruction, and to the degree that Emerson helps us see this, we should thank him.

EPILOGUE

A man's manners, to be radiant, must announce his reality.
—*JMN13*, 393

I began this book hoping to articulate, defend, and conduct Emersonian self-culture. In both my thematic reflections and my rhetorical performances, I wanted to proceed in a manner true to its course, full of honor for its friends, and consistently equal to whatever occasions arose. What I found was a practice concerned with our bearings in nearly every sense that word provides. The object of self-culture's receptive-reflective striving is the manner in which we carry ourselves and in how that manner bears witness to the world it quotes, whether in dependence or influence. Moreover, in each moment, Emersonian self-culture is oriented toward eloquence; that is, it bears toward a life that says, as well as it can, its way or ways of abandonment. More specifically, it bears witness to prospects, rooted in the involuntary sallies of genius, native or ecstatic. But more than that, it affirms them, without undue apology, and in aversion to conformities and foolish consistencies.

Carried out under a law of metamorphosis, Emersonian self-culture endures a soul that perpetually becomes, in part through a succession of moods that orient one in the world. Among those many moods, Emersonian self culture, in its ethos of the moment, favors youth for its energy, sense of possibility, and resilience, for such capacities are integral to a project requiring perseverance along paths that twist and turn. Moreover, should we bear our projects to term, should we give birth to unforeseen futures, say, a future beyond those theistic shadows

[195]

that haunt Emerson's texts, then our youth will find another version of itself around the bend.

I speak of an "ethos" because the issue is character, a manner of being that is, in part, born of the strivings of Emersonian self-culture. The ethos is "of the moment" because, in a double consciousness, it attends to who we've been and who we are becoming. Ready to let the former drop if the latter announces a redirection, it thus bears upon our lives and world, more praxis than attitude, though the former includes the latter in a way that European modernity seems bent on forgetting. In the practice of philosophy, such an ethos asks us to tarry at our limits, to prove reticent when tempted to finalize ourselves, to remain observant of the difference that marks our being in the world—what I have, following Dewey, termed the difference between primary and secondary experience, the world as pre-reflectively given and as reflectively thought.

The ethos of Emersonian self-culture is also schooled in friendship, where it discovers a sociality in genius and thus a way for our many relations to bear upon our eloquence. Influencing and being influenced among those who might prove friend and/or enemy, we are led to consider, in a once again doubled consciousness, whether our bearing is exemplary, whether the character we cannot help but publish is worthy of (because it tends to and toward) a noble life. Moreover, friendship multiplies our opportunities for exceeding the dictates of native genius, thus enlarging our prospects for an eloquent life. And this enables self-culture to better pursue a principal goal, namely, checking any mastertones that ineloquently corner us.

Not that our friends can resolve our being for us. Emersonian self-culture remains an irreducibly personal project, grounded and ungrounded by events and projects than no one can undergo or pursue for us. It is thus simultaneously a practice of society and solitude, and how we conspire with our quoting condition bears upon the eloquence to which our works and days bear witness.

Grasping how our being involves an insurmountable play of society and solitude also makes plain that self-culture and reform are not contraries. Because more than our friends bear our impress, a wish to be eloquent will lead us to wonder whether all of our footfalls announce, in our what and how, that which we aspire to be. In fact, like it or not, the cultivation of a life reforms the conditions on which that life depends. Knowing this, Emersonian self-culture assumes responsibility for its various influences and dependencies, as near and as far as *my* reach can be said to extend. In fact, insofar as our condition implicates us on many fronts, our efforts at reformation should prove as catholic as our character, that is, equal to the full occasion of our condition, intertwined, as it is, with so much more than you or I.

NOTES

1. Self-culture is a watchword of the nineteenth century. One finds texts devoted to self-culture, from W. E. Channing's 1838 lecture to Blackie's *On Self-Culture* (1874) and Clarke's *Self-Culture* (1880). One could just translate *Bildung* as "culture," as many did and do, Emerson included, but the English term now denotes little more than the social fabric that backgrounds and foregrounds human life. Not that the ambiguity is new. Even Emerson suffered the problem as he notes in a journal of 1837: "Culture—how much meaning the Germans affix to the word & how unlike to the English sense" (*JMN5*, 303). For clarity, then, and to acknowledge my inheritance of a project that captivated nineteenth-century America, "self-culture" orients these reflections.

2. That the two should be tied is unsurprising, given that Emerson regards history as a matter of biography, both in its production and in its reception (*EL1*, 79; *EL2*, 12–14; *CW2*, 6). For him, cultural traits are merely conglomerations of individual traits. As he says in "Self-Reliance," "All history resolves itself very easily into the biography of a few stout and earnest persons" (*CW2*, 36).

3. My reading of Emerson thus runs counter to those who limit the question of *Bildung* to a point in Emerson's career. Whicher, for example, claims that: "Culture is a term that one associates more with his later thought than with the years of transcendental protest" (1953, 84). I think the early lectures render this view untenable. Not that I'm the first to make this point. David Robinson's two books (1982 and 1993) also find the practice of self-culture throughout Emerson's career.

4. Regarding this last point, I am echoing Rawls's compelling observation that utilitarianism does not take seriously the distinction between persons (1971, 183–92).

5. Steven Lukes (1973) has argued that the term "individualism" was initially championed by Catholic Restoration theorists like Joseph de Maistre, who wanted to villainize social atomism and egoism. Later British theorists like Matthew Arnold and Samuel Smiles kept the term but championed its referent, a self-sufficient agent unbound by tradition. Because I don't regard the self of self-culture as such a being, it seems prudent to mark my turf with a different concept.

6. This marks a change from my essay "Relentless Unfolding," where I em-

braced the term "individuation" (Lysaker 2004). I am not denying that the term has a certain felicity in this context, only that it also risks saying precisely what I don't want to say, and thus I've elected to let it go.

7. For an intense discussion of Nietzsche's relation to Emerson, consult *ESQ: A Journal of the American Renaissance* 43 (1997):1–4. For a provocative reading of one thinker into the other, see David Mikics's *The Romance of Individualism in Emerson and Nietzsche* (2003).

8. The initial point is made again in Journal V: "In reading there is a sort of half & half mixture. The book must be good, but the reader must also be active" (*JMN9*, 106).

9. Christina Kirklighter has drawn some of these connections, and summarized those drawn by others (2002, 1–11, 39–58). According to some accounts, however, Emerson's essays are less than typical. R.D. O'Leary insists that the essay is designed for amusement rather than instruction, thus defining Emerson out of the genre, at least on this score (1928, 23). O'Leary's position seems out of step with its own period, however. In an Oxford Reading Course text from 1927, M. Edmund Speare insists upon the contrary, suggesting that an essay is designed to win the heart of the reader (1927, 10).

10. Gass himself terms Emerson's essays "aggressive," but he reads this as evidence of an ambivalent relation to audience and not as pedagogically informed. Robert Atwan (1989) also notes that Emerson's essays agitate, citing a "notorious inconsistency and self-contradiction" as examples. While these traits may agitate, I would stress that Emerson's essays as a whole are bent on agitation, on engaging us to the point of ignition so that we might continue on our own. His texts should thus be read as he himself approached books: "Books are the best of things, well used; abused, among the worst. What is the right use? What is the one end which all means go to effect? They are for nothing but to inspire" (*CW1*, 56).

11. For all his achievement, Gass couldn't be more wrong when he says that "what Emerson intended to do when he spoke was wipe away his audience like smoke from a blackboard, and replace it with his essay, heard in their hearts like an adopted beat" (Gass 1982, 362). As Emerson tells an audience gathered in 1867, "A fatal disservice does this Swedenborg or other lawyer who offers to do my thinking for me" (*LL2*, 385).

12. Emerson writes of witness with regard to our deeper inspirations. "With every influx of light, comes new danger. Has he light? He must bear witness to the light, and always outrun the sympathy which gives him such keen satisfaction, by his fidelity to new revelations of the incessant soul" (*CW2*, 58–59).

13. At several places, Socrates suggests that one seek ennobling company, for corrupt company only leads to one's own undoing. This is perhaps most famously advanced in the *Apology* (25c–e).

14. With this kind of process in mind, I appreciate Whitman's remark that "the best part of Emersonianism is, it breeds the giant that destroys itself" (1982, 1055).

15. A passage from Journal E (1839) articulates well both sides of this phenomenon: "Let those then make much of the different genius of different periods who suffer them. I who seek enjoyments which proceed not out of time, but out of thought, will celebrate on this lofty Sabbath Morn the day without night, the beautiful Ocean which hath no tides. And yet literature too, this magical man-provoking talisman is in some sort a creature of time. It is begotten by Time on the Soul" (*JMN7*, 266). See also the suggestion in Journal G (1841) that: "the best books are the dullest if read out of time. If I read Plato when I am not bright, I go over the words sometimes of a page without any meaning & must read it again" (*JMN8*, 45).

2. THE GENIUS OF NATURE

1. The thought also appears in a lecture from 1848: "Man is rich as he is much related" (*LL1*, 170).

2. One finds a similar thought in the late lecture, "The Progress of Culture": "Depth of character, height of genius, can only find nourishment in this soil. The miracles of genius always rest on profound convictions which refuse to be analyzed. Enthusiasm is the leaping lightning, not to be measured by the horsepower of the understanding" (*CE8*, 229).

3. With equal vehemence and with similar import, Emerson records in a journal entry of 1857: "I find no more flagrant proof of skepticism than the toleration of slavery" (*JMN14*, 129). In this context, I take "skepticism" to name positions that one entertains only counter-factually, and thus they can never truly reconcile one to the position they espouse.

4. Emerson's commitment to a notion like intentionality is evident when he asserts in "The Transcendentalist" that "thought only appears in the objects it classifies" (*CW1*, 201). In Husserl's language, this is to say that the intentional act (what Heidegger regards as the *intentio*) cannot be explored independently of the corresponding intentional object (what Heidegger regards as the *intentum*).

5. Consider also this later journal entry: "A Mr. Schaad who printed an orthodox pamphlet lately at Pittsburgh, PA. says that 'Mr. Emerson is a pantheist by intuition, rather than by argument.' So it seems our *intuitions* are mistaken. Who then can set us right?" (*JMN13*, 105).

6. While we'll return to this issue in later chapters, it is worth noting now that reflection's dependence on involuntary perception adds epistemic import to Emerson's claim that involuntary perceptions stand as the "last fact behind which analysis cannot go." On Emerson's view, which West (1989)

rightly marks as an evasion of certain epistemological conundrums, involuntary perceptions are only displaced in the order of justification by other involuntary perceptions, and thus reflection never wins itself from them by analyzing their reliability, or to use more contemporary language, by articulating those qualities that they must have if it they are to stand as true.

7. Pardon the deluge, but I want to show how mistaken it would be to presume that a relatively early piece like "Self-Reliance" (1841) favors intuition, while a later piece like "Quotation and Originality" (first delivered in 1859) favors quotation. The first passage is from a lecture of 1833, the second from a lecture of 1837. The journal entry, later used in "Quotation and Originality," is from 1844. The lines from *Representative Men,* the latter part of which serves as an epigram to "Quotation and Originality," were published in 1850.

8. Here I have in mind a series of Kittay's responses to the work of Carol Gilligan, beginning with *Women and Moral Theory* (1987), *Love's Labor* (1998), and *The Subject of Care* (1998).

9. I take Emerson to be the latter sort in both instances: synthetic and meliorist. His synthetic cast of mind is evident in the sheer wealth of his interlocutors and the broad yet fluid way in which he moves among them. Regarding the second, I find it in his approach to "representative men" who meliorate each other's excesses and in his claim that "it needs the whole society, to give the symmetry we seek" (*CW3*, 34).

10. The lecture from which this line is drawn, "Genius and Temperament," actually substitutes "talent" for "temperament" in everything but the title. It is thus not a stretch to regard the two terms as interchangeable for Emerson.

11. I invoke "Circles" at this juncture because it shortcuts the objection that my use of categories from "Experience," mood and temperament, introduces a kind of doubt absent from *Essays: First Series.* "Circles" not only invokes the notion of moods, stressing that they "do not believe in each other," but posits a relentless becoming that maroons us from time to time with as much abandon as "Experience" does (*CW2,* 182). "In nature, every moment is new; the past is always swallowed and forgotten; the coming is only sacred. Nothing is secure but life, transition, the energizing spirit. No love can be bound by oath or covenant to secure it against a higher love. No truth so sublime but it may be trivial tomorrow in the light of new thoughts. People wish to be settled: only as far as they are unsettled, is there any hope for them" (*CW2,* 189).

12. A passage from Journal HO complicates matters. Emerson writes: "I adjourn the question of race, for it is too early. When we have got the names Celt, Saxon, Roman, we are still only using an arbitrary/idle/& superficial distinction, as if we classified people by the street in which they lived. The foundations of race are not in anatomy, but in metaphysics. Temperament which tyrannizes over family-lines derives from moral & elemental causes, &

the existence of individual men as of man himself shrouds the moral laws. There is a profound instinct stirring all the new interest of mankind in race, and which, beginning at the most outward facts, will shed one after another the covers of the question, until it reaches the spiritual causes" (*JMN13*, 233 and 234). This holds open the possibility that Emerson preserves a thick notion of race on the basis of a teleological philosophy of history. Such a view runs counter to one side of his more general conception of nature, however, so there remain Emersonian reasons for seeking a kind of eloquence that eschews the rhetoric of race. Of course, questions concerning the usefulness of racial categories are more complicated than this brief discussion lets on. Like my colleague Naomi Zack, I take it as a matter of course that races have no biological foundations. But given that people experience themselves and others as raced, and given that such experiences determine in part their self-regard and their regard for others and thus their treatment of themselves and others, it does seem that race is "real" when considered as a subjective and an intersubjective phenomenon. As to whether this reality does more harm than good, that is a matter to be considered elsewhere.

3. REFLECTING ELOQUENCE

1. If one traces the distinction between standing upright and quadruped life, one finds, I think, Emerson's debt to renaissance humanism, e.g., Pico della Mirandola's "On the Dignity of Man" and its insistent distinction between man and animal (1998, 6). Emersonian self-culture is not inextricably bound to this dichotomy, however, and thus I note it in order to let it go.

2. Kateb (2002, 26–27) worries that the image of the rose keeps alive an impossible dream, that of a life directed only toward the present. My concern is in keeping with his, although I am less concerned with memory's inescapable role in our lives than with the place of a whole series of reflective acts in Emersonian self-culture.

3. The language of conversion also can be found in "The American Scholar" and "The Divinity School Address" (*CW1*, 59 and 86). It also occurs in "Fate," where we find: "Insight is not will, nor is affection will. Perception is cold, and goodness dies in wishes. . . . There can be no driving force, except through the conversion of the man into his will, making him the will, and the will him" (*CW6*, 16).

4 In a later lecture, "Classes of Men," Emerson claims that there are "two classes, into one of which each individual will be thrown," and he specifies them as will, which is masculine, and sympathy, which is feminine (*LL2*, 170). Similarly, the 1855 lecture "Woman," if we can trust the Centenary Edition version, aligns men with will and intellect, and women with sentiment and affection for goodness (*CE11*, 407 and 628).

[203]

5. In chapter 6, I will return to this line and consider what it means to regard one's own thoughts as "true for all men," and not solely men.

6. Chapter 7 will discuss the line that I'm invoking: "Then again, do not tell me, as a good man did to-day, of my obligation to put all poor men in good situations. Are they *my* poor? I tell thee, thou foolish philanthropist, that I grudge the dollar, the dime, the cent I give to such men as do not belong to me and to whom I do not belong" (*CW2*, 30–31).

7. I know that several scholars consider this question of the times to be the question of slavery. I do not. Rather, I consider it to be a question of the *Zeitgeist*, of an era's basic principles, axes around which it revolves. One sees precisely this kind of concern in Emerson's 1848 lecture "The Spirit of the Times," where he reviews various epochal principles—Greek, Christian, and Modern—considering the third in terms of commerce, tools, and science (*LL1*, 106–25).

8. Provocatively, "Power," which follows "Fate" in *The Conduct of Life*, identifies imbecility as "the key to all ages" (*CW6*, 29). On its face, it thus seems to offer what "Fate" avoids, i.e., a theory of the age. And yet I find something else here, a "key" that unlocks history and navigates it. The charge in "Power" thus continues the trajectory of "Fate," one that resolves the question of the times into questions of conduct. In fact, even the substance of the charge, imbecility, directs us toward questions of conduct, given that it denotes weakness and infirmity, and thus an inability to resolve problems into questions concerning our bearings.

9. In less prosaic terms, Emerson proclaims in "Human Life": "He is encumbered by his own past. His past hour mortgages the present hour. Yesterday is the enemy of today. His deed hinders him from doing, his thought from thinking; his former virtue is apt to become an impediment to new virtue" (*EL3*, 87).

10. Note also how "The American Scholar" closes with various prospects—"I read with joy some of the auspicious signs of coming days as they glimmer already through poetry and art, through philosophy and science, through church and state" (*CW1*, 67). To these specific examples I would add that in many ways "The American Scholar" is itself a kind of prospecting with regard to the force of self-trust within scholarly practices, just as the Divinity School Address runs self-trust through spiritual practice in general and ministering in particular.

11. The thought is seconded in the 1867 lecture "The Progress of Culture": "Culture implies all which gives the mind possession of its own powers; as languages to the critic, telescope to the astronomer" (*CE8*, 217).

4. DIVINING BECOMING

1. A late journal entry underscores the temporal limits of our condition: "It occurs that the short limit of human life is set in relation to the instruction

man can draw of Nature. No one has lived long enough to exhaust its laws" (*JMN16*, 308).

2. For a similar point of connection between Emerson and Dewey, see Naoko Saito's *The Gleam of Light* (2005), although Saito aligns the two thinkers by way of "impulse," not primary and secondary experience. See also Doug Anderson's *Philosophy Americana* (2006).

3. At this point my reading folds into and moves about Cavell's "Finding as Founding." I think his claim that "Experience" is a text of recovery, "a finding of the world, a returning of it, to it," is of lasting value (2003, 138).

4. I draw what follows from Robert Richardson's remarkably comprehensive biography, *Emerson: The Mind on Fire* (1995).

5. A similar thought can be found in Journal W: "I suppose that all that is done in ploughing & sowing & reaping & storing is repeated in finer sort in the life of men who never touch the plough handles. The essence of those manipulations is subtle & reappears in countinghouses & council boards, in games of cards & chess, in conversations, correspondences, & in poets' rhymes" (*JMN9*, 226).

6. Note the unwitting noble savage figure in this passage, one that presents indigenous people as mostly unconscious and thus unlikely candidates for self-culture. It is worth attending to such exclusions in order to register the fact of their presence in the prose of a justly celebrated writer, to observe them as the unconscious prejudices they are, and to take a step toward letting them go.

7. This sentiment is apparent as early as 1830. "Every moral agent is a temple which he hath built for himself, and his spirit dwelleth therein, forever and ever" (*CS2*, 150).

8. I think Emerson finds this solace lacking in Shakespeare, hence his criticisms in *Representative Men*: "He converted the elements which waited on his command, into entertainments. . . . One remembers again the trumpet text in the Koran,—'The Heavens and the earth and all that is between them, think ye we have created them in jest?'" (*CW4*, 124). In this regard, Emerson seems to favor Milton, whose "gifts are subordinated to his moral sentiments," and with a particular eye for humanity's role in the universe (*EL1*, 154 and 162). Similarly, he esteems Michelangelo for whom "perfect beauty and goodness are one" on a cosmic scale (*EL1*, 100).

9. Within such a mindset, one can see why Emerson claims in "Compensation" that he is "never a real sufferer but by my own fault" (*CW2*, 71). Such suffering strikes him as a kind of selfishness, a siding with one's own dæmon over God.

10. Referring to Emerson's early lectures, David Robinson has also noted that "self-culture is really Self-culture, that the formation of the soul necessitates a surrender to the generic soul" (1982, 106). His analysis of Emerson's

later work (1993, 57) does not, however, set the double-consciousness within this line of thought.

11. At this point, Emersonian self-culture draws near Wilhelm von Humboldt's conception of *Bildung,* which, Gadamer says, "evokes the ancient mystical tradition according to which man carries in his soul the image of God, after whom he is fashioned, and which man must cultivate in himself" (1992, 11). For Emerson, however, divine images shine everywhere, and thus one must also know nature in order to divine oneself.

12. I have in mind the account offered in the third essay of *On the Genealogy of Morals* (1967), where Nietzsche presents the ascetic ideal as an "artifice for the *preservation* of life," one that converts a world without meaning, a *horror vacui,* into a stage on which our striving and suffering find justification and purpose.

13. Surprisingly, at least to me, Emerson has little to say about Job. In a very early journal he notes his solitude, and then in the late 1830s, he names him in a list of "oriental" men (*JMN1,* 98; *JMN5,* 103). In the various essay collections, I find only a passing mention of the book of Job in "Books" (*CE7,* 198). True, there is a sermon devoted to a passage from Job, but it does not concern Job's plight (*CS2,* 144–50). And while one finds several references to Job in the sermons, these mostly paraphrase lines regarding human infirmity (e.g., *CS2,* 51; *CS3,* 29) and divine omnipotence (e.g., *CS1,* 57). Or, when they do engage Job's despair, it is repudiated (*CS1,* 132; *CS3,* 40; *CS4,* 122). Joel Porte finds what I miss in the opening of "Literary Ethics," where Emerson apparently is "identifying with the beleaguered Job and preparing to redeem him from sorrow" (1979, 149). But there Emerson invokes the "beleaguered Job" to characterize those whom the scholar should elevate, not the scholar, and thus I don't see much by way of self-identification.

14. One finds a similar problem in reverse when Emerson insists, "The earth has lost no virtues, the sun no beams; seed time and harvest punctually return" (*LL2,* 191). The history of the victor may erase not only violence and injustice but also alien modes of attunement and knowledge that, in its arrogance, it fails to recognize.

15. This turn of thought certainly does not begin in Emerson. It has obvious roots in Luther's doctrine concerning the priesthood of all believers, and, as David Robinson (1982) has shown, Emerson's thought is also working out problems inherited from Unitarian theology. In addition, Emerson himself notes the Quaker roots of his radical self-trust (*EL1,* 172; *LL2,* 381; *CE11,* 488).

16. Robinson (1982, 56) notes how this bold move distinguishes Emerson from Ware and Channing. Moreover, he too believes that a "struggle with Christology was part of a process of secularization in Emerson's thought that was based upon the elevation of the nature of man" (59). With the exception

of its invocation of necessity, I think this line from "The Uses of Great Men" further evidences this movement: "Our colossal theologies of Judaism, Christism, Buddhism, Mahometism are the necessary and structural action of the human mind" (*CW5*, 4).

17. Crowley, born Edward Alexander (1875–1947), was an occultist who self-identified as "the Beast" of Revelation and developed a "spiritist" tradition (Emerson's term) that sought personal growth and power through gnostic teachings, meditation, and magic, including ritualized sex acts.

18. I have in mind the early lecture devoted to Milton and the essay published shortly thereafter in the *North American Review* (*EL1*, 144–63; *CE12*, 245–79).

19. Even in "Worship" one finds this kind of confidence. Emerson writes: "I would not degrade myself by casting about in my memory for a thought, nor by waiting for one. If the thought come, I would give it entertainment. It should, as it ought, go into my hands and feet; but if it come not spontaneously, it comes not rightly at all. If it can spare me, I am sure I can spare it" (*CW6*, 263 and 125).

20. In affirming genius as the seat of revelation, Emerson abandons the posture that Sampson Reed (1800–1880) relied on to keep inspiration pious: "Know, then, that genius is divine, not when man thinks that he is God, but when he acknowledges that his powers are from God. Here is the link of the finite with the infinite, of the divine with the human, this is the humility which exalts" (Peabody 1967, 60)

21. One finds a similar smear at the opening of "Experience." Emerson locates a "Genius" at the opening of the "door by which we enter" the ascending and descending steps of experience, a door he later figures as the threshold of ecstatic genius, that is, as one "through which the creator passes" beyond the reach of temperament (*CW3*, 27 and 32).

22. One finds a more direct displacement of final causes in "Circles," where Emerson announces, "There is no outside, no enclosing wall, no circumference to us" (*CW2*, 181).

23. "Self-overcoming" figures prominently in *Beyond Good and Evil* (1966), and my reading of it continually quotes and translates the opening essay of Charles Scott's *Language of Difference* (1987).

24. The initial passage is drawn from the lecture "Fate," first delivered in December of 1851. In full, it reads: "It seems to me that he has learned its [life's—JTL] lesson, who has come to feel so assured of his well-being as to hold lightly all particulars of today and tomorrow, and to count death amongst the particulars. He must have such a grasp of the whole, as to preserve it when he is ridiculous and unfortunate" (*LL1*, 251–52).

25. I am again citing Book III of Nietzsche's *Gay Science*, this time §108,

where Nietzsche proclaims for the first time the death of God and adds that "given the way of men, there may still be caves for thousands of years in which his shadow will be shown. And we—we still have to vanquish his shadow, too" (1974, 167).

5. ON THE EDGES OF OUR SOULS

1. It is worth noting that Emerson's own peers had similar worries, and without even considering the implications of divine decomposition. Francis Bowen, in a review of *Nature*, laments Emerson's high regard for intuition, arguing, as Barbara Packer reports, that it undermines the possibility of a rational Christian faith (Bercovitch 1999, 392–93).

2. Over the next several pages I will quote, without direct citation, from sections 4 and 5 of Emerson's "Experience" (*CW3*, 34–39). I will, however, indicate the section in question.

3. Here I follow the translation of Hippocrates Apostle, although Peter Warnek was instrumental in directing me to this passage from Aristotle's *Nichomachean Ethics* (1984, 21 [1103a]). I should also note that given what we've seen about character and quotation in chapter 2, the recollection of custom in this context is certainly pertinent, although I won't do much to render it explicit or explore its import. Finally, I do not invoke "ethos" in order to claim Emerson for virtue ethics, and my use of "maxim" is intended in part to make that clear. Emerson's thought shows signs of too many schools of ethical thought to fit neatly into any one.

4. In deferring to mood in this context, I thus set aside any talk of criteria employed in a judgment and thus any discursive criteria that might categorically resolve disagreements. In this I think I depart from Naoko Saito's attempt to wed Emersonian self-culture to Dewey's language of "directive criteria," although in a more general way, I find her ability to move between Emerson and Dewey without reducing one to the other compelling and productive. See Saito 2005, 99–119.

5. I take this poverty and the humility it presumably instills to be the "present of philosophy" that Cavell finds represented in and gifted by Wittgenstein, though I would add that it is no less Cavell's gift to us (1989, 72). I stress this and my debt to it because in other areas—for example, with regard to Emerson's devotion to intuition and his philosophy of nature—I find little compatibility between Emerson and Wittgenstein or ordinary language philosophy in general.

6. One finds something of this mood in "The Uses of Great Men," and amid images that directly recall "Experience" and its doubts. "We swim, day by day, on a river of delusions, and are effectually amused with houses and towns in the air, of which the men about us are dupes. But life is a sincerity. In lucid inter-

vals, we say, 'Let there be an entrance opened for me into realities; I have worn the fool's cap too long'" (*CW4*, 12).

7. Walt Whitman, *Complete Poetry and Collected Prose* (New York: Literary Classics of the United States, 1982), 120.

8. Denis Johnson, *The Throne of the Third Heaven of the Nations Millennium General Assembly* (New York: HarperCollins, 1995), 162.

6. COMMENDED STRANGERS, BEAUTIFUL ENEMIES

1. This line echoes what Montaigne attributes to Aristotle, and what Emerson records: "O my friends, there is no friend" (*JMN6*, 161). One also finds the line quoted in Sermon CXL, a text that introduces several of the themes we'll consider (*CS4*, 51).

2. Consider this as well: "Especially if any one show me a stroke of courage, a piece of inventive wit, a trait of character, or a pure delight in character when shown by others, always must I be that man's or that woman's debtor as one who has discovered to me among the perishing men somewhat more clean & incorruptible than the eternal light of these midnight stars" (*CL2*, 341).

3. A similar sentiment arises in "Considerations by the Way": "Our chief want in life is, somebody who shall make us do what we can. This is the service of a friend. With him we are easily great. There is a sublime attraction in him to whatever virtue is in us. How he flings wide the doors of existence!" (*CW6*, 143).

4. Calvin Trillin, "Alice, Off the Page," *The New Yorker*, 27 March 2006, 44–57.

5. One meets this thought again in a letter of 1853: "I suppose the only secret that gives us power over social nature, as over all nature, is, worth; is to deserve" (*CL4*, 365).

6. Cavell observes, rightly I think, that for Emerson, the "moral is not a separate realm or a separate branch of philosophical study, but one in which each assertion is a moral act (intrusive or not, magnanimous or not, heartfelt or not, kind or cutting, faithful or treacherous, promising cheer or chagrin, acknowledging or denying) . . ." (1990, xxix). The same thought occurs again in "Emerson's Constitutional Amending," reprinted in *Emerson's Transcendental Etudes* (Cavell 2003, 204).

7. A degree of alertness is all the more important, given the flighty nature of genius, social or otherwise. "It is full of mysteries, it is full of fate. Our dæmons or genii have obviously more to do with it than the measure-loving intellect, and what most of all fascinates me in my friend is not permanently in him, but comes & goes, a light that plays about his head, but does not always dip so low as into his eyes" (*CL8*, 12–13).

8. In a different context, my concerns replay the spirit of Sharon Camer-

on's unease in "The Way of Life by Abandonment: Emerson's Impersonal" (1998), and this time with greater sympathy.

9. The association is predictable, given Emerson's regard for books. "The truth is all works of literature are Janus faced and look to the future and to the past. . . . There never was an original writer. Each is a link in an endless chain. To receive and impart are the talents of the poet and he ought to possess both in equal degrees. . . . This is but the nature of man, universal receiving to the end of universal giving" (*EL1*, 284).

10. "Conversation is the last flower of civility," Emerson tells his audience in 1855, "and the best result which life has to offer us; a cup for gods, which has no repentance. It is our account of ourselves. All we have, all we can do, all we know, is brought into play, and is the reproduction in finer form of all our havings" (*LL2*, 20).

11. So too, when I read Emerson informing Caroline Sturgis: "Present, you shall be present only as an angel might be, & absent you shall not be absent from me" (*CL2*, 334).

12. Robert N. Hudspeth, *The Letters of Margaret Fuller* (Ithaca, N.Y.: Cornell University Press, 1983), 2:341.

13. Others have considered this troubled relationship on its own terms and in far greater depth. See Joan Von Mehren's *Minerva and the Muse: A Life of Margaret Fuller* (1996); Caleb Crain's *American Sympathy* (2001); and an earlier article by Carl Strauch, "Hatred's Swift Repulsions: Emerson, Margaret Fuller, and Others" (1968). Thanks to David Robinson for directing me towards these discussions.

7. TENDING TO REFORM

1. Excepting the issue of Native America, several studies pursue such questions, most notably Len Gougeon's *Virtue's Hero* (1990), as well as Michael Gilmore's "Emerson and the Persistence of the Commodity" and Robert Milder's "The Radical Emerson?" A recent, judicious study of Emerson's confrontation with slavery can be found in Maurice Lee's *Slavery, Philosophy, and American Literature* (2005, 165–209).

2. I take my question to share the spirit in which Buell writes: "But in order to grasp what is most distinctive and instructive about Emerson as an intellectual who (eventually) entered the political arena, we must focus less on adjudicating what he did when and more on what he thought and said about what he was doing, or not doing" (2003, 280).

3. As usual, Emerson invokes "race" as a kind of macro-temperament. As I argued in chapter 2, this figure is excisable from Emersonian self-culture without deforming its overall trajectory.

4. John Brown (1800–1859) was a radical player in the 1850s. He participated

in violent clashes with pro-slavery forces as Kansas prepared to become a state. Brown is most famous, however, for his raid on the federal armory at Harper's Ferry, which ended in his capture and eventual execution. During the 1850s, Brown visited Emerson, who helped provide him with 200 rifles for his efforts in Kansas and who later, following his failed raid, spoke publicly on his behalf.

5. One reason for focusing on exemplarity is that, like Plato, Emerson fears the corrupting power of ill behavior. He is reported as declaring during an attempted address to the Massachusetts Anti-Slavery Society: "I think it is the same with the moral pestilence under which the country has suffered so long; it actually decomposes mankind. This institution of slavery is based on a crime of that fatal character that decomposes men" (*EAW*, 126).

6. The inverse is offered in Journal W: "Poltroonery is in acknowledging an inferiority as incurable" (*JMN9*, 226).

7. In Journal O, Emerson asserts: "There ought to be in every town a permanent proprietor which should hold library, picture & sculpture gallery, museum, &c." (*JMN9*, 372). And, speaking at the dedication of Concord's public library, he observes: "The chairman of Mr. Munroe's trustees has told you how old is the foundation of our own village library, and we think we can trace in our modest records a correspondent effect of culture amidst our citizens" (*CE11*, 497).

8. One finds this sense of complicity in Emerson's letter to Martin Van Buren regarding the forced removal of the Cherokee, when he asks, "How could we call this conspiracy that should crush these poor Indians our Government?" and in his recoil from the Fugitive Slave Act, which leads him to tell his fellow citizens: "We do not breathe well. . . . I wake in the morning with a painful sensation, which I carry about all day" (*EAW*, 3 and 53). One also finds an inverse directive in some late remarks from 1867: "It is only by good works, it is only on the basis of active duty, that worship finds expression" (*CE11*, 480).

9. For discussions of this painful story, see *Making a Better World* (Parson 2005) and *Chavez Ravine, 1949* (Normark 1999). Thanks to José Mendoza for reminding me of this bleak fact of U.S. history.

10. Emerson makes the same point five years later in a letter protesting the kidnapping of a runaway slave. "If it shall turn out, as desponding men say, that our people do not really care whether Boston is a slave-port or not, provided our trade thrives, then we may, at least, cease to dread hard times and ruin. It is high time our bad wealth came to an end" (*EAW*, 45).

11. Journal O provides a complementary observation: "We are slain by indirections. Give us the question of slavery,—yea or nay; Texas, yea or nay; War, yea or nay; we should all vote right. But we accept the devil himself in an indirection. What taxes will we not pay in coffee, sugar, &c but spare us a direct tax" (*JMN9*, 422).

12. As I observed in chapter 4, Emerson also will not completely leave reform in the hands of a theodical divinity, even though he does believe that "Fate involves melioration" (*CW6*, 19). As he suggests in antislavery remarks: "There is a Divine Providence in the world which will not save us but through our own co-operation" (*EAW*, 89).

13. I am begging the question of revolution, of course. But if one rejects reform in favor of revolution, then one must, sooner or later, explain what revolutionary steps should be taken. Otherwise, I'm not sure holding out for revolution is distinguishable from cynicism.

14. Gougeon's study of Emerson's reform activities led me to this event (1990, 104–107).

15. Consider also this praise for Confucius: "At the same time, he abstained from paradox and met the ingrained prudence of his nation by saying always, 'Bend one cubit to straighten eight'" (*CE11*, 473).

16. In the context of *Representative Men*, Sam Worley regards this as an "immanent criticism," one that needn't appeal to transcendent values in order to praise and criticize because it relies instead on reinterpretations of what had been the general will (2001, 25–49). I'm sympathetic with the suggestion, though I wouldn't term this "immanent critique," given that term's place in Hegelian-Marxist thought (where it involves illustrating how a given practice fails to be true to its own discourse of legitimation). I also think Emerson's enduring relation to divinity renders the "immanence" of his thought a thorny issue. Thus, rather than asserting Emerson's "immanence," I think it behooves a reader to inherit him as such, which is to say, to help him banish the theological shadows haunting his work.

17. The previous sentence paraphrases "The Poet" (*CW3*, 7, 4, and 11).

18. Here I think of lines like: "Nature offers all her creatures to him as a picture-language" (*CW3*, 8); and: "There is no word in our language that can not become to us typical of nature by giving it emphasis" (*EL3*, 352).

19. Something like this occurs in Journal SO, when Emerson writes: "Now & then leaps a word or a fact to light which is no man's invention, but the common instinct. Thus, 'all men are born free and equal'—though denied by all politics, is the key-word of our modern civilization" (*JMN14*, 42).

20. If it bases itself on the dictates of genius, Emersonian self-culture can maintain a "dual accountability to independent integrity and to addressing social wrongs," to use Buell's apt phrase (2003, 286). And it is obedience to genius, to what proclaims the "duty of the day," which allows Emersonian self-culture to answer the following in the affirmative: "Can you be politically active and still self-reliant?" (Kateb 2002, 178).

BIBLIOGRAPHY

Adorno, Theodor. 1991. *Notes to Literature*. Vol. 1. New York: Columbia University Press.

Allen, Gay Wilson. 1981. *Waldo Emerson*. New York: Viking.

Anderson, Douglas. 2006. *Philosophy Americana*. New York: Fordham University Press.

Aristotle. 1984. *Nicomachean Ethics*. Grinnell, Iowa: Peripatetic Press.

Atkins, G. W. 1992. *Estranging the Familiar*. Athens: University of Georgia Press.

Atwan, Robert. 1989. "Ecstasy and Eloquence: The Method of Emerson's Essays." In *Essays on the Essay: Redefining the Genre*, ed. Alexander J. Butrym. Athens: University of Georgia Press.

Baker, Carlos. 1997. *Emerson Among the Eccentrics*. New York: Penguin Books.

Benjamin, Walter. 2003. *Selected Writings*, Vol. 4. Cambridge, Mass.: Harvard University Press.

Bercovitch, Sacvan. 1995. *The Cambridge History of American Literature*, Vol. 2: *1820–1865*. Cambridge: Cambridge University Press.

Bishop, Jonathan. 1964. *Emerson on the Soul*. Cambridge, Mass.: Harvard University Press.

Blackie, John Stuart. 1874. *Self-Culture*. New York: Scribner, Armstrong, and Co.

Bloom, Harold. 1976. *Figures of Capable Imagination*. New York: Seabury, 1976.

———. 1997. *Agon*. Oxford: Oxford University Press.

———. 2003. *A Map of Misreading*. Oxford: Oxford University Press.

Buell, Lawrence. 1993. *Ralph Waldo Emerson: A Collection of Critical Essays*. Englewood Cliffs, N.J.: Prentice-Hall.

———. 2003. *Emerson*. Cambridge, Mass.: Harvard University Press.

Butrym, Alexander J. 1989. *Essays on the Essay*. Athens: University of Georgia Press.

Cadava, Eduardo. 1997. *Emerson and the Climates of History*. Stanford, Calif.: Stanford University Press.

Cameron, Sharon. 1986. "Representing Grief: Emerson's 'Experience'." *Representations* 15 (Summer): 15–41.

——. 1998. "The Way of Life by Abandonment: Emerson's Impersonal." *Critical Inquiry* 25 (Fall).

Cavell, Stanley. 1989. *This New Yet Unapproachable America.* Albuquerque, N.M.: Living Batch Press.

——. 1990. *Conditions Handsome and Unhandsome.* Chicago: University of Chicago Press.

——. 1994. *A Pitch of Philosophy.* Cambridge, Mass.: Harvard University Press.

——. 2003. *Emerson's Transcendental Etudes.* Stanford, Calif.: Stanford University Press.

——. 2004. *Cities of Words.* Cambridge, Mass.: Harvard University Press.

——. 2005. *Philosophy the Day After Tomorrow.* Cambridge, Mass.: Harvard University Press.

Celan, Paul. 1983. *Gesammelte Werke in fünf Bänden.* Frankfurt am Main: Suhrkamp Verlag.

Channing, William Ellery. 1970. *The Works of William E. Channing.* New York: Burt Franklin.

Clarke, James Freeman. 1900. *Self-Culture.* Boston: Houghton, Mifflin, and Co.

Crain, Caleb. 2001. *American Sympathy: Men, Friendship, and Literature in the New Nation.* New Haven, Conn.: Yale University Press.

Field, Susan. 1997. *The Romance of Desire.* Teaneck, N.J.: Fairleigh Dickinson University Press.

Foucault, Michel. 1970. *The Order of Things.* New York: Random House.

Gadamer, Hans-Georg. 1981. *Reason in the Age of Science.* Cambridge: MIT Press.

——. 1992. *Truth and Method.* New York: Crossroad.

Gass, William H. 1982. "Emerson and the Essay." *Yale Review* 71:3.

Gilmore, Michael T. 1982. "Emerson and the Persistence of the Commodity." In *Emerson: Prospect and Retrospect,* ed. Joel Porte. Harvard English Studies 10.

Gonnaud, Maurice. 1987. *An Uneasy Solitude.* Princeton, N.J.: Princeton University Press.

Goodman, Russell. 1985. *American Philosophy and the Romantic Tradition.* New York: Cambridge University Press.

Gougeon, Len. 1990. *Virtue's Hero.* Athens: University of Georgia Press.

Harding, Walter. 1967. *Emerson's Library.* Charlottesville: University of Virginia Press.

Heidegger, Martin. 1980. *Gesamtausgabe: Band 39.* Frankfurt am Main: Vittorio Klostermann.

Hudspeth, Robert N. 1983. *The Letters of Margaret Fuller,* Vol. 2. Ithaca, N.Y.: Cornell University Press.

Johnson, Denis. 1995. *The Throne of the Third Heaven of the Nations Millennium General Assembly.* New York: HarperCollins.

Kateb, George. 2002. *Emerson and Self-Reliance.* 2nd ed. Lanham, Md.: Rowman and Littlefield.

Kirklighter, Christina. 2002. *Traversing the Democratic Borders of the Essay.* Albany: SUNY Press.

Kitay, Eva Feder. 1999. *Love's Labor.* New York: Routledge.

Kitay, Eva Feder, and Ellen Feder. 2002. *The Subject of Care: Feminist Perspectives on Dependency.* Lanham, Md.: Rowman and Littlefield.

Kittay, Eva Feder, and Diana T. Meyers. 1987. *Women and Moral Theory.* Savage, Md.: Rowman and Littlefield.

Konvitz, Milton, ed. 1972. *The Recognition of Ralph Waldo Emerson.* Ann Arbor: University of Michigan Press.

Lee, Maurice. 2005. *Slavery, Philosophy, and American Literature.* Cambridge: Cambridge University Press.

Levinas, Emmanuel. 1969. *Totality and Infinity.* Pittsburgh: Duquesne University Press.

Liebman, Sheldon. 1969. "The Development of Emerson's Theory of Rhetoric." *American Literature* 41, no. 2 (May): 178–206.

Lukes, Stephen. 1973. *Individualism.* New York: Harper and Row.

Lysaker, John. 1996. "Friendship at the End of Metaphysics." *Soundings* 79, no. 3–4: 511–40.

———. 1998. "Binding the Beautiful: Art as Criticism in Adorno and Dewey." *Journal of Speculative Philosophy* 12, no. 4: 233–44.

———. 2002. *You Must Change Your Life.* State College: Penn State Press.

———. 2003. "Relentless Unfolding: Emerson's Individualism." *Journal of Speculative Philosophy* 17, no. 3: 155–63.

———. 2004. "Taking Emerson Personally." *Georgia Review* 58, no. 4 (Winter): 832–50.

Mandelstam, Osip. 1979. *The Complete Critical Prose and Letters.* Ann Arbor: Ardis.

McDermott, John Joseph. 1986. *Streams of Experience.* Amherst: University of Massachusetts Press.

Mikics, David. 2003. *The Romance of Individualism in Emerson and Nietzsche.* Athens: Ohio University Press.

Milder, Robert. 1999. "The Radical Emerson?" In *The Cambridge Companion to Ralph Waldo Emerson,* ed. Joel Porte et al. Cambridge: Cambridge University Press.

Milton, John. *Paradise Lost.* 1957. *Complete Poems and Major Prose.* Edited by Merritt Y. Hughes. New York: Odyssey Press.

Mirandola, Pico della. 1998. *On the Dignity of Man.* Indianapolis, Ind.: Hackett Publishing Co.

Mitchell, Stephen. 1982. *The Selected Poetry of Rainer Maria Rilke.* New York: Random House.

Newfield, Christopher. 1996. *The Emerson Effect.* Chicago: University of Chicago Press.

Nietzsche, Friedrich. 1966. *Beyond Good and Evil.* New York: Random House.

———. 1967. *On the Genealogy of Morals.* New York: Random House.

———. 1974. *The Gay Science.* New York: Random House.

Normark, Don. 1999. *Chávez Ravine, 1949.* San Francisco: Chronicle Books.

Obaldia, Claire de. 1995. *The Essaying Spirit.* Oxford: Clarendon Press.

O'Leary, R. D. 1928. *The Essay.* New York: Thomas Y. Crowell.

Packer, Barbara. 1982. *Emerson's Fall.* New York: Continuum.

Parson, Don. 2005. *Making a Better World: Public Housing, the Red Scare, and the Direction of Modern Los Angeles.* Minneapolis: University of Minnesota Press.

Peabody, Elizabeth. 1967. *Aesthetic Papers.* New York: AMS Press.

Peirce, Charles S. 1960. *Collected Papers,* Vols. 5 and 6. Cambridge: Harvard University Press.

Poirier, Richard. 1987. *The Renewal of Literature.* New York: Random House.

———. 1992. *Poetry and Pragmatism.* Cambridge, Mass.: Harvard University Press.

Porte, Joel. 1979. *Representative Man.* New York: Oxford University Press.

Porte, Joel, ed. 1982. "Emerson: Prospect and Retrospect." *Harvard English Studies* 10.

Porte, Joel, et al., eds. 1999. *The Cambridge Companion to Ralph Waldo Emerson.* New York: Cambridge University Press.

Porter, David. 1978. *Emerson and Literary Change.* Cambridge, Mass.: Harvard University Press.

Rawls, John. 1971. *Theory of Justice.* Cambridge, Mass.: Harvard University Press.

Richardson, Robert. 1996. *Emerson: The Mind on Fire.* Berkley: University of California Press.

Roberson, Susan. 1995. *Emerson in His Sermons.* Columbia: University of Missouri Press.

Robinson, David. 1982. *Apostle of Culture.* Philadelphia: University of Pennsylvania Press.

———. 1993. *Emerson and the Conduct of Life.* New York: Cambridge University Press.

Rosenwald, Lawrence. 1988. *Emerson and the Art of the Diary.* Oxford: Oxford University Press.

Sachs, Kenneth. 2003. *Understanding Emerson.* Princeton, N.J.: Princeton University Press.

Saito, Naoko. 2005. *The Gleam of Light.* New York: Fordham University Press.

Schirmeister, Pamela. 1999. *Less Legible Meanings.* Stanford, Calif.: Stanford University Press.

Scott, Charles. 1987. *Language of Difference.* Atlantic Highlands, N.J.: Humanities Press.

Sealts, Merton. 1992. *Emerson on the Scholar.* Columbia: University of Missouri Press.

Speare, M. Edmund. 1927. *The Essay.* New York: Oxford University Press.

Carl Strauch. 1968. "Hatred's Swift Repulsions: Emerson, Margaret Fuller, and Others." *Studies in Romanticism* 7: 65–103.

Van Cromphout, Gustaaf. 1999. *Emerson's Ethics.* Columbia: University of Missouri Press.

Van Leer, David. 1986. *Emerson's Epistemology.* New York: Cambridge University Press.

Von Mehren, Joan. 1996. *Minerva and the Muse: A Life of Margaret Fuller.* Amherst: University of Massachusetts Press.

West, Cornel. 1989. *American Evasion of Philosophy.* Madison: University of Wisconsin Press.

Whicher, Stephen. 1953. *Freedom and Fate.* Philadelphia: University of Pennsylvania Press.

Whitman, Walt. 1982. *Complete Poetry and Collected Prose.* New York: Literary Classics of the United States.

Wittenberg, David. 2001. *Philosophy, Revision, Critique.* Stanford, Calif.: Stanford University Press.

Worley, Sam. 2001. *Emerson, Thoreau, and the Role of the Culture Critic.* Albany: SUNY Press.

INDEX

abandonment, 66, 117–118, 120, 122, 134, 145, 195; reform and, 171, 173, 176

Adorno, Theodor, 9–10, 122–123

affinity, 30, 37–38, 40, 46, 74, 78–80, 197. *See also* Ralph Waldo Emerson

Alcott, Bronson, 163

amor fati, 137

apology, 60–65, 71, 76, 100, 103–104, 120, 195

Aristotle, 126, 146, 208n3

asceticism, 103–104

atomism, 7–8

authorship, 11. *See also* writing

autonomy, 8

bearing (*Haltung*), 157–159, 161, 166, 175, 195

Benjamin, Walter, 23, 135

books, 74–75, 161, 200n10, 210n9. *See also* Ralph Waldo Emerson

Brown, John, 171, 173, 182, 187, 210n4. *See also* Ralph Waldo Emerson

Buell, Lawrence, 16, 65, 180, 210n2, 212n20

Cameron, Sharon, 69, 209–210n8

casualty, 33–34, 78, 87, 90, 117–118, 133, 153. *See also* Ralph Waldo Emerson

causality, 33–34, 118, 183; efficient,

85–87, 117; final, 92, 105, 114, 207n22

Cavell, Stanley, x, 41, 115, 128, 183–184, 205n3, 209n6; on Emerson and Wittgenstein, 16, 121, 129, 208n5; on Emerson and writing, 16, 186

Celan, Paul, 12, 22–23

character (ηθοV), 2–3, 52, 54–55, 69, 81, 131, 136; Aristotelian ethos and, 126–127, 146, 196, 208n3; constant expression of, 3, 52, 54–55, 69, 167; friendship and, 146–148, 154–155, 167; race and, 50; reform and, 182–184, 194, 197; reflective mediation of, 54–55, 69, 81. *See also* Ralph Waldo Emerson

commerce, 28, 43. *See also* Ralph Waldo Emerson

commodities, 5, 188

conduct, 30–31, 67, 103, 127, 173, 204n8; of life, 66–70, 89, 103, 135, 150, 173; writing and, 79

conformity, 66, 68, 71; aversion to, 60, 120, 184, 195. *See also* Ralph Waldo Emerson

consciousness, 54–56, 72; *See also* Ralph Waldo Emerson

consistency, 70, 185

conspiring, 20, 67–69, 81, 142, 168, 179–180

conversation, 161, 185. *See also* Ralph Waldo Emerson

JOHN LYSAKER
is Associate Professor and Head of
the Philosophy Department at the University of Oregon.